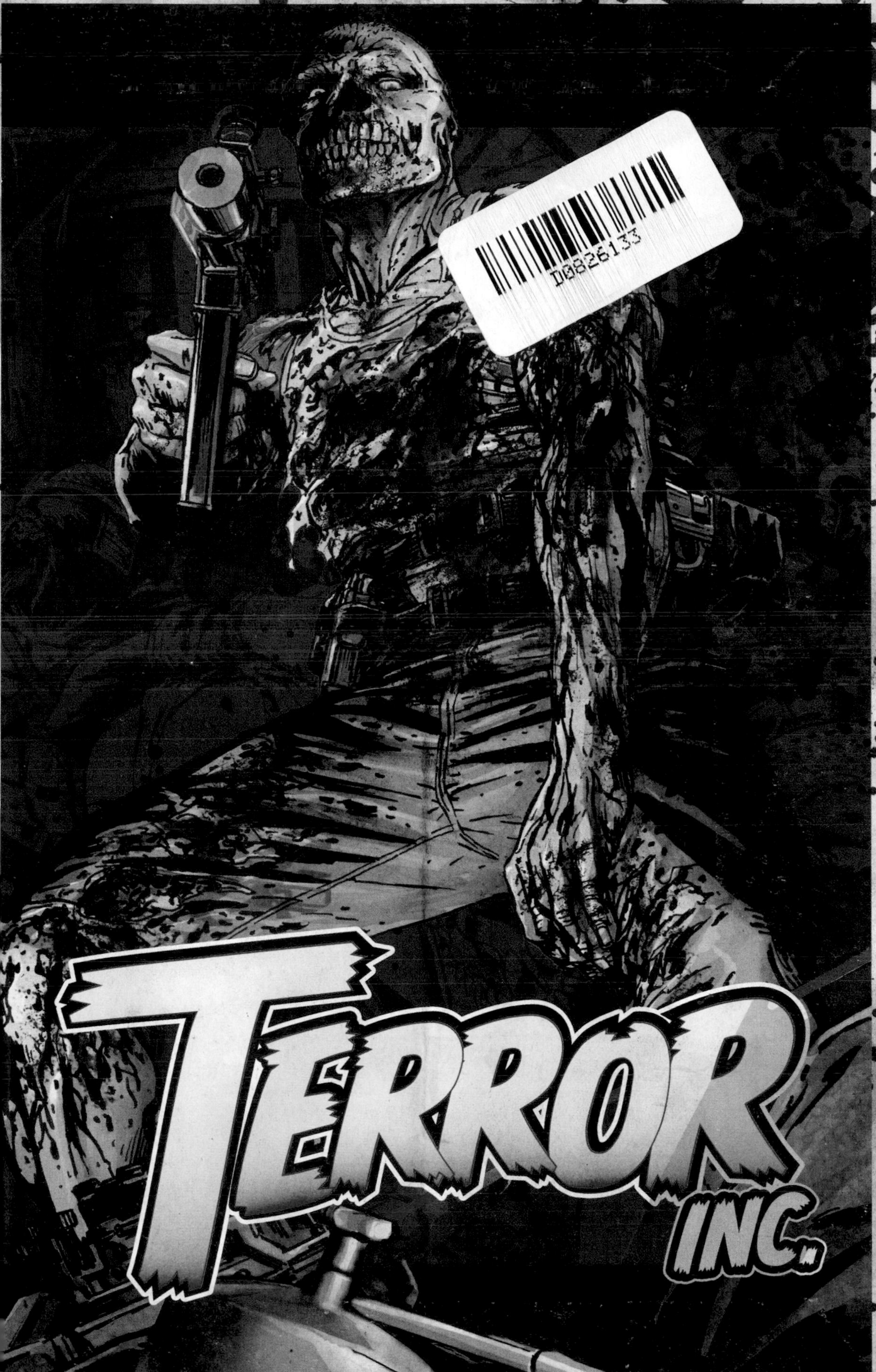
TERROR
INC.

WRITER: DAVID LAPHAM ART: PATRICK ZIRCHER

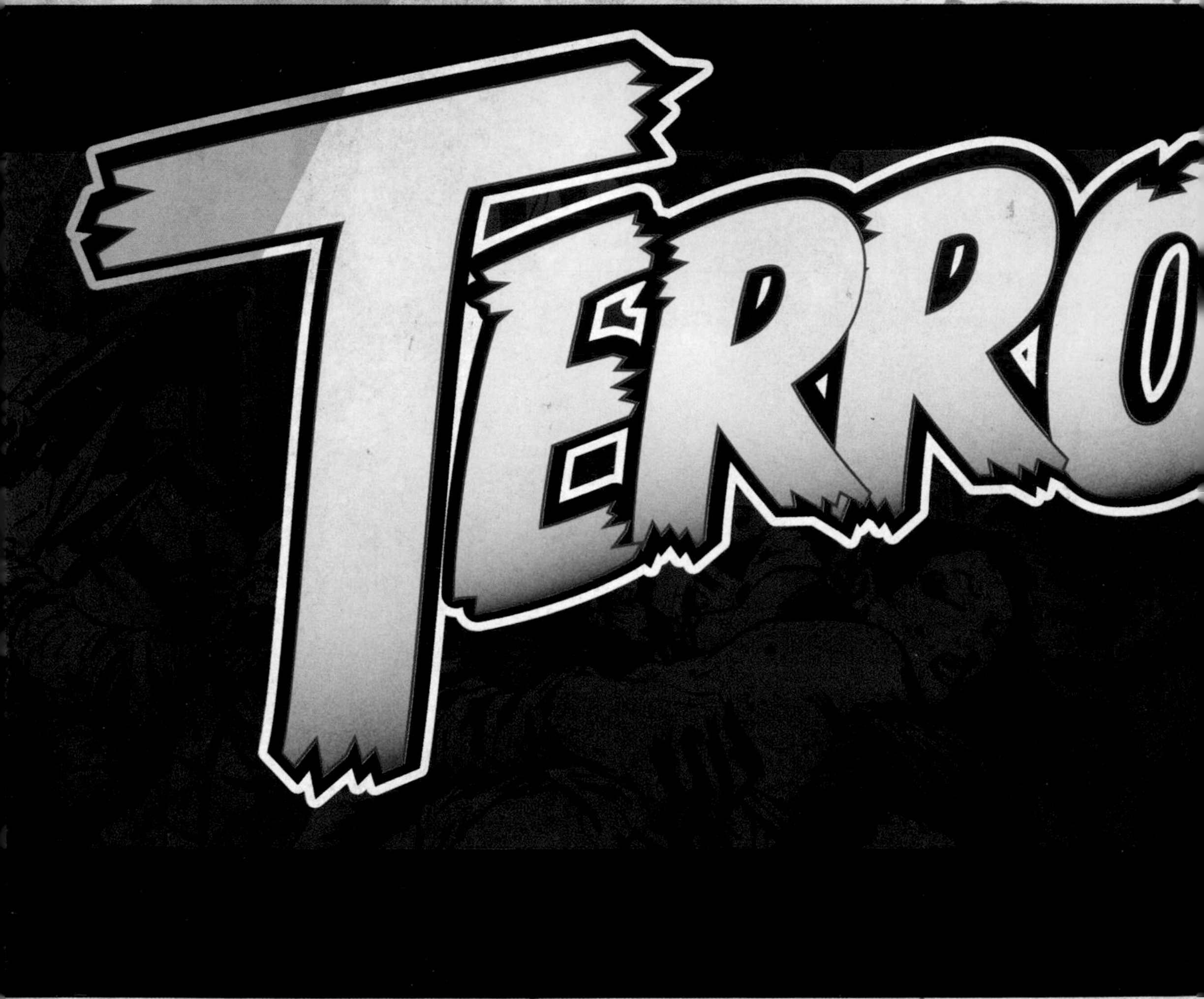
TERRO

COLOR ART: JUNE CHUNG LETTERS: VC'S JOE CARAMAGNA COVER ART: JELENA KEVIC DJURDJEVIC

ASSISTANT EDITOR: ALEJANDRO ARBONA EDITOR: WARREN SIMONS

TERROR, INC. CREATED BY D.G. CHICHESTER, MARGARET CLARK & KLAUS JANSON

COLLECTION EDITOR: JENNIFER GRÜNWALD ASSISTANT EDITORS: CORY LEVINE & JOHN DENNING

EDITOR, SPECIAL PROJECTS: MARK D. BEAZLEY SENIOR EDITOR, SPECIAL PROJECTS: JEFF YOUNGQUIST

SENIOR VICE PRESIDENT OF SALES: DAVID GABRIEL BOOK DESIGNER: RODOLFO MURAGUCHI

EDITOR IN CHIEF: JOE QUESADA PUBLISHER: DAN BUCKLEY

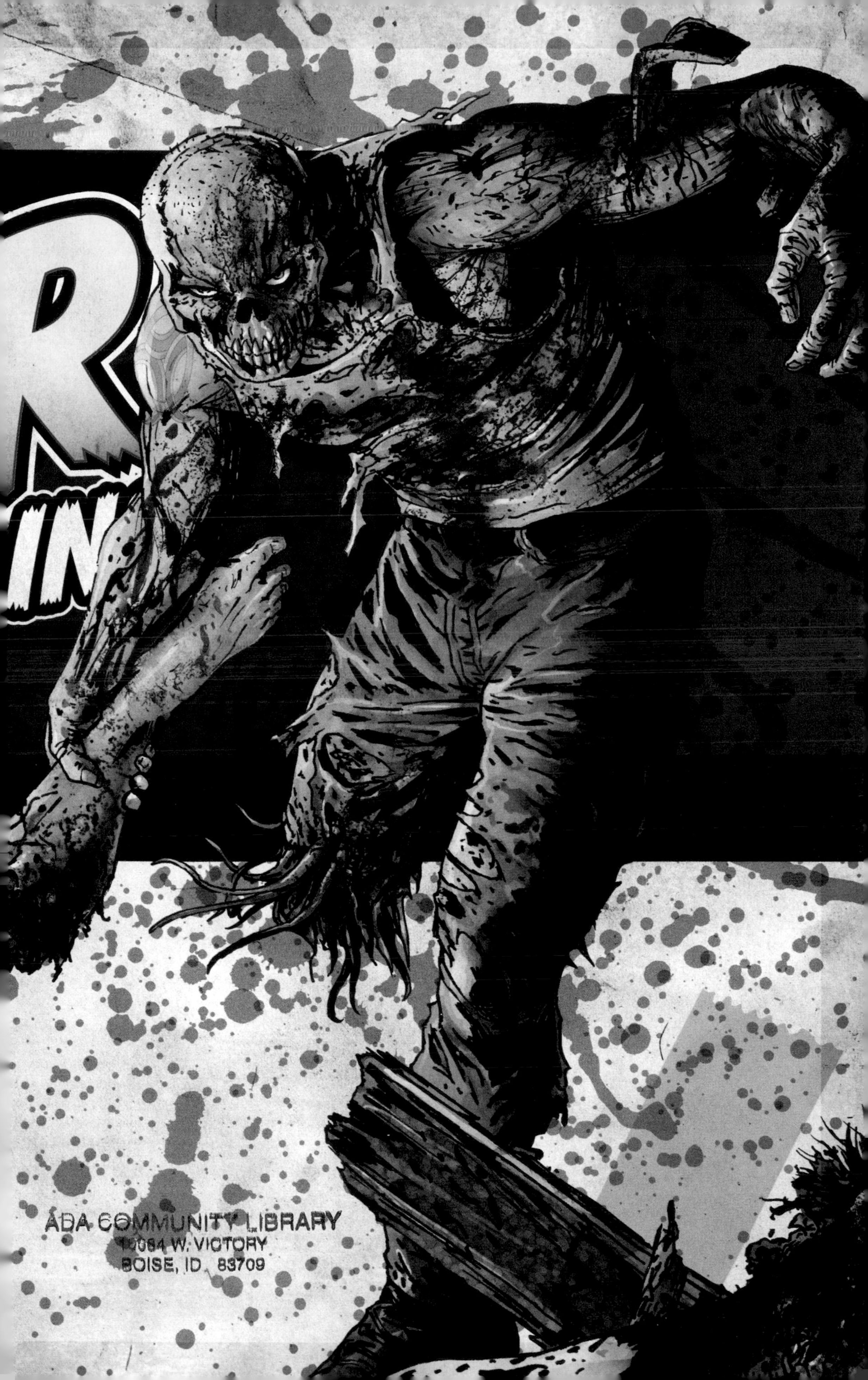

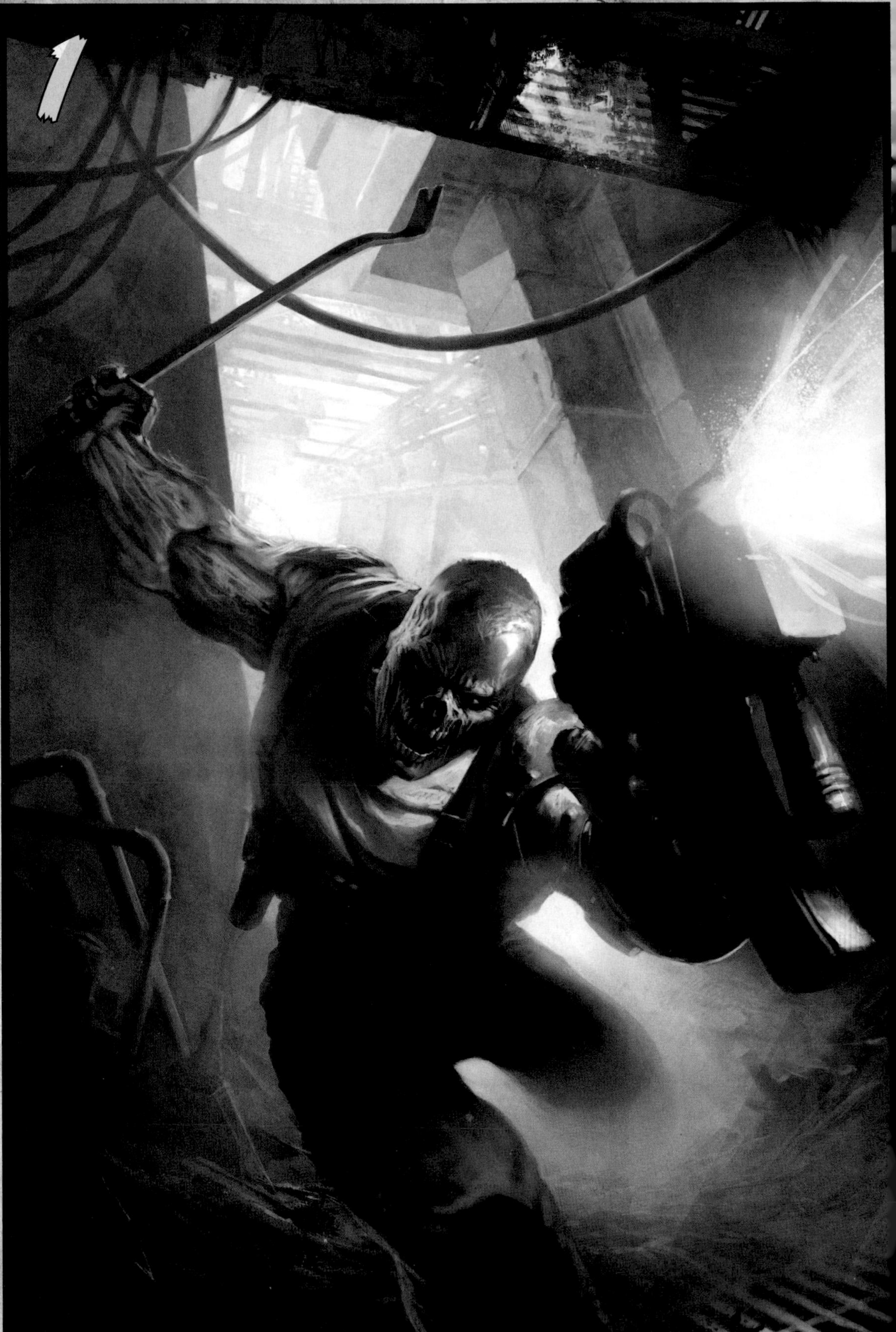
1

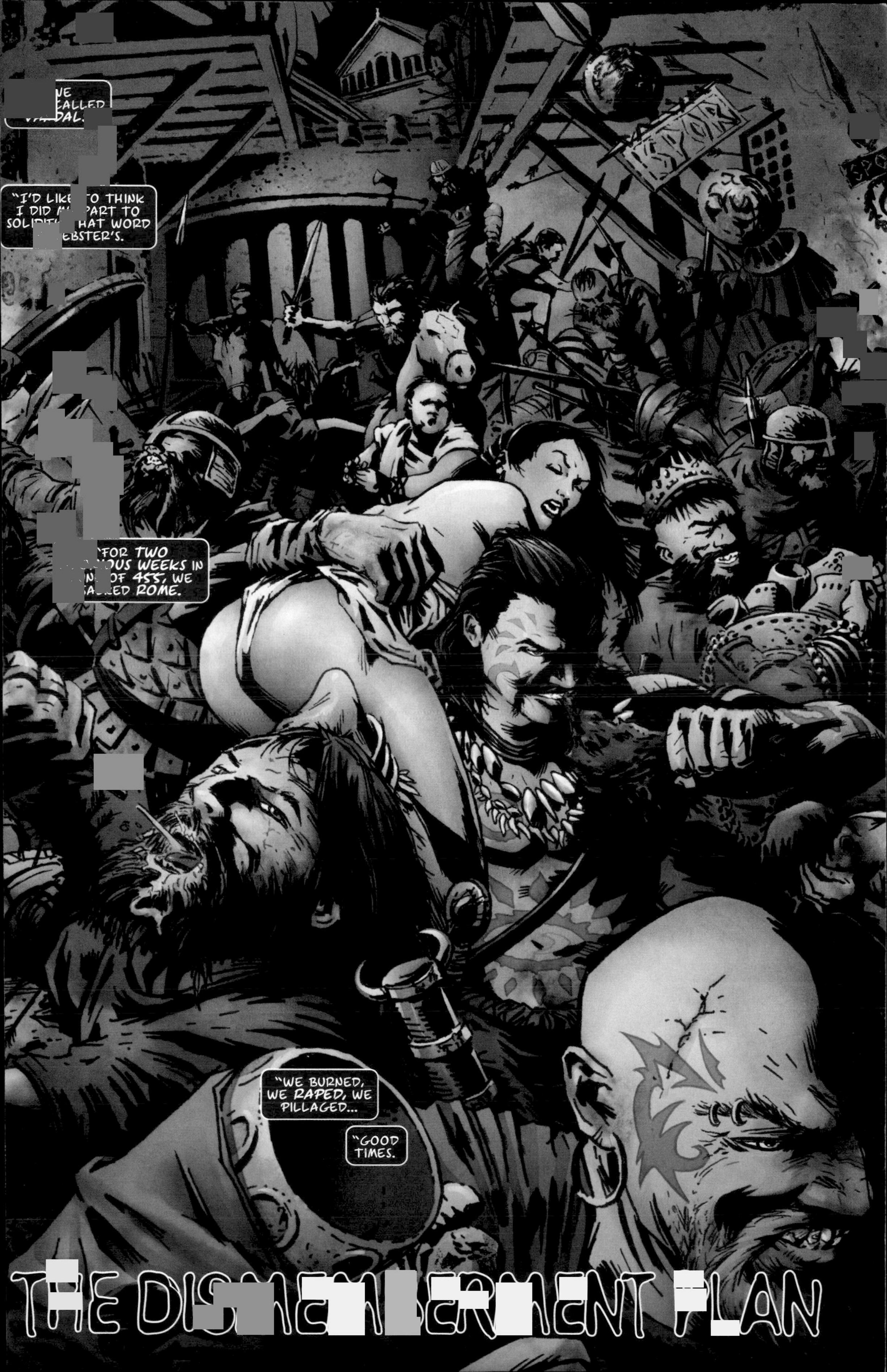
WE ... CALLED ...
“I'D LIKE TO THINK I DID ... PART TO SOLIDIF... HAT WORD ... EBSTER'S.
...FOR TWO ...OUS WEEKS IN ... OF 455, WE ...ACKED ROME.
“WE BURNED, WE RAPED, WE PILLAGED...
“GOOD TIMES.
THE DIS... ME... ERMENT ...LAN

"...COURSE OUR [...]SY OF A KING [...]ET [...]E POPE [...]ALK [...]IM INTO SIGNING [...] TREATY."

"WE PACKED OUR NEWFOUND BELONGINGS AND HEADED HOME."

"I NEVER HAD [...]CH AT HOME. [...] WIFE WAS A [...]ORE, AND AFTER [...]ASTING THOSE [...]ROMAN LADIES, WELL..."

"...SHE DIDN'T EVEN SEEM APPEALING IN THE DARK."

"[...]IKE [...] KNEW IT WOULD[...] THE TREATY CAM[...] BACK TO BITE US [...]N THE ASS."

"[...]HEIR ARMY FILLED [...]ITH A BUNCH OF [...]WEAK-ASSED NANCY BOYS, [...]E ROMANS TURNED [...]O WITCHCRAFT."

"OR MAYBE THE POPE CALLED IN A FAVOR."

"A MARE."

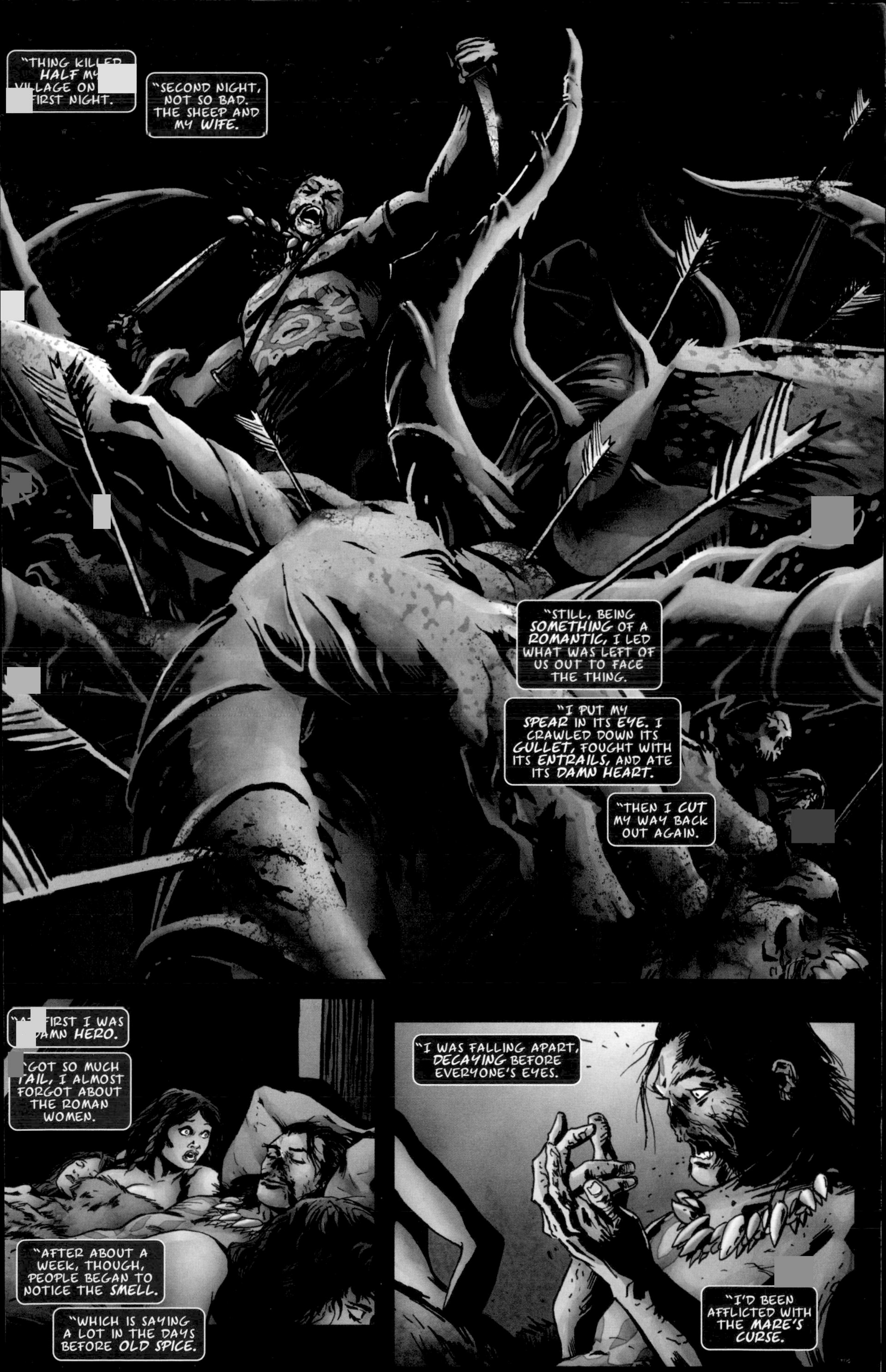
"THING KILLED HALF MY VILLAGE ON FIRST NIGHT.
"SECOND NIGHT, NOT SO BAD. THE SHEEP AND MY WIFE.
"STILL, BEING SOMETHING OF A ROMANTIC, I LED WHAT WAS LEFT OF US OUT TO FACE THE THING.
"I PUT MY SPEAR IN ITS EYE. I CRAWLED DOWN ITS GULLET, FOUGHT WITH ITS ENTRAILS, AND ATE ITS DAMN HEART.
"THEN I CUT MY WAY BACK OUT AGAIN.
FIRST I WAS DAMN HERO.
GOT SO MUCH TAIL, I ALMOST FORGOT ABOUT THE ROMAN WOMEN.
"AFTER ABOUT A WEEK, THOUGH, PEOPLE BEGAN TO NOTICE THE SMELL.
"WHICH IS SAYING A LOT IN THE DAYS BEFORE OLD SPICE.
"I WAS FALLING APART, DECAYING BEFORE EVERYONE'S EYES.
"I'D BEEN AFFLICTED WITH THE MARE'S CURSE.

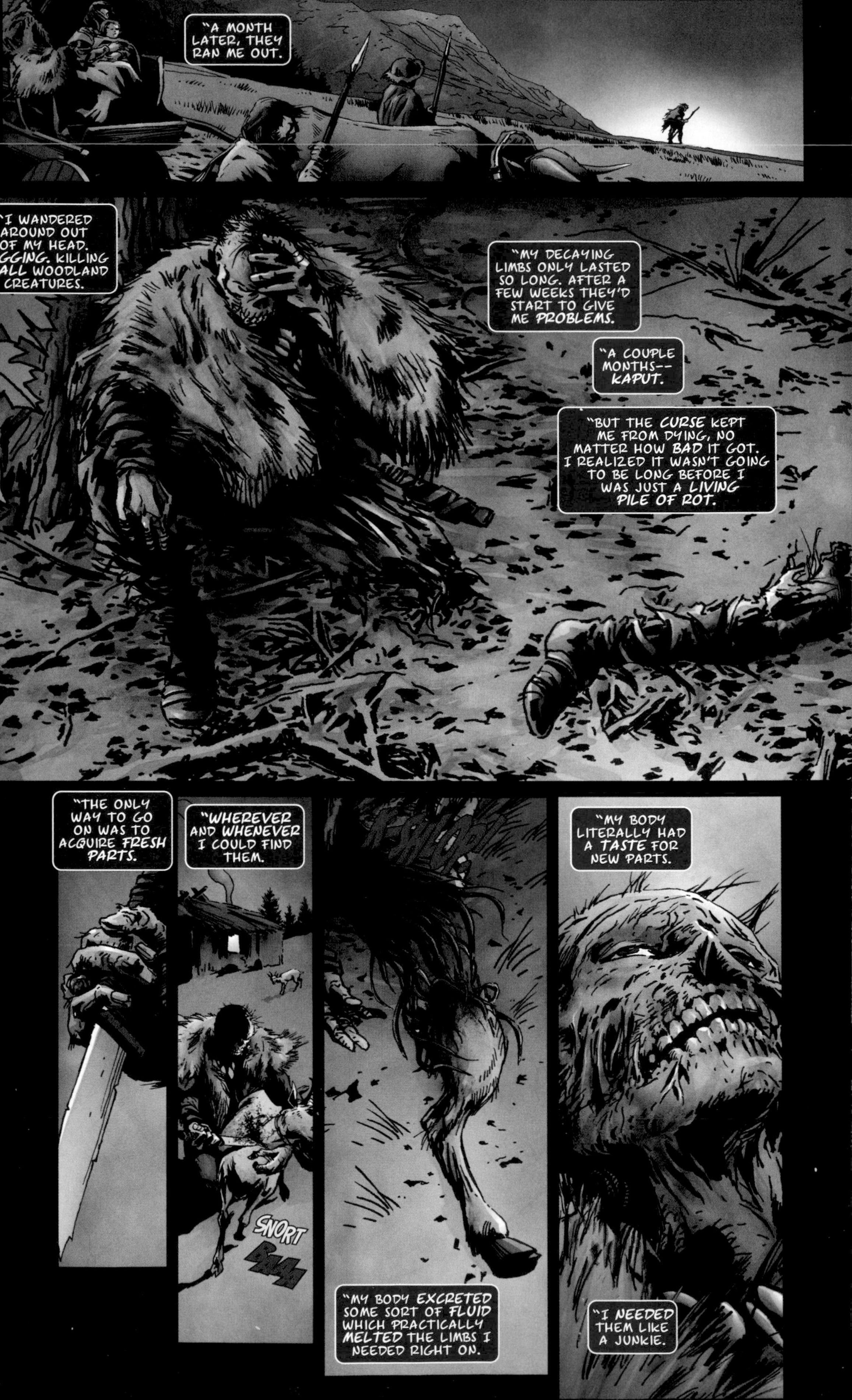
"A MONTH LATER, THEY RAN ME OUT.
"I WANDERED AROUND OUT OF MY HEAD. BEGGING. KILLING SMALL WOODLAND CREATURES.
"MY DECAYING LIMBS ONLY LASTED SO LONG. AFTER A FEW WEEKS THEY'D START TO GIVE ME PROBLEMS.
"A COUPLE MONTHS-- KAPUT.
"BUT THE CURSE KEPT ME FROM DYING, NO MATTER HOW BAD IT GOT. I REALIZED IT WASN'T GOING TO BE LONG BEFORE I WAS JUST A LIVING PILE OF ROT.
"THE ONLY WAY TO GO ON WAS TO ACQUIRE FRESH PARTS.
"WHEREVER AND WHENEVER I COULD FIND THEM.
SNORT
"MY BODY EXCRETED SOME SORT OF FLUID WHICH PRACTICALLY MELTED THE LIMBS I NEEDED RIGHT ON.
"MY BODY LITERALLY HAD A TASTE FOR NEW PARTS.
"I NEEDED THEM LIKE A JUNKIE.

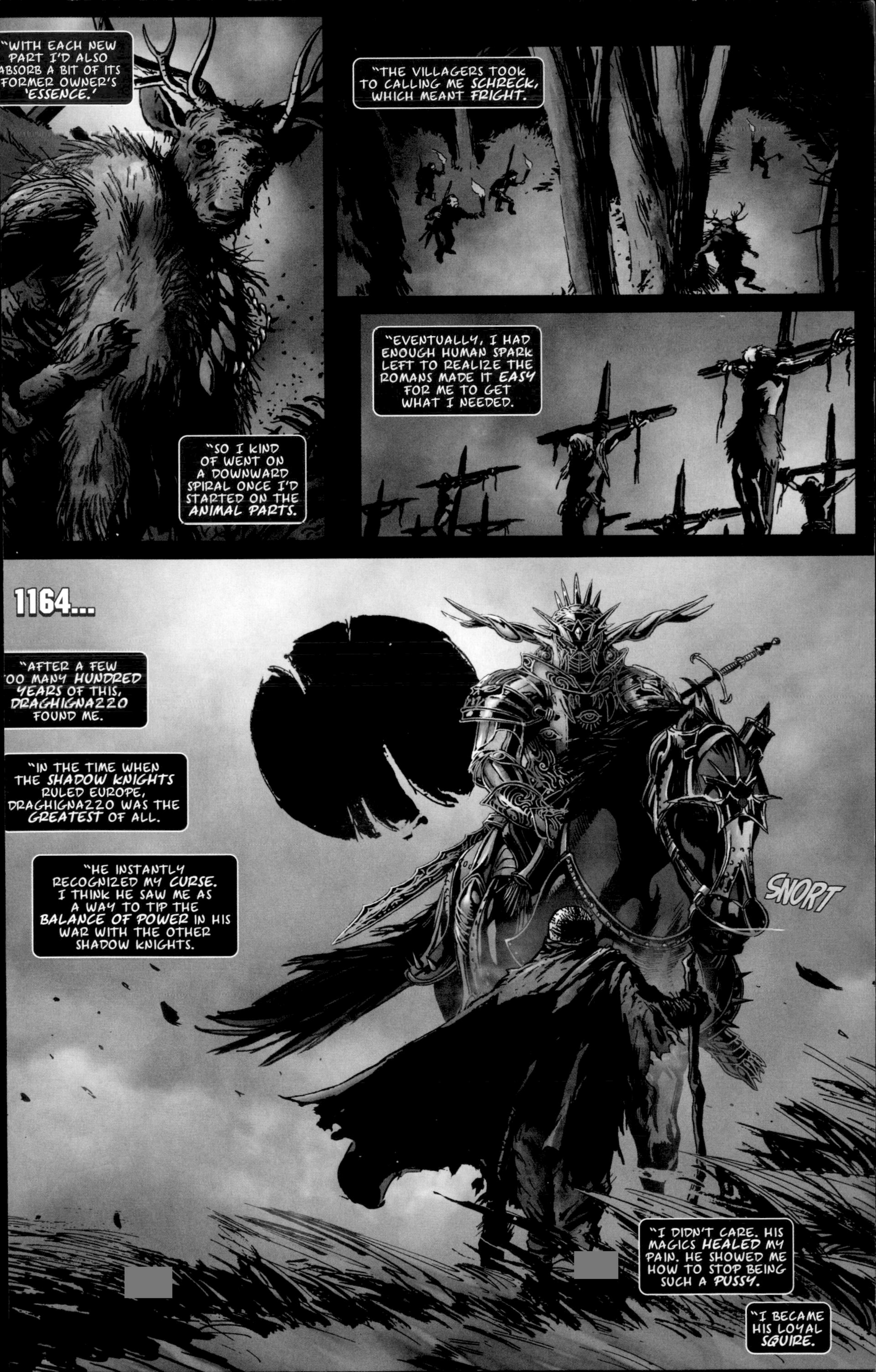
"WITH EACH NEW PART I'D ALSO ABSORB A BIT OF ITS FORMER OWNER'S 'ESSENCE.'
"SO I KIND OF WENT ON A DOWNWARD SPIRAL ONCE I'D STARTED ON THE ANIMAL PARTS.
"THE VILLAGERS TOOK TO CALLING ME SCHRECK, WHICH MEANT FRIGHT.
"EVENTUALLY, I HAD ENOUGH HUMAN SPARK LEFT TO REALIZE THE ROMANS MADE IT EASY FOR ME TO GET WHAT I NEEDED.
1164...
"AFTER A FEW TOO MANY HUNDRED YEARS OF THIS, DRAGHIGNAZZO FOUND ME.
"IN THE TIME WHEN THE SHADOW KNIGHTS RULED EUROPE, DRAGHIGNAZZO WAS THE GREATEST OF ALL.
"HE INSTANTLY RECOGNIZED MY CURSE. I THINK HE SAW ME AS A WAY TO TIP THE BALANCE OF POWER IN HIS WAR WITH THE OTHER SHADOW KNIGHTS.
SNORT
"I DIDN'T CARE. HIS MAGICS HEALED MY PAIN. HE SHOWED ME HOW TO STOP BEING SUCH A PUSSY.
"I BECAME HIS LOYAL SQUIRE.

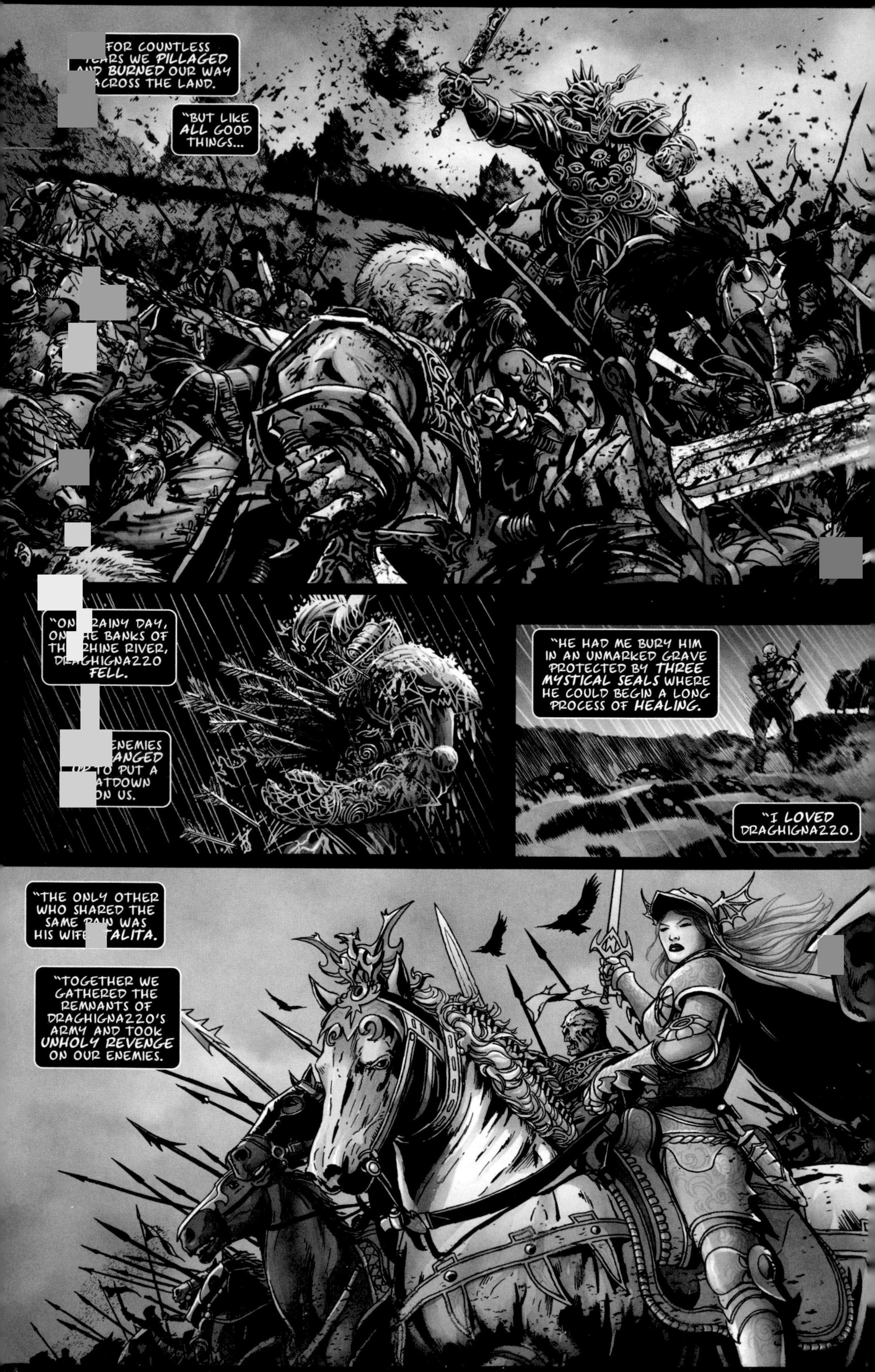
FOR COUNTLESS EARS WE PILLAGED AND BURNED OUR WAY ACROSS THE LAND.
"BUT LIKE ALL GOOD THINGS...
"ON RAINY DAY, ON HE BANKS OF TH RHINE RIVER, DRAGHIGNAZZO FELL.
ENEMIES ANGED UP TO PUT A ATDOWN ON US.
"HE HAD ME BURY HIM IN AN UNMARKED GRAVE PROTECTED BY THREE MYSTICAL SEALS WHERE HE COULD BEGIN A LONG PROCESS OF HEALING.
"I LOVED DRAGHIGNAZZO.
"THE ONLY OTHER WHO SHARED THE SAME PAIN WAS HIS WIFE TALITA.
"TOGETHER WE GATHERED THE REMNANTS OF DRAGHIGNAZZO'S ARMY AND TOOK UNHOLY REVENGE ON OUR ENEMIES.

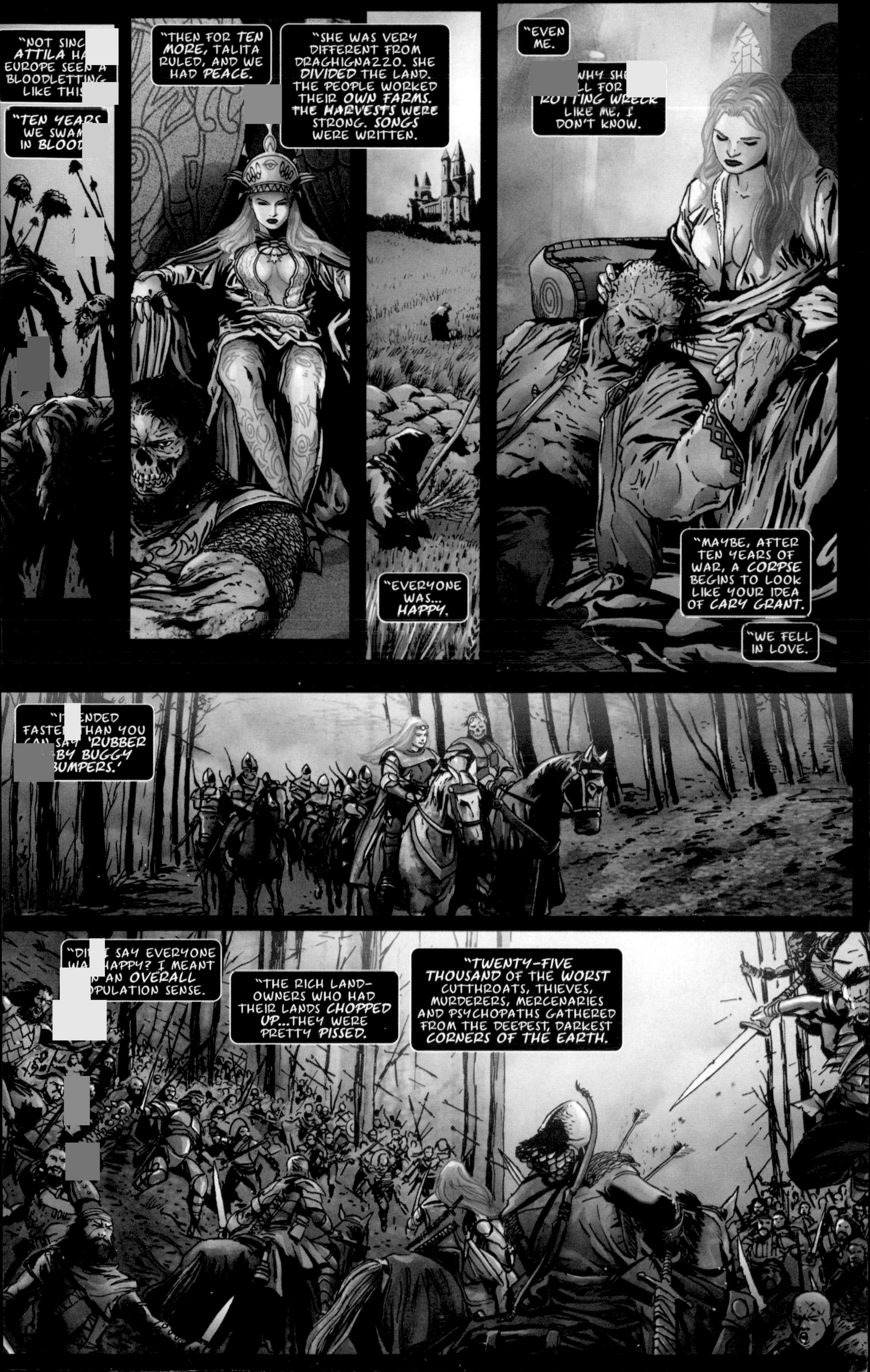
"NOT SINC ATTILA HA EUROPE SEEN A BLOODLETTING LIKE THIS
"TEN YEARS WE SWAM IN BLOOD
"THEN FOR TEN MORE, TALITA RULED, AND WE HAD PEACE.
"SHE WAS VERY DIFFERENT FROM DRAGHIGNAZZO. SHE DIVIDED THE LAND. THE PEOPLE WORKED THEIR OWN FARMS. THE HARVESTS WERE STRONG. SONGS WERE WRITTEN.
"EVERYONE WAS... HAPPY.
"EVEN ME.
WHY SHE LL FOR ROTTING WRECK LIKE ME, I DON'T KNOW.
"MAYBE, AFTER TEN YEARS OF WAR, A CORPSE BEGINS TO LOOK LIKE YOUR IDEA OF CARY GRANT.
"WE FELL IN LOVE.
ENDED FASTE THAN YOU CAN SAY 'RUBBER BY BUGGY BUMPERS.'
"DI SAY EVERYONE WA HAPPY? I MEANT N AN OVERALL OPULATION SENSE.
"THE RICH LAND-OWNERS WHO HAD THEIR LANDS CHOPPED UP...THEY WERE PRETTY PISSED.
"TWENTY-FIVE THOUSAND OF THE WORST CUTTHROATS, THIEVES, MURDERERS, MERCENARIES AND PSYCHOPATHS GATHERED FROM THE DEEPEST, DARKEST CORNERS OF THE EARTH.

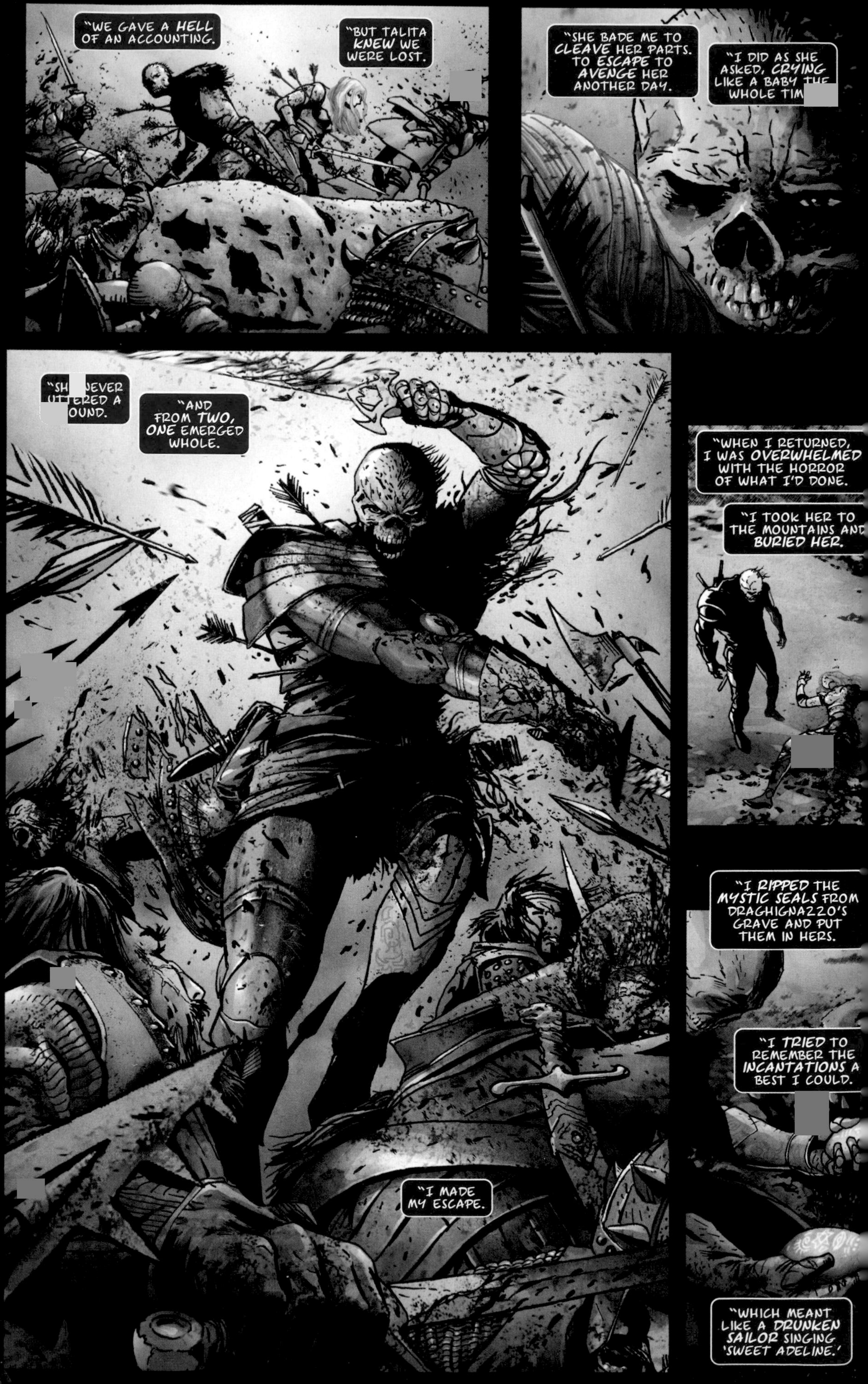

“WE GAVE A HELL OF AN ACCOUNTING.
“BUT TALITA KNEW WE WERE LOST.
“SHE BADE ME TO CLEAVE HER PARTS. TO ESCAPE TO AVENGE HER ANOTHER DAY.
“I DID AS SHE ASKED, CRYING LIKE A BABY THE WHOLE TIM
“SH EVER TERED A OUND.
“AND FROM TWO, ONE EMERGED WHOLE.
“I MADE MY ESCAPE.
“WHEN I RETURNED, I WAS OVERWHELMED WITH THE HORROR OF WHAT I'D DONE.
“I TOOK HER TO THE MOUNTAINS AND BURIED HER.
“I RIPPED THE MYSTIC SEALS FROM DRAGHIGNAZZO'S GRAVE AND PUT THEM IN HERS.
“I TRIED TO REMEMBER THE INCANTATIONS A BEST I COULD.
“WHICH MEANT LIKE A DRUNKEN SAILOR SINGING 'SWEET ADELINE.'

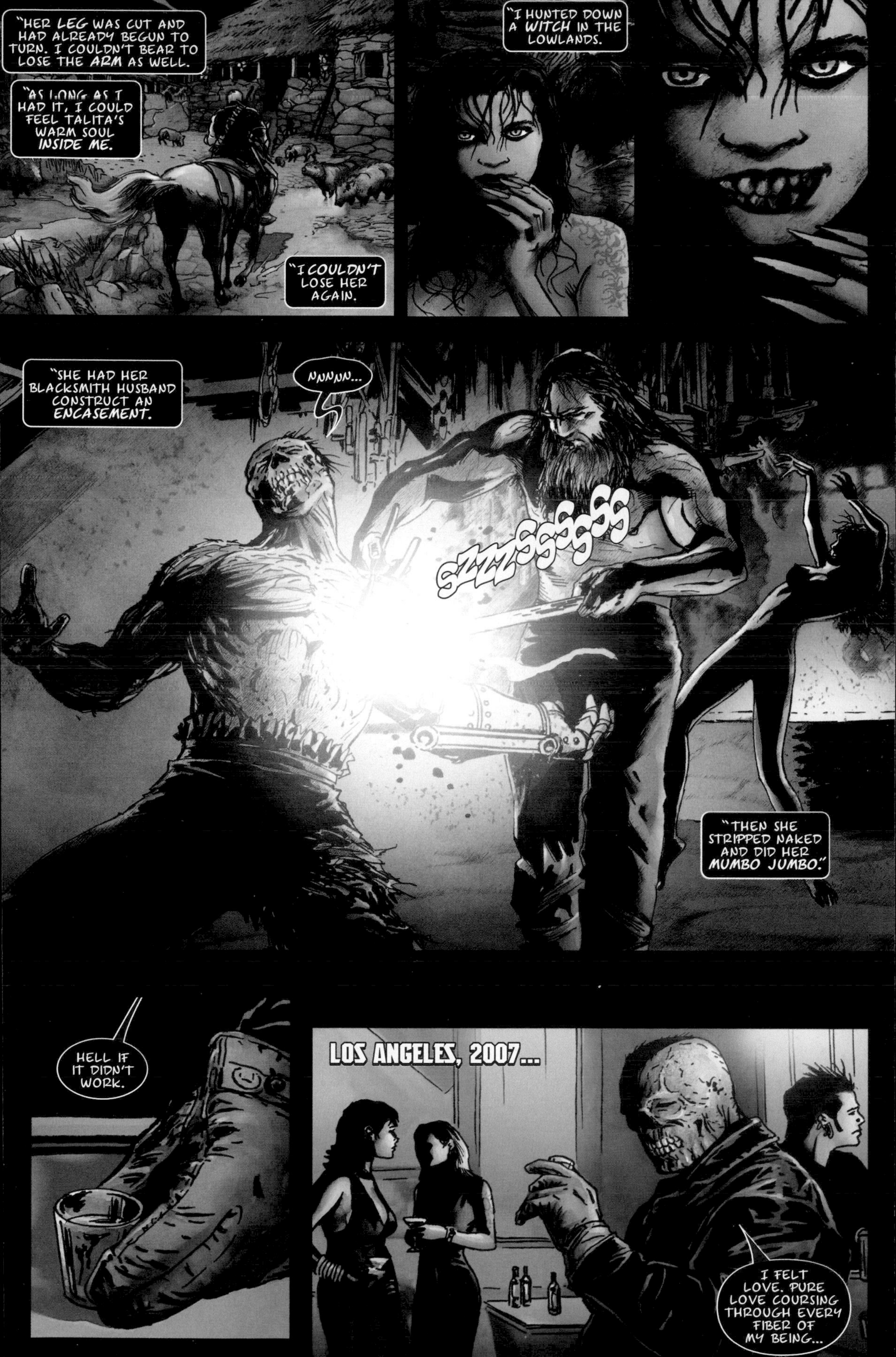
"HER LEG WAS CUT AND HAD ALREADY BEGUN TO TURN. I COULDN'T BEAR TO LOSE THE ARM AS WELL.
"AS LONG AS I HAD IT, I COULD FEEL TALITA'S WARM SOUL INSIDE ME.
"I COULDN'T LOSE HER AGAIN.
"I HUNTED DOWN A WITCH IN THE LOWLANDS.
"SHE HAD HER BLACKSMITH HUSBAND CONSTRUCT AN ENCASEMENT.
NNNNN...
SZZZSSSSSSS
"THEN SHE STRIPPED NAKED AND DID HER MUMBO JUMBO."
HELL IF IT DIDN'T WORK.
LOS ANGELES, 2007...
I FELT LOVE. PURE LOVE COURSING THROUGH EVERY FIBER OF MY BEING...

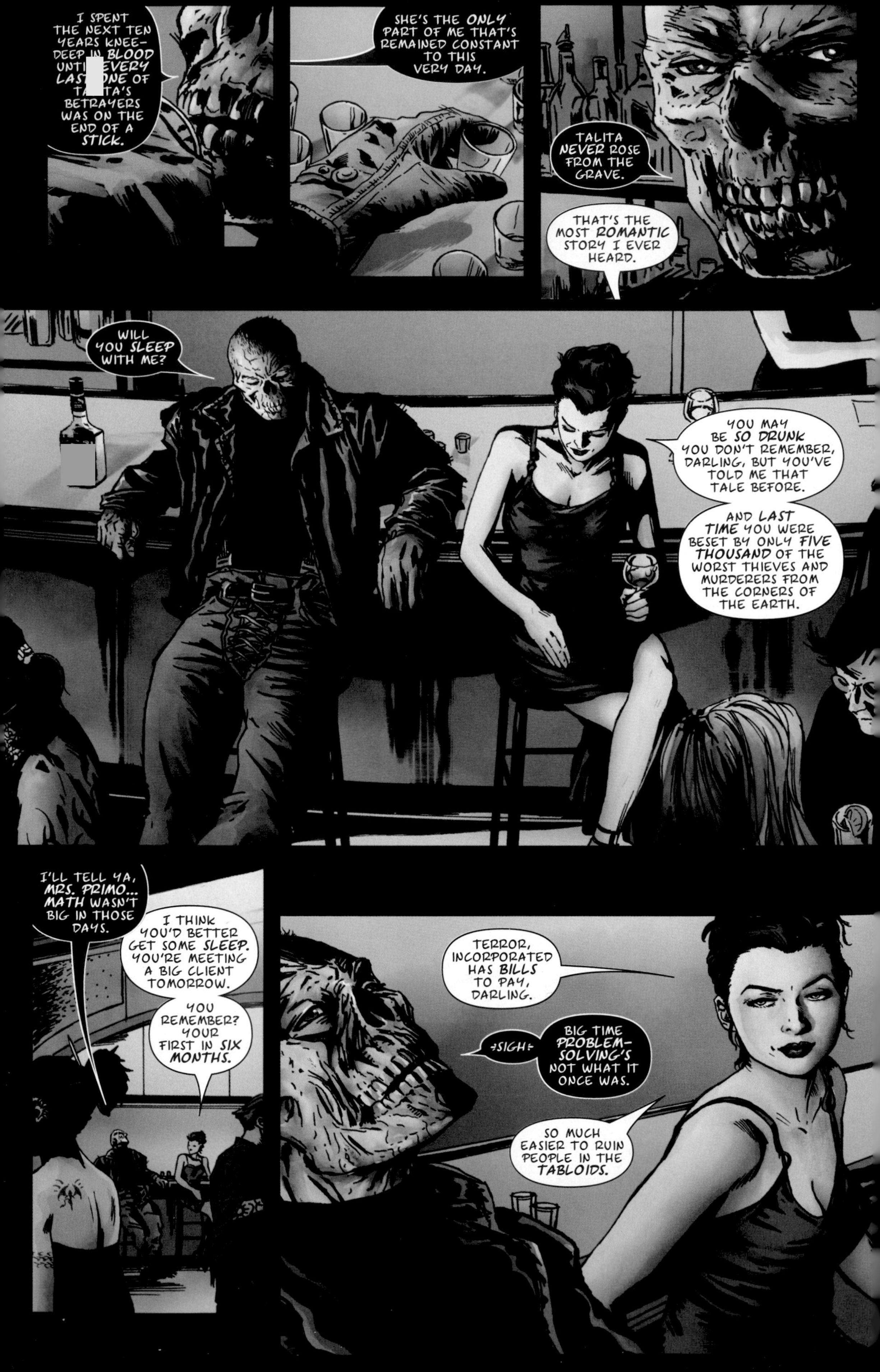
I SPENT THE NEXT TEN YEARS KNEE-DEEP IN BLOOD UNTI EVERY LAS ONE OF TA ITA'S BETRAYERS WAS ON THE END OF A STICK.
SHE'S THE ONLY PART OF ME THAT'S REMAINED CONSTANT TO THIS VERY DAY.
TALITA NEVER ROSE FROM THE GRAVE.
THAT'S THE MOST ROMANTIC STORY I EVER HEARD.
WILL YOU SLEEP WITH ME?
YOU MAY BE SO DRUNK YOU DON'T REMEMBER, DARLING, BUT YOU'VE TOLD ME THAT TALE BEFORE.
AND LAST TIME YOU WERE BESET BY ONLY FIVE THOUSAND OF THE WORST THIEVES AND MURDERERS FROM THE CORNERS OF THE EARTH.
I'LL TELL YA, MRS. PRIMO... MATH WASN'T BIG IN THOSE DAYS.
I THINK YOU'D BETTER GET SOME SLEEP. YOU'RE MEETING A BIG CLIENT TOMORROW.
YOU REMEMBER? YOUR FIRST IN SIX MONTHS.
TERROR, INCORPORATED HAS BILLS TO PAY, DARLING.
+SIGH+
BIG TIME PROBLEM-SOLVING'S NOT WHAT IT ONCE WAS.
SO MUCH EASIER TO RUIN PEOPLE IN THE TABLOIDS.

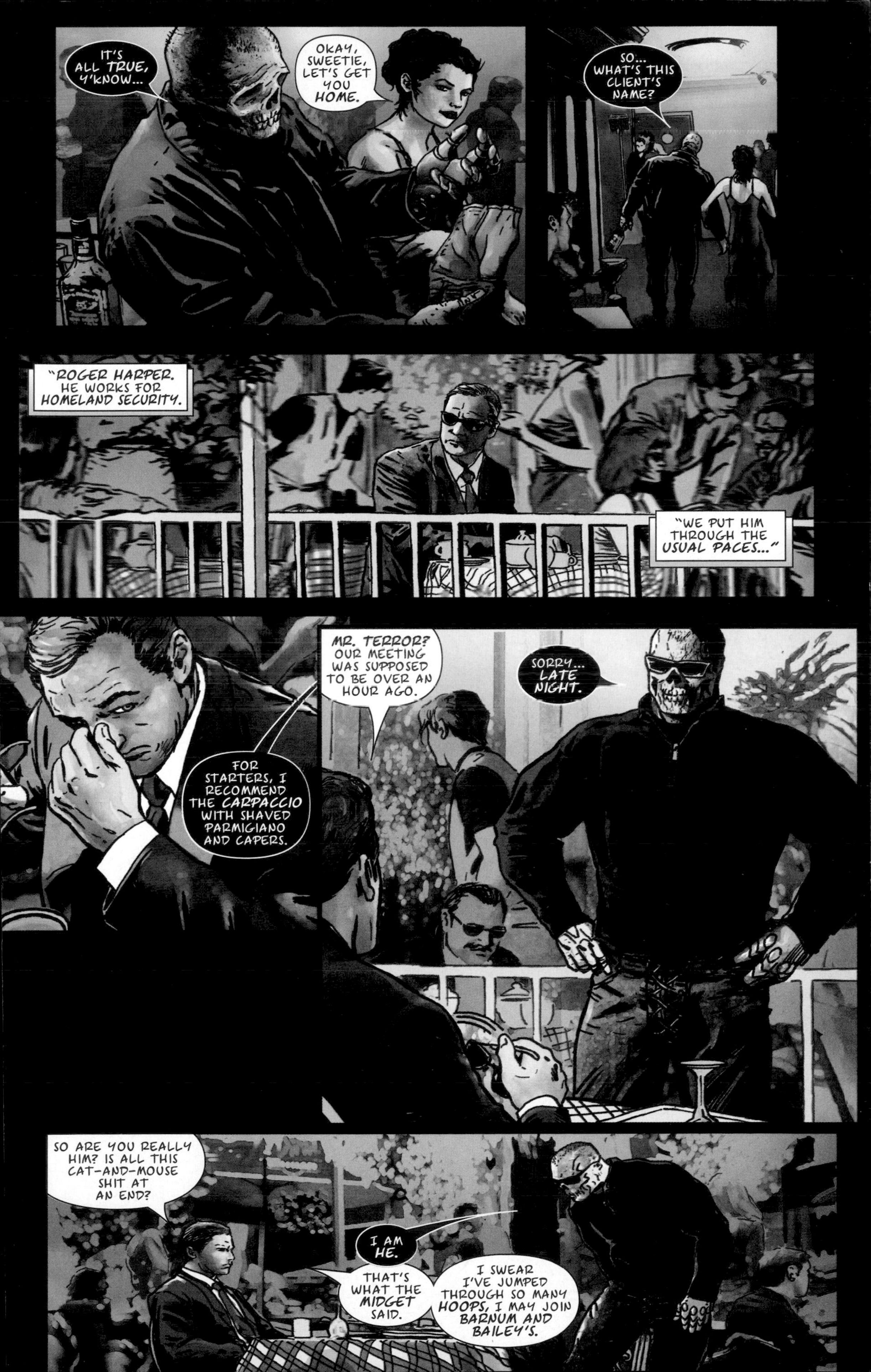
IT'S ALL TRUE, Y'KNOW...
OKAY, SWEETIE, LET'S GET YOU HOME.
SO... WHAT'S THIS CLIENT'S NAME?
"ROGER HARPER. HE WORKS FOR HOMELAND SECURITY.
"WE PUT HIM THROUGH THE USUAL PACES..."
FOR STARTERS, I RECOMMEND THE CARPACCIO WITH SHAVED PARMIGIANO AND CAPERS.
MR. TERROR? OUR MEETING WAS SUPPOSED TO BE OVER AN HOUR AGO.
SORRY... LATE NIGHT.
SO ARE YOU REALLY HIM? IS ALL THIS CAT-AND-MOUSE SHIT AT AN END?
I AM HE.
THAT'S WHAT THE MIDGET SAID.
I SWEAR I'VE JUMPED THROUGH SO MANY HOOPS, I MAY JOIN BARNUM AND BAILEY'S.

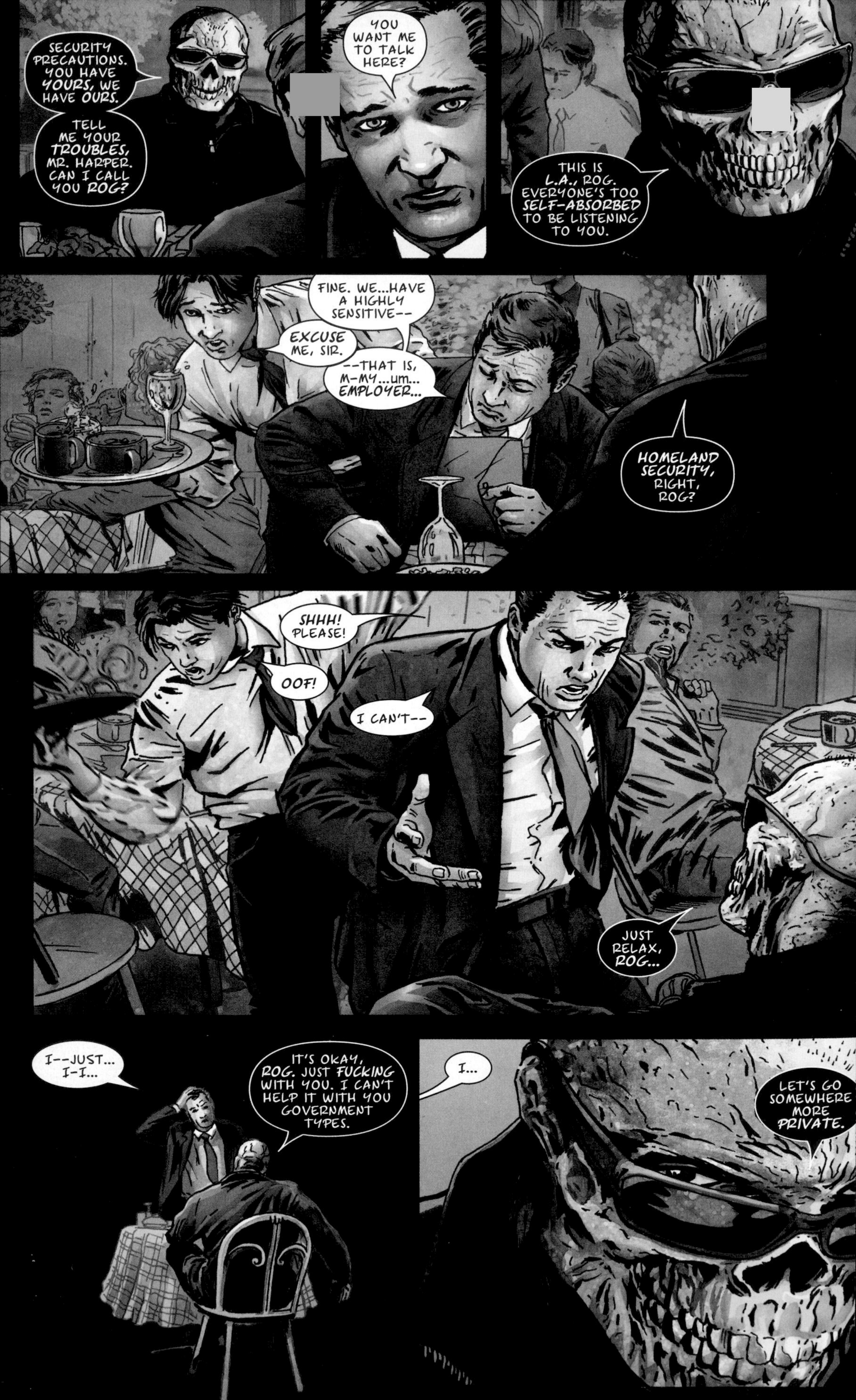
SECURITY PRECAUTIONS. YOU HAVE YOURS, WE HAVE OURS.
TELL ME YOUR TROUBLES, MR. HARPER. CAN I CALL YOU ROG?
YOU WANT ME TO TALK HERE?
THIS IS L.A., ROG. EVERYONE'S TOO SELF-ABSORBED TO BE LISTENING TO YOU.
FINE. WE...HAVE A HIGHLY SENSITIVE--
EXCUSE ME, SIR.
--THAT IS, M-MY...UM... EMPLOYER...
HOMELAND SECURITY, RIGHT, ROG?
SHHH! PLEASE!
OOF!
I CAN'T--
JUST RELAX, ROG...
I--JUST... I-I...
IT'S OKAY, ROG. JUST FUCKING WITH YOU. I CAN'T HELP IT WITH YOU GOVERNMENT TYPES.
I...
LET'S GO SOMEWHERE MORE PRIVATE.

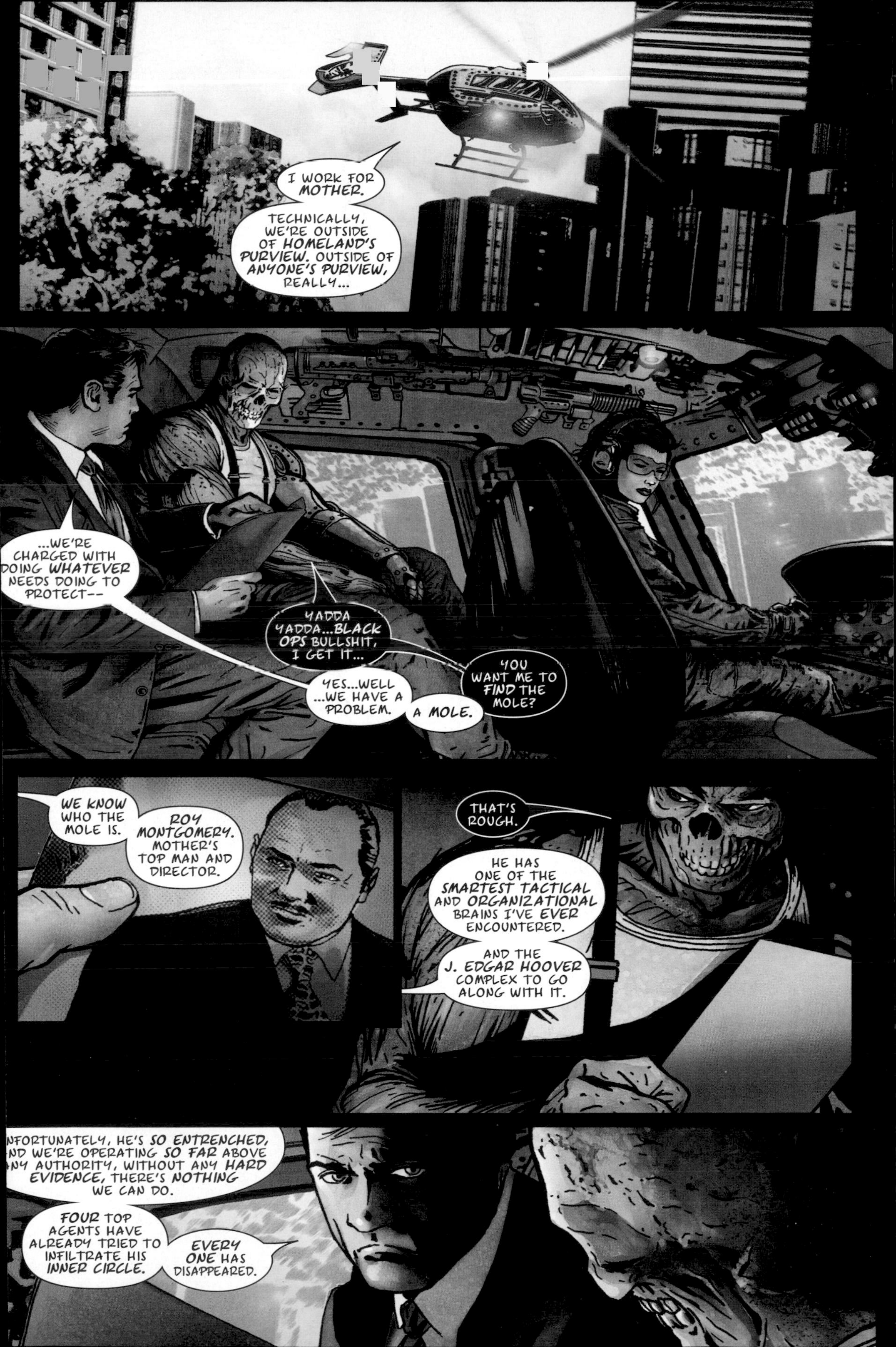
I WORK FOR MOTHER.
TECHNICALLY, WE'RE OUTSIDE OF HOMELAND'S PURVIEW. OUTSIDE OF ANYONE'S PURVIEW, REALLY...
...WE'RE CHARGED WITH DOING WHATEVER NEEDS DOING TO PROTECT--
YADDA YADDA...BLACK OPS BULLSHIT, I GET IT...
YES...WELL ...WE HAVE A PROBLEM.
A MOLE.
YOU WANT ME TO FIND THE MOLE?
WE KNOW WHO THE MOLE IS.
ROY MONTGOMERY. MOTHER'S TOP MAN AND DIRECTOR.
THAT'S ROUGH.
HE HAS ONE OF THE SMARTEST TACTICAL AND ORGANIZATIONAL BRAINS I'VE EVER ENCOUNTERED.
AND THE J. EDGAR HOOVER COMPLEX TO GO ALONG WITH IT.
NFORTUNATELY, HE'S SO ENTRENCHED, ND WE'RE OPERATING SO FAR ABOVE NY AUTHORITY, WITHOUT ANY HARD EVIDENCE, THERE'S NOTHING WE CAN DO.
FOUR TOP AGENTS HAVE ALREADY TRIED TO INFILTRATE HIS INNER CIRCLE.
EVERY ONE HAS DISAPPEARED.

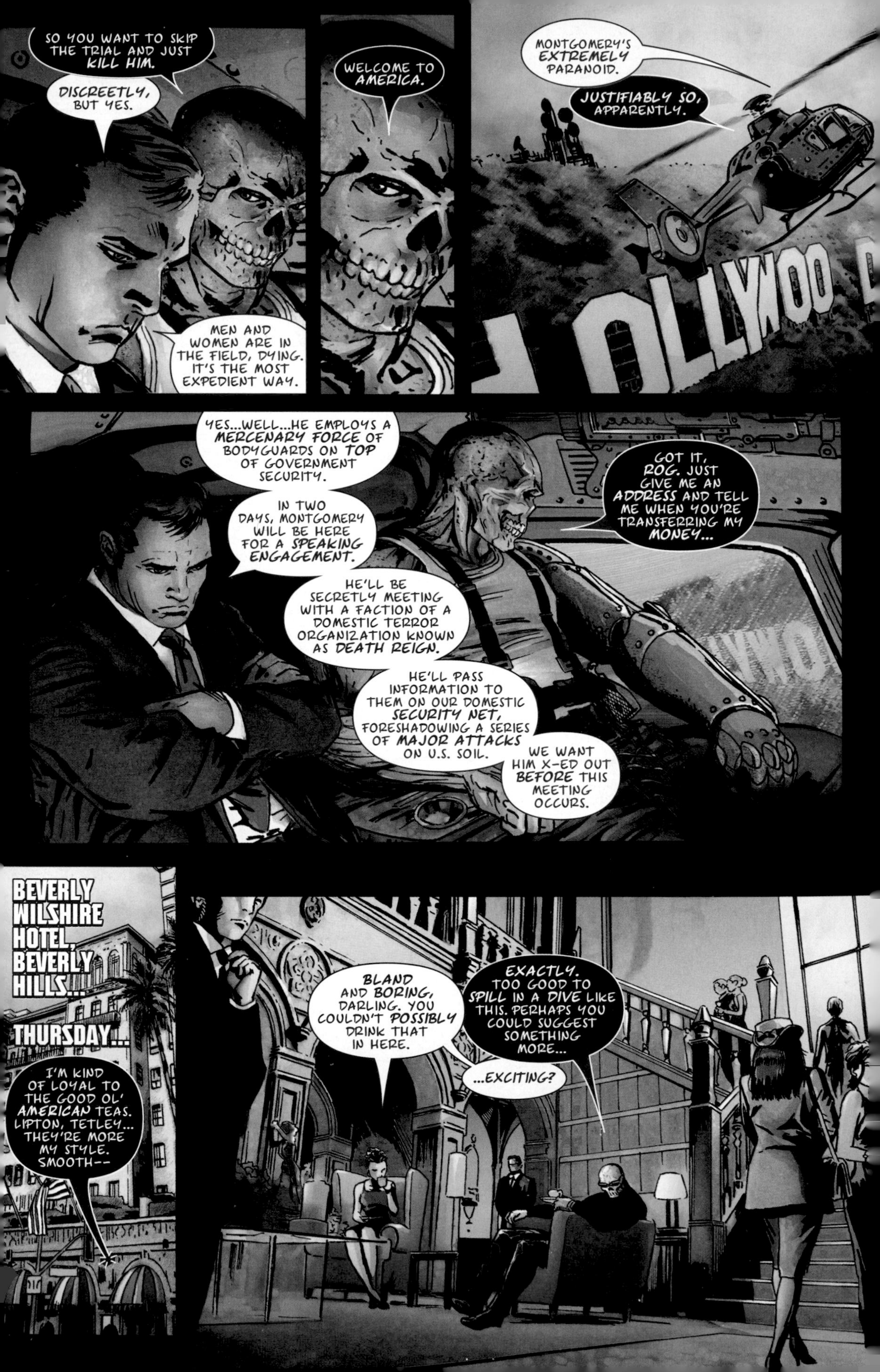
SO YOU WANT TO SKIP THE TRIAL AND JUST KILL HIM.
DISCREETLY, BUT YES.
MEN AND WOMEN ARE IN THE FIELD, DYING. IT'S THE MOST EXPEDIENT WAY.
WELCOME TO AMERICA.
MONTGOMERY'S EXTREMELY PARANOID.
JUSTIFIABLY SO, APPARENTLY.
OLLYWOO
YES...WELL...HE EMPLOYS A MERCENARY FORCE OF BODYGUARDS ON TOP OF GOVERNMENT SECURITY.
IN TWO DAYS, MONTGOMERY WILL BE HERE FOR A SPEAKING ENGAGEMENT.
HE'LL BE SECRETLY MEETING WITH A FACTION OF A DOMESTIC TERROR ORGANIZATION KNOWN AS DEATH REIGN.
HE'LL PASS INFORMATION TO THEM ON OUR DOMESTIC SECURITY NET, FORESHADOWING A SERIES OF MAJOR ATTACKS ON U.S. SOIL.
WE WANT HIM X-ED OUT BEFORE THIS MEETING OCCURS.
GOT IT, ROG. JUST GIVE ME AN ADDRESS AND TELL ME WHEN YOU'RE TRANSFERRING MY MONEY...
BEVERLY WILSHIRE HOTEL, BEVERLY HILLS...
THURSDAY...
I'M KIND OF LOYAL TO THE GOOD OL' AMERICAN TEAS. LIPTON, TETLEY... THEY'RE MORE MY STYLE. SMOOTH--
BLAND AND BORING, DARLING. YOU COULDN'T POSSIBLY DRINK THAT IN HERE.
EXACTLY. TOO GOOD TO SPILL IN A DIVE LIKE THIS. PERHAPS YOU COULD SUGGEST SOMETHING MORE...
...EXCITING?

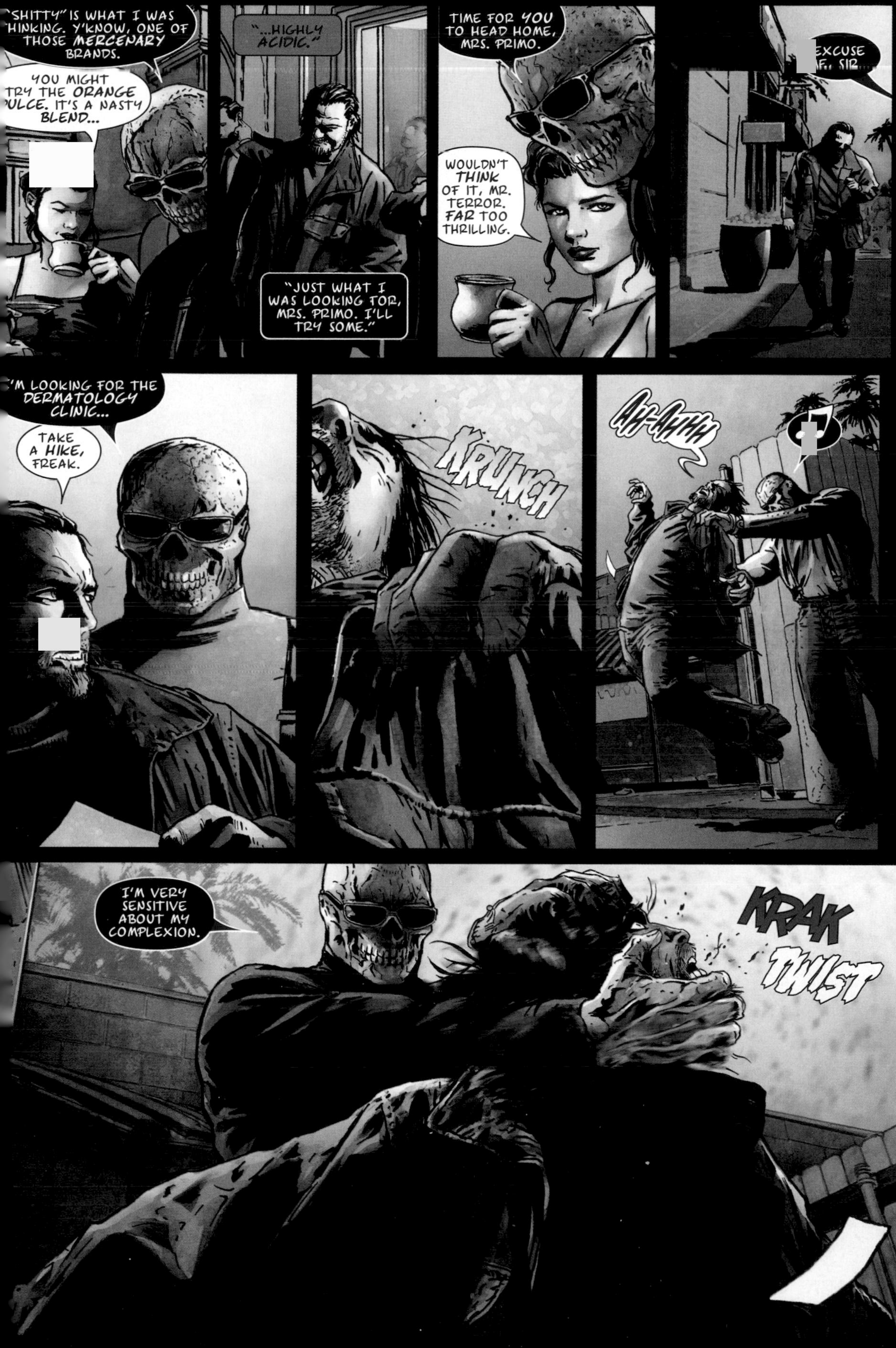
"SHITTY" IS WHAT I WAS HINKING. Y'KNOW, ONE OF THOSE MERCENARY BRANDS.
YOU MIGHT TRY THE ORANGE ULCE. IT'S A NASTY BLEND...
"...HIGHLY ACIDIC."
"JUST WHAT I WAS LOOKING FOR, MRS. PRIMO. I'LL TRY SOME."
TIME FOR YOU TO HEAD HOME, MRS. PRIMO.
WOULDN'T THINK OF IT, MR. TERROR. FAR TOO THRILLING.
EXCUSE E, SIR
'M LOOKING FOR THE DERMATOLOGY CLINIC...
TAKE A HIKE, FREAK.
KRUNCH
AH-AHHH
I'M VERY SENSITIVE ABOUT MY COMPLEXION.
KRAK
TWIST

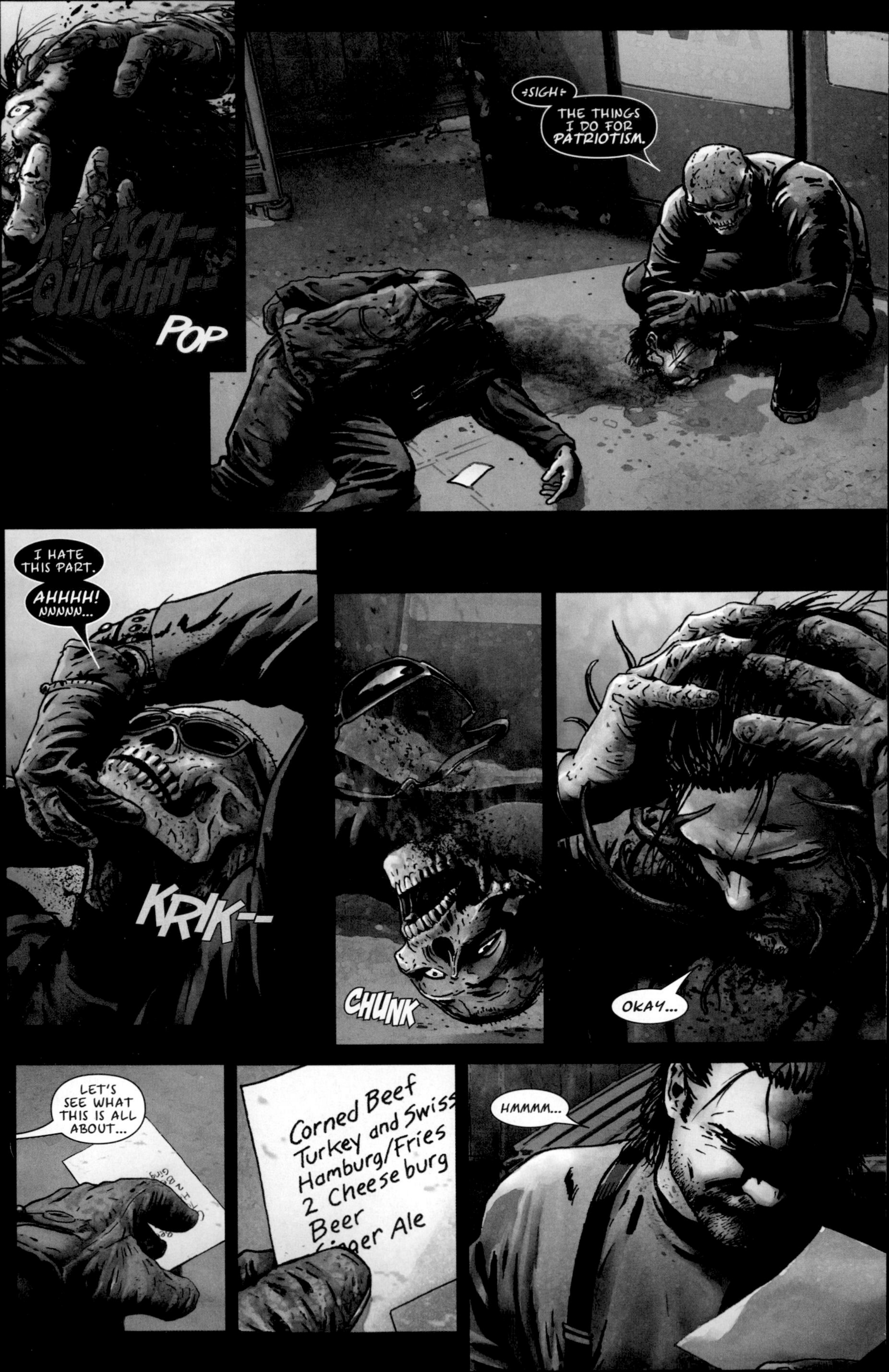
K-K-KCH--
QUICHHH--
POP
-SIGH-
THE THINGS I DO FOR PATRIOTISM.
I HATE THIS PART.
AHHHH! NNNNN...
KRIK--
CHUNK
OKAY...
LET'S SEE WHAT THIS IS ALL ABOUT...
Corned Beef
Turkey and Swiss
Hamburg/Fries
2 Cheese burg
Beer
Ginger Ale
HMMMM...

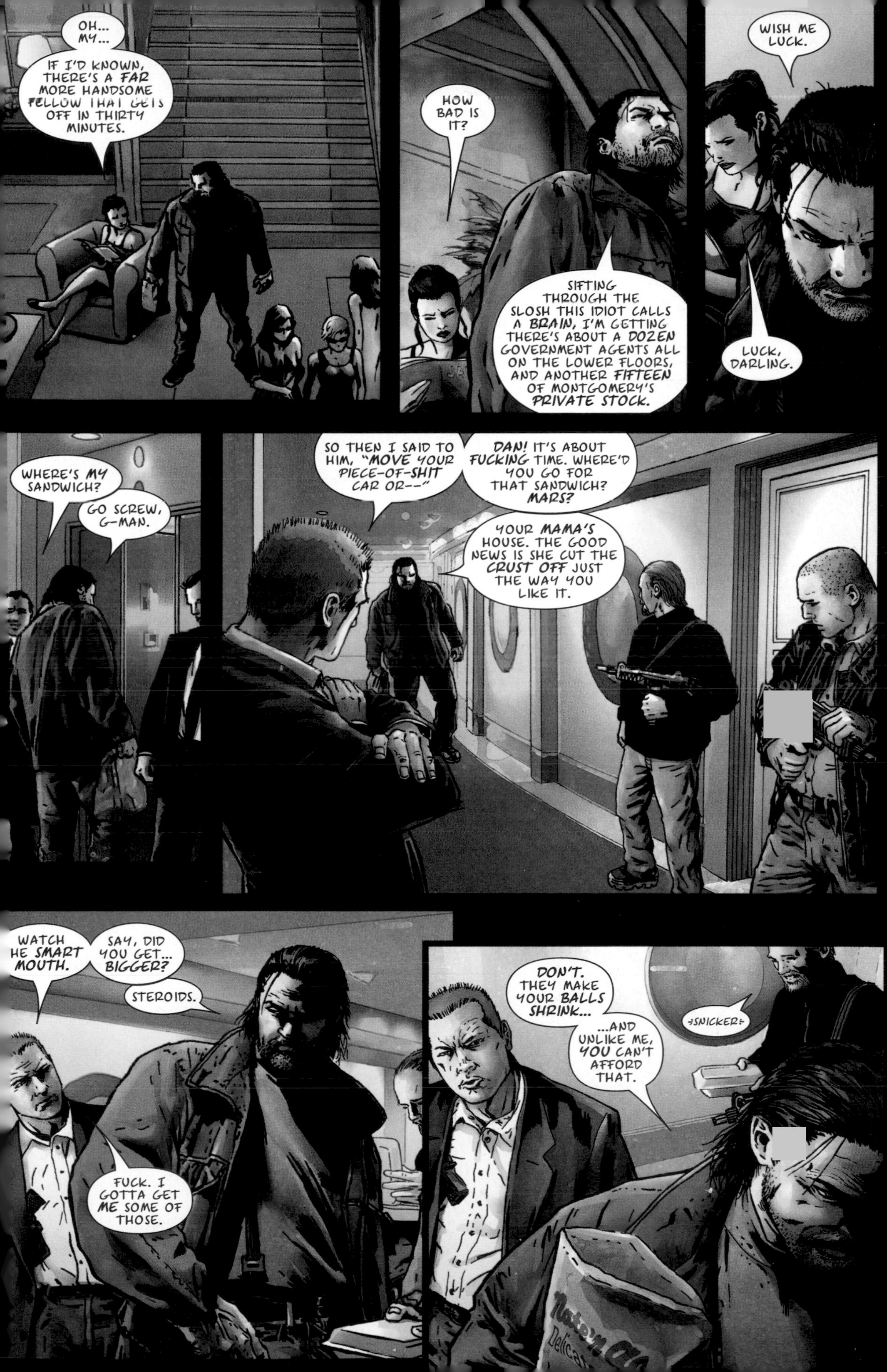
OH... MY...
IF I'D KNOWN, THERE'S A FAR MORE HANDSOME FELLOW THAT GETS OFF IN THIRTY MINUTES.
HOW BAD IS IT?
SIFTING THROUGH THE SLOSH THIS IDIOT CALLS A BRAIN, I'M GETTING THERE'S ABOUT A DOZEN GOVERNMENT AGENTS ALL ON THE LOWER FLOORS, AND ANOTHER FIFTEEN OF MONTGOMERY'S PRIVATE STOCK.
WISH ME LUCK.
LUCK, DARLING.
WHERE'S MY SANDWICH?
GO SCREW, G-MAN.
SO THEN I SAID TO HIM, "MOVE YOUR PIECE-OF-SHIT CAR OR--"
DAN! IT'S ABOUT FUCKING TIME. WHERE'D YOU GO FOR THAT SANDWICH? MARS?
YOUR MAMA'S HOUSE. THE GOOD NEWS IS SHE CUT THE CRUST OFF JUST THE WAY YOU LIKE IT.
WATCH HE SMART MOUTH.
SAY, DID YOU GET... BIGGER?
STEROIDS.
FUCK. I GOTTA GET ME SOME OF THOSE.
DON'T. THEY MAKE YOUR BALLS SHRINK...
...AND UNLIKE ME, YOU CAN'T AFFORD THAT.
=SNICKER=

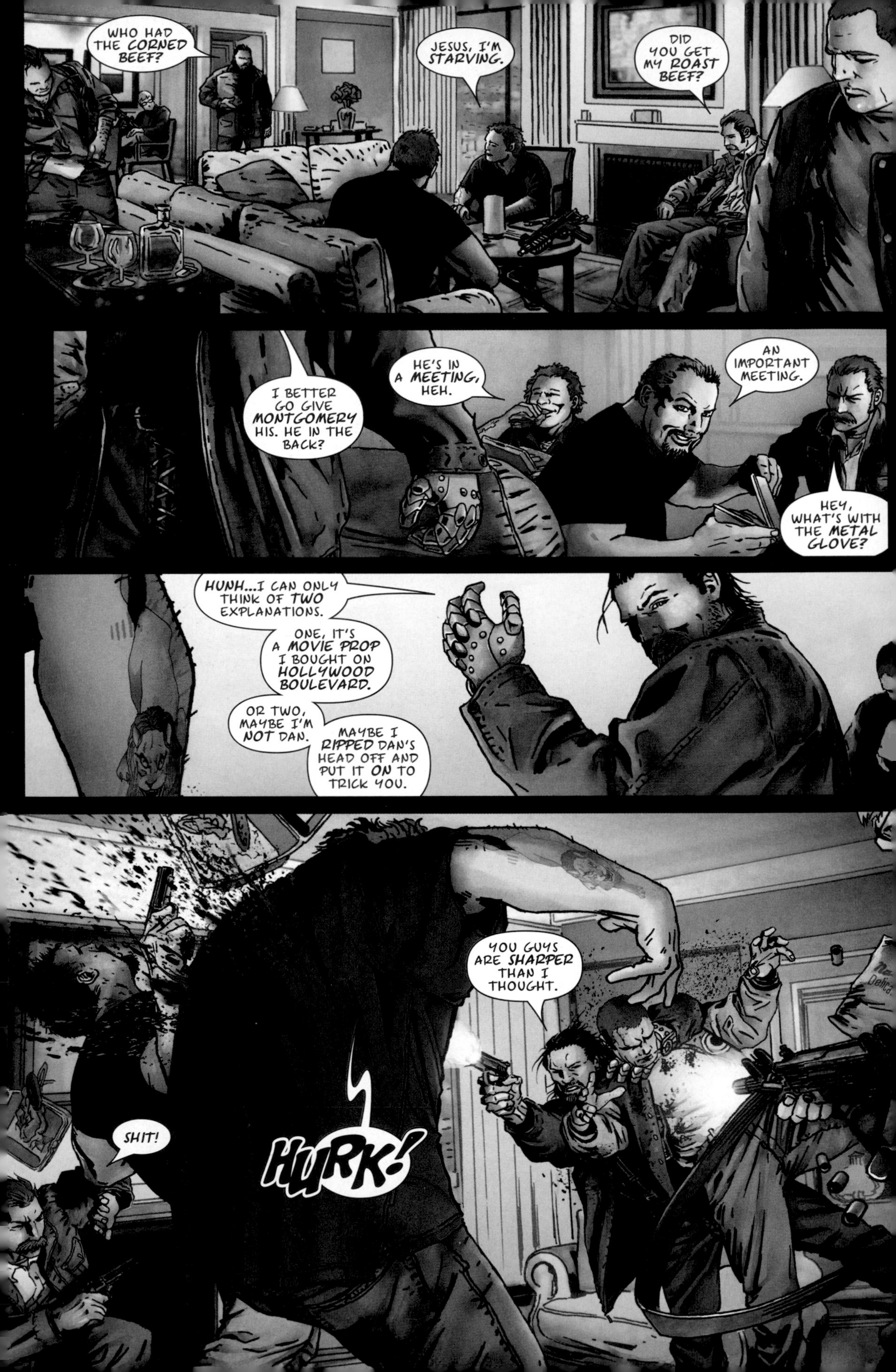
WHO HAD THE CORNED BEEF?
JESUS, I'M STARVING.
DID YOU GET MY ROAST BEEF?
I BETTER GO GIVE MONTGOMERY HIS. HE IN THE BACK?
HE'S IN A MEETING, HEH.
AN IMPORTANT MEETING.
HEY, WHAT'S WITH THE METAL GLOVE?
HUNH...I CAN ONLY THINK OF TWO EXPLANATIONS.
ONE, IT'S A MOVIE PROP I BOUGHT ON HOLLYWOOD BOULEVARD.
OR TWO, MAYBE I'M NOT DAN.
MAYBE I RIPPED DAN'S HEAD OFF AND PUT IT ON TO TRICK YOU.
YOU GUYS ARE SHARPER THAN I THOUGHT.
SHIT!
HURK!

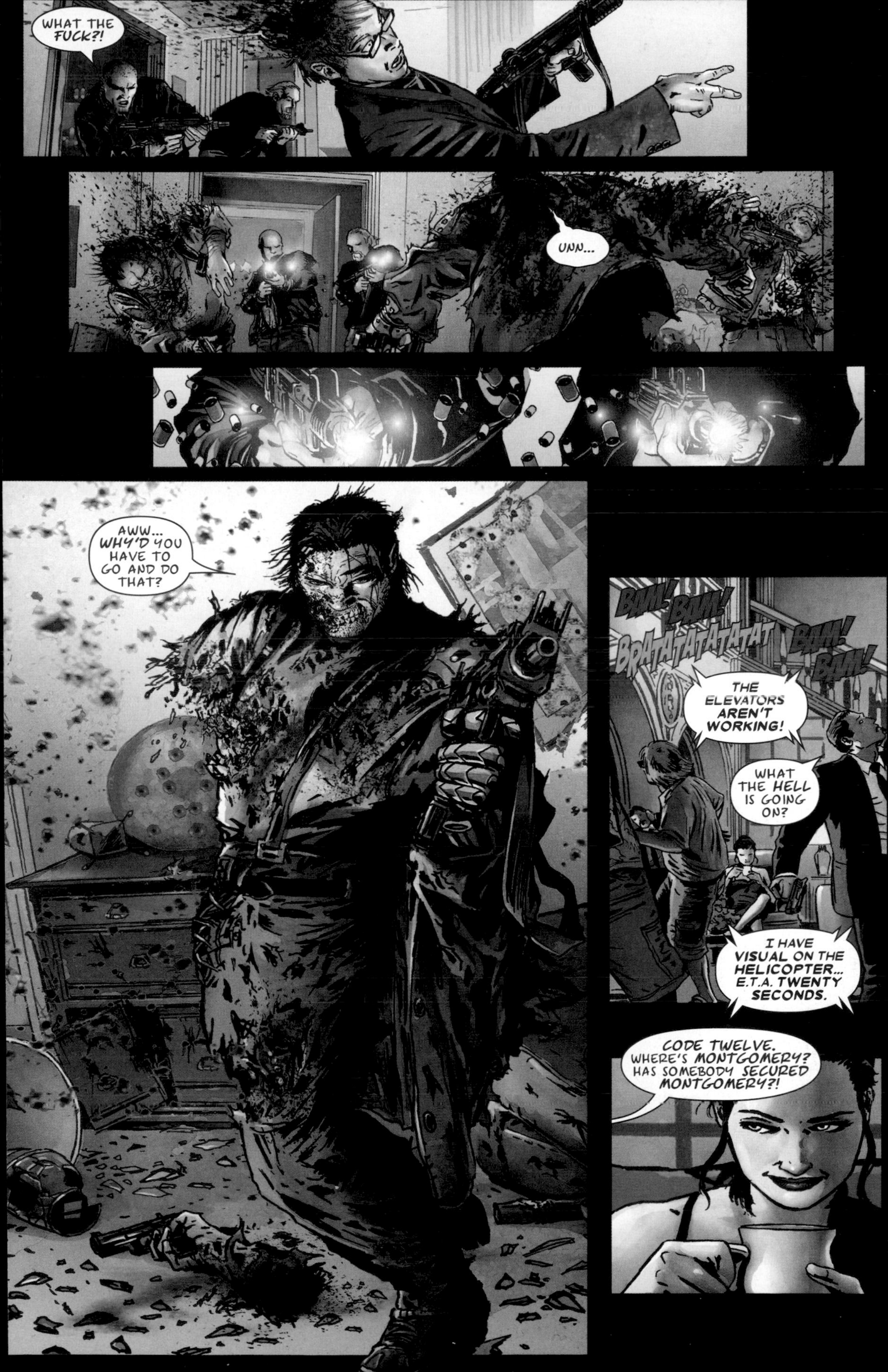
WHAT THE FUCK?!
UNN...
AWW... WHY'D YOU HAVE TO GO AND DO THAT?
BAM! BAM! BRATATATATATAT BAM! BAM!
THE ELEVATORS AREN'T WORKING!
WHAT THE HELL IS GOING ON?
I HAVE VISUAL ON THE HELICOPTER... E.T.A. TWENTY SECONDS.
CODE TWELVE. WHERE'S MONTGOMERY? HAS SOMEBODY SECURED MONTGOMERY?!

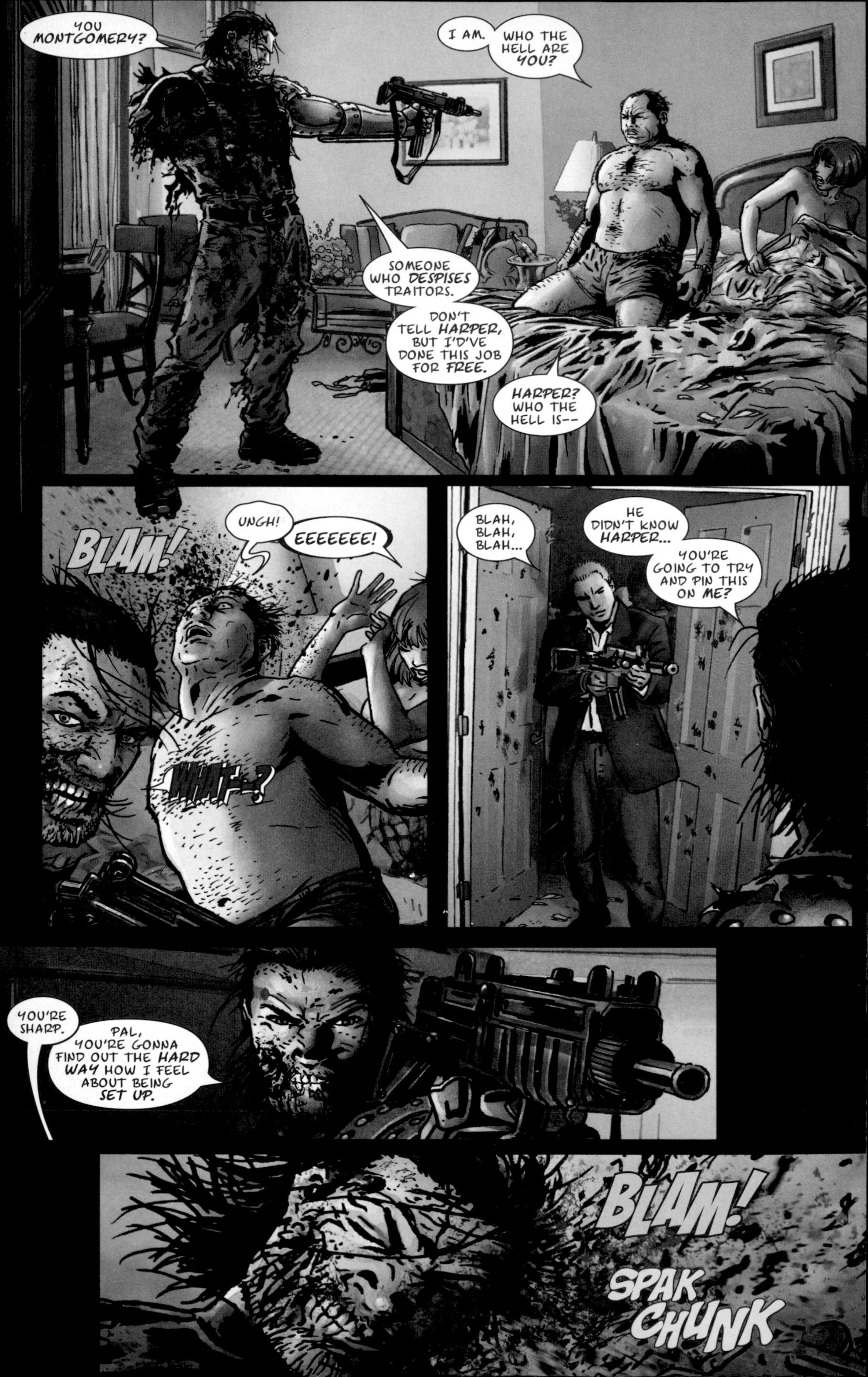
YOU MONTGOMERY?
I AM.
WHO THE HELL ARE YOU?
SOMEONE WHO DESPISES TRAITORS.
DON'T TELL HARPER, BUT I'D'VE DONE THIS JOB FOR FREE.
HARPER? WHO THE HELL IS--
BLAM!
UNGH!
EEEEEEE!
WHAT--?
BLAH, BLAH, BLAH...
HE DIDN'T KNOW HARPER...
YOU'RE GOING TO TRY AND PIN THIS ON ME?
YOU'RE SHARP.
PAL, YOU'RE GONNA FIND OUT THE HARD WAY HOW I FEEL ABOUT BEING SET UP.
BLAM!
SPAK
CHUNK

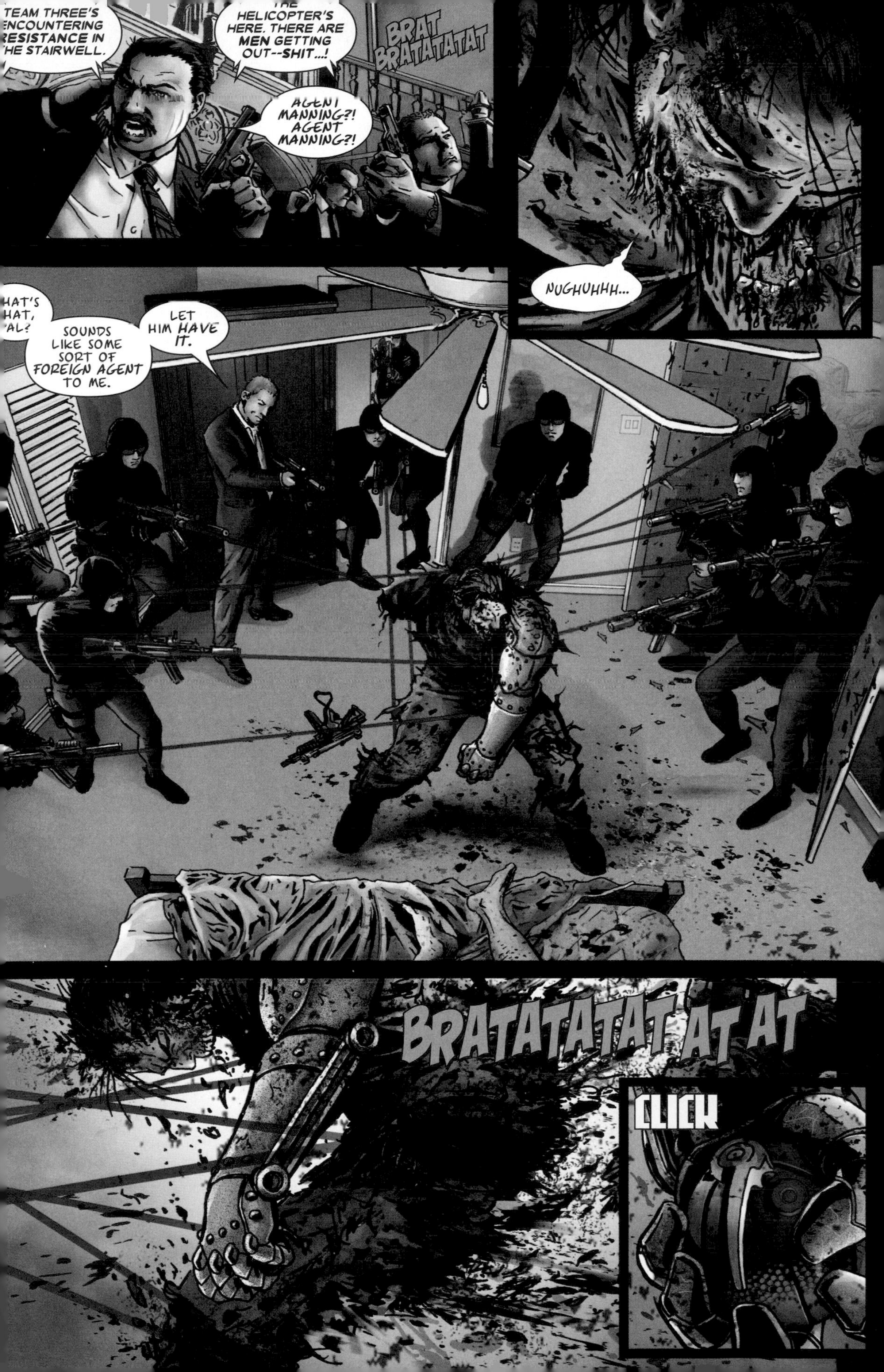
TEAM THREE'S ENCOUNTERING RESISTANCE IN THE STAIRWELL.
THE HELICOPTER'S HERE. THERE ARE MEN GETTING OUT--SHIT...!
BRAT BRATATATAT
AGENT MANNING?! AGENT MANNING?!
NUGHUHHH...
SOUNDS LIKE SOME SORT OF FOREIGN AGENT TO ME.
LET HIM HAVE IT.
BRATATATAT AT AT
CLICK

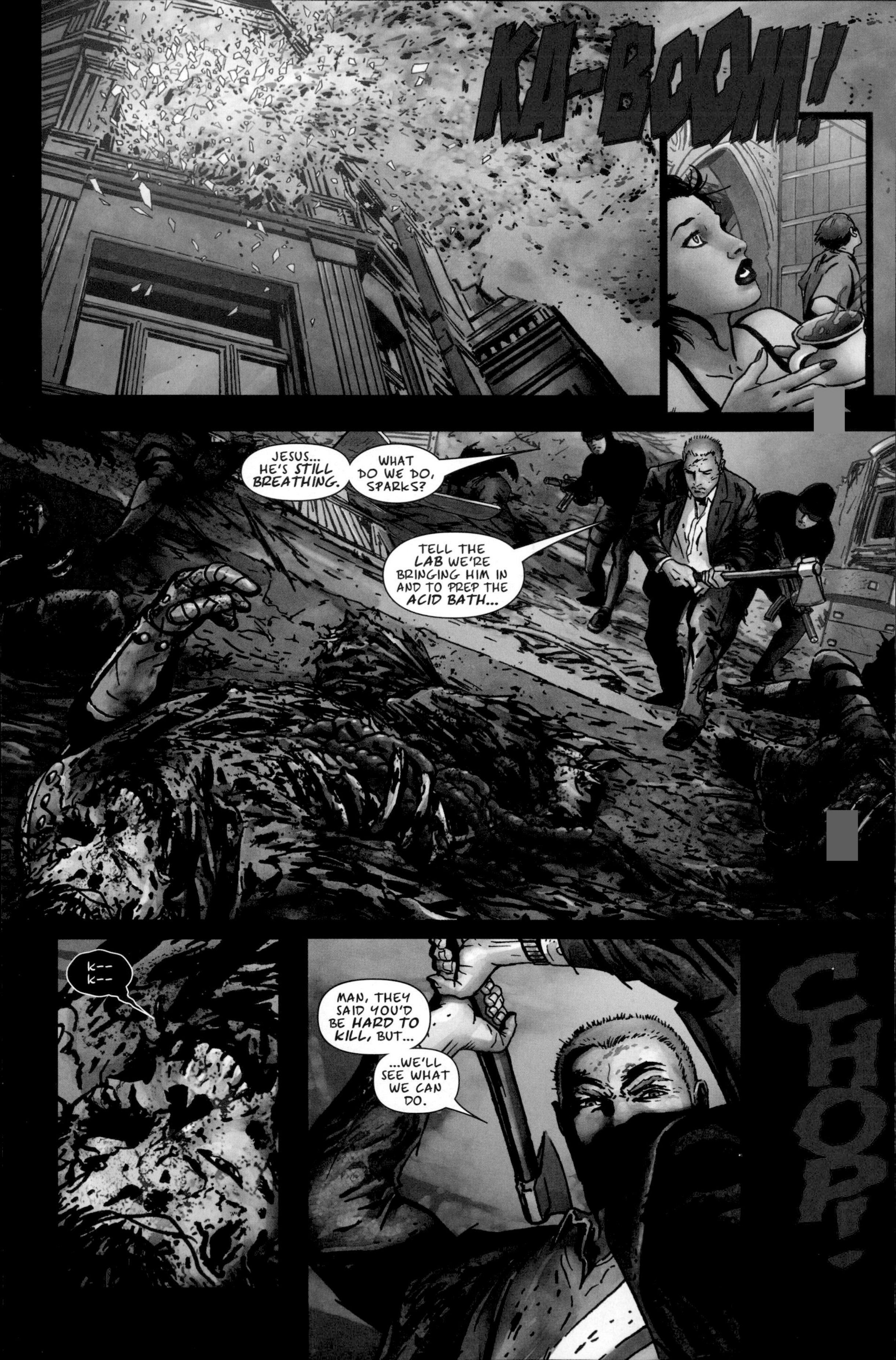
KA-BOOM!
JESUS... HE'S STILL BREATHING.
WHAT DO WE DO, SPARKS?
TELL THE LAB WE'RE BRINGING HIM IN AND TO PREP THE ACID BATH...
K-- K--
MAN, THEY SAID YOU'D BE HARD TO KILL, BUT...
...WE'LL SEE WHAT WE CAN DO.
CHOP!

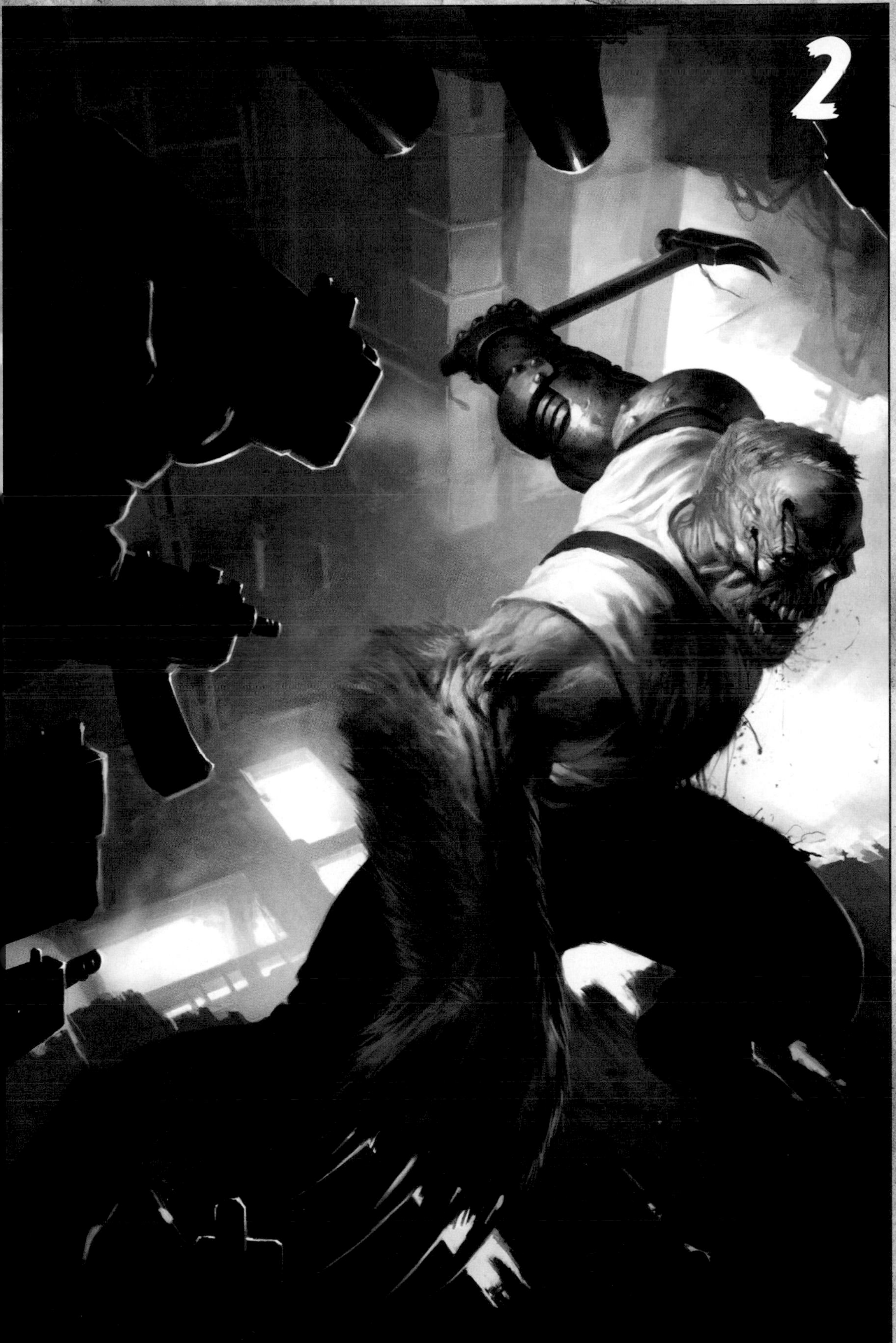
2

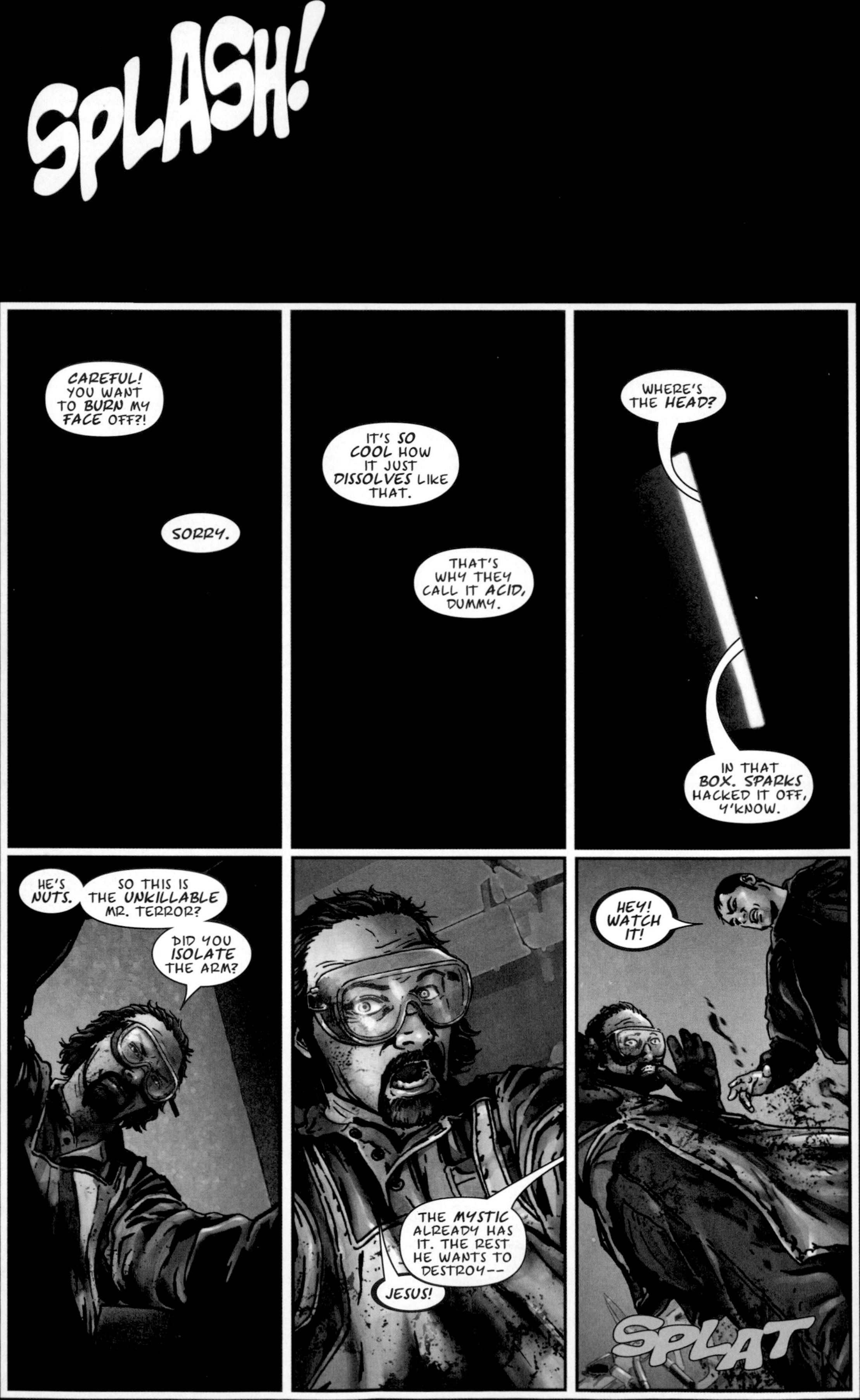
SPLASH!
CAREFUL! YOU WANT TO BURN MY FACE OFF?!
SORRY.
IT'S SO COOL HOW IT JUST DISSOLVES LIKE THAT.
THAT'S WHY THEY CALL IT ACID, DUMMY.
WHERE'S THE HEAD?
IN THAT BOX. SPARKS HACKED IT OFF, Y'KNOW.
HE'S NUTS.
SO THIS IS THE UNKILLABLE MR. TERROR?
DID YOU ISOLATE THE ARM?
THE MYSTIC ALREADY HAS IT. THE REST HE WANTS TO DESTROY--
JESUS!
HEY! WATCH IT!
SPLAT

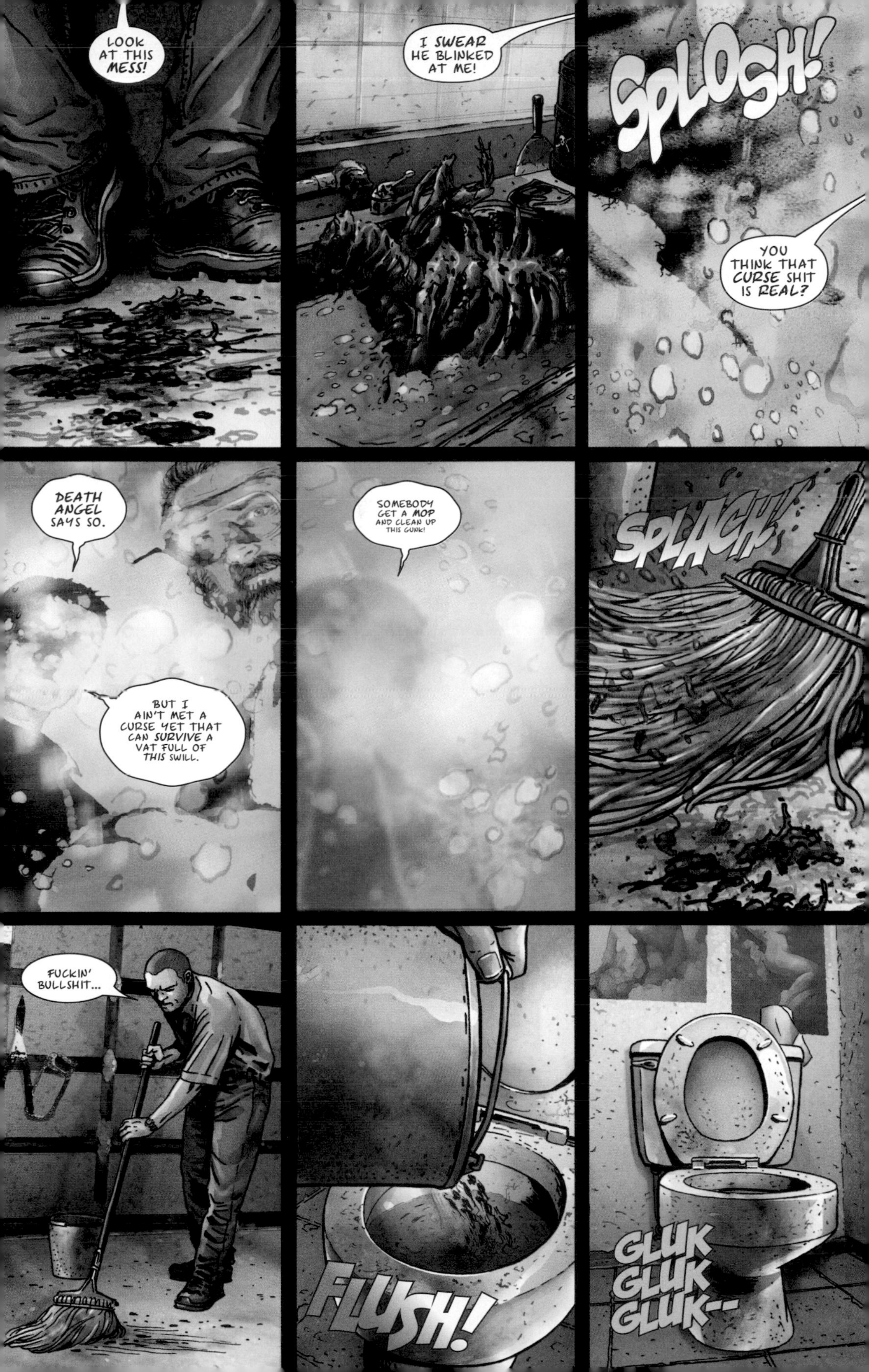
LOOK AT THIS MESS!
I SWEAR HE BLINKED AT ME!
SPLOSH!
YOU THINK THAT CURSE SHIT IS REAL?
DEATH ANGEL SAYS SO.
BUT I AIN'T MET A CURSE YET THAT CAN SURVIVE A VAT FULL OF THIS SWILL.
SOMEBODY GET A MOP AND CLEAN UP THIS GUNK!
SPLACH!
FUCKIN' BULLSHIT...
FLUSH!
GLUK GLUK GLUK--

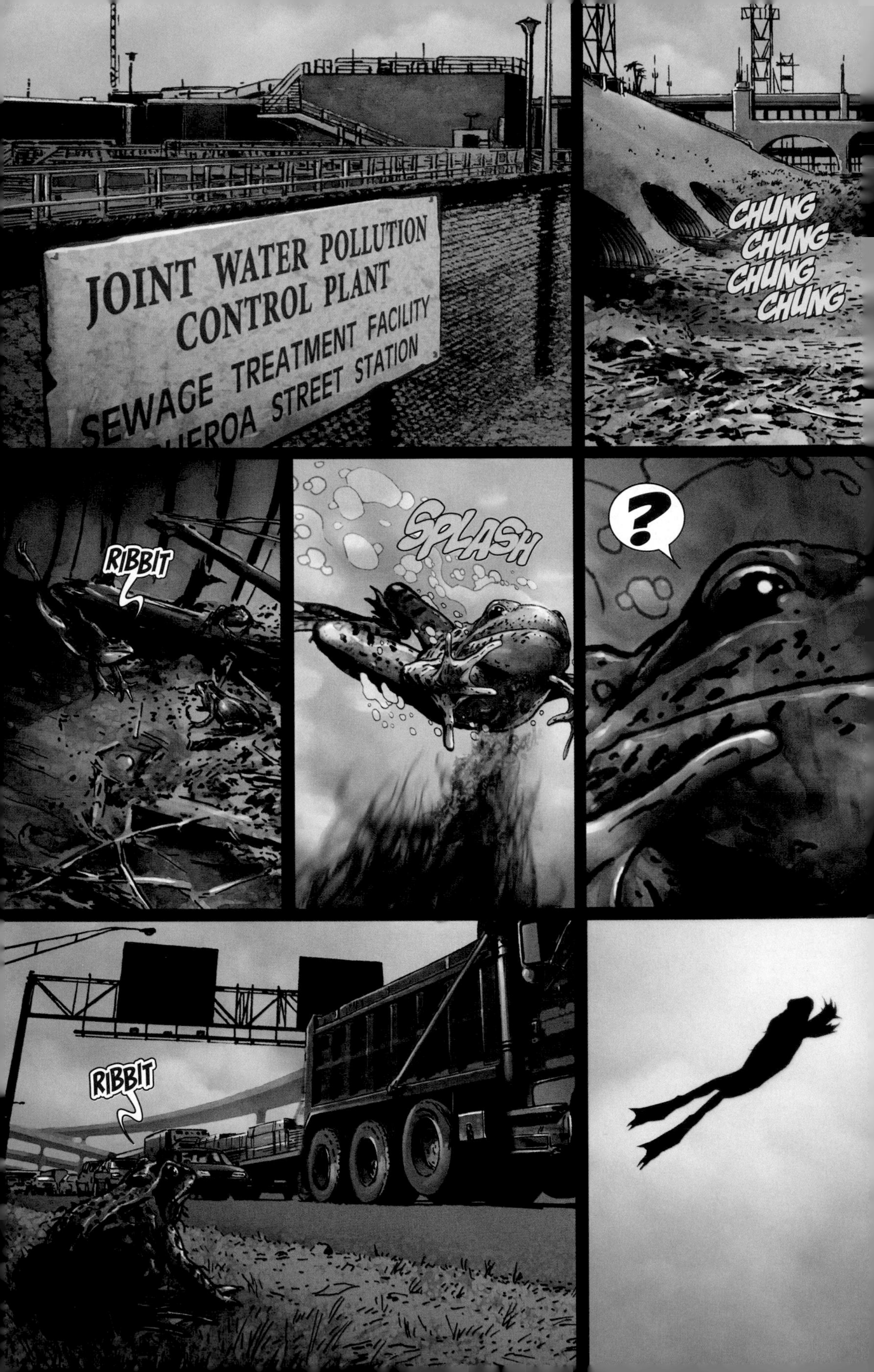
JOINT WATER POLLUTION
CONTROL PLANT
SEWAGE TREATMENT FACILITY
STREET STATION
CHUNG
CHUNG
CHUNG
CHUNG
RIBBIT
SPLASH
?
RIBBIT

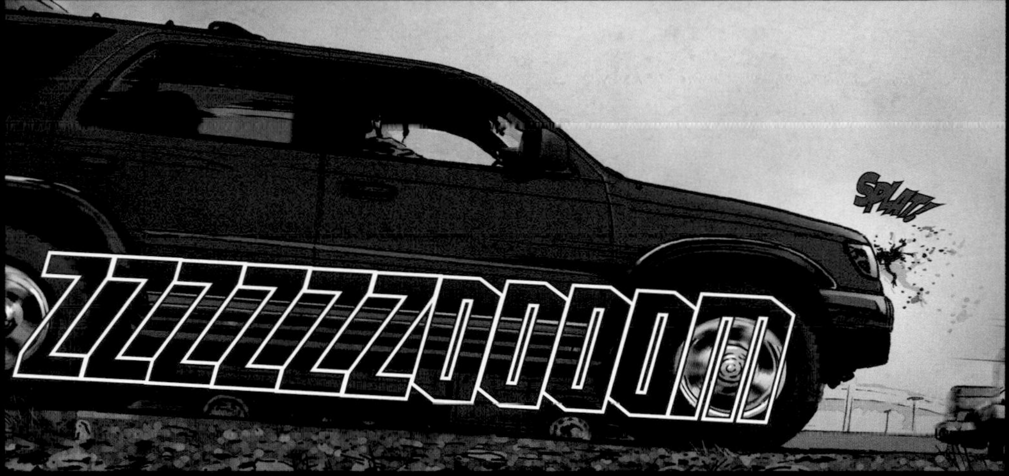
SPLATT
ZZZZZZZOOOOOM

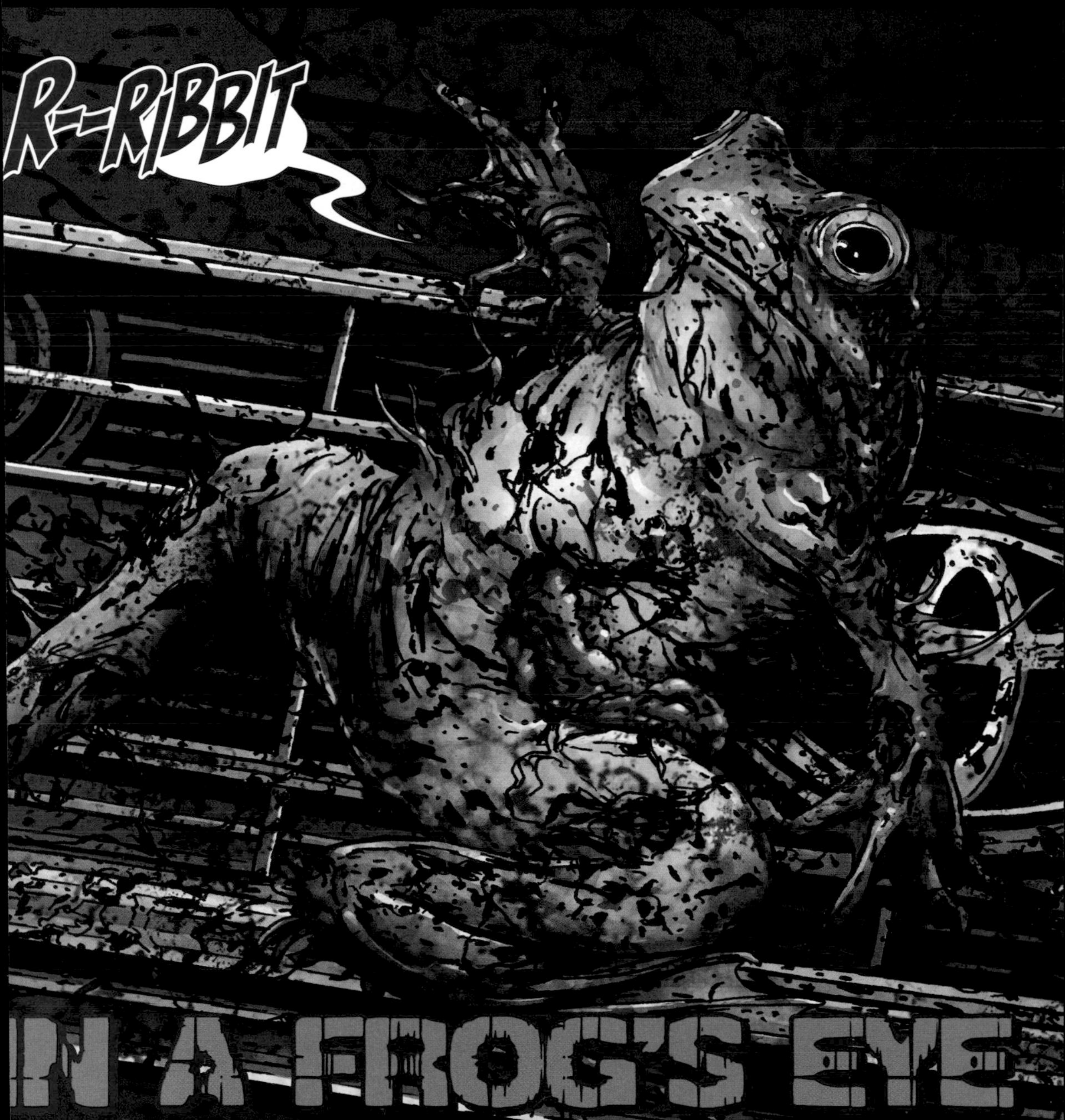
R--RIBBIT
IN A FROG'S EYE

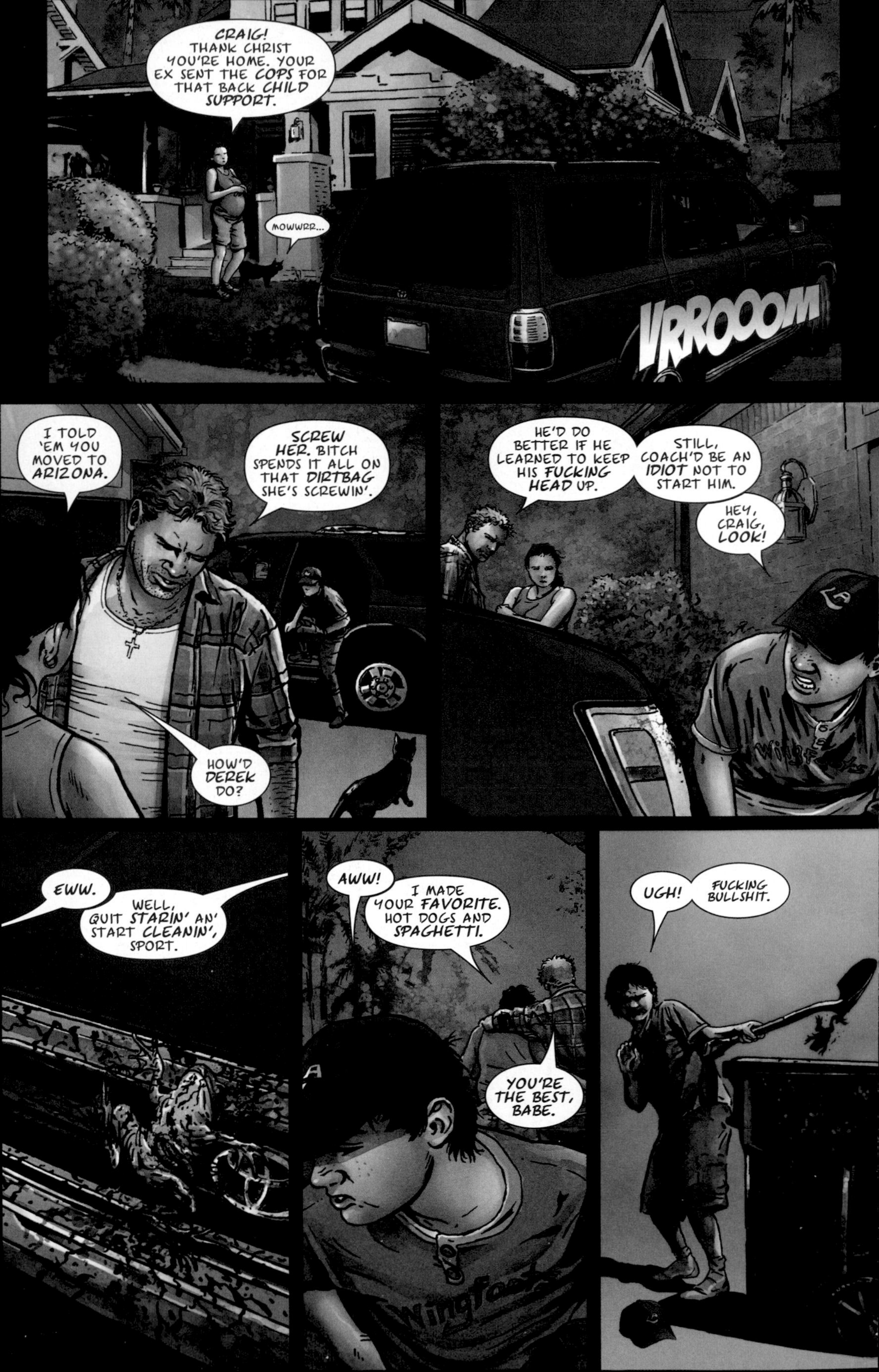
CRAIG! THANK CHRIST YOU'RE HOME. YOUR EX SENT THE COPS FOR THAT BACK CHILD SUPPORT.
MOWWRR...
VRROOOM
I TOLD 'EM YOU MOVED TO ARIZONA.
SCREW HER. BITCH SPENDS IT ALL ON THAT DIRTBAG SHE'S SCREWIN'.
HOW'D DEREK DO?
HE'D DO BETTER IF HE LEARNED TO KEEP HIS FUCKING HEAD UP.
STILL, COACH'D BE AN IDIOT NOT TO START HIM.
HEY, CRAIG, LOOK!
EWW.
WELL, QUIT STARIN' AN' START CLEANIN', SPORT.
AWW!
I MADE YOUR FAVORITE. HOT DOGS AND SPAGHETTI.
YOU'RE THE BEST, BABE.
UGH!
FUCKING BULLSHIT.

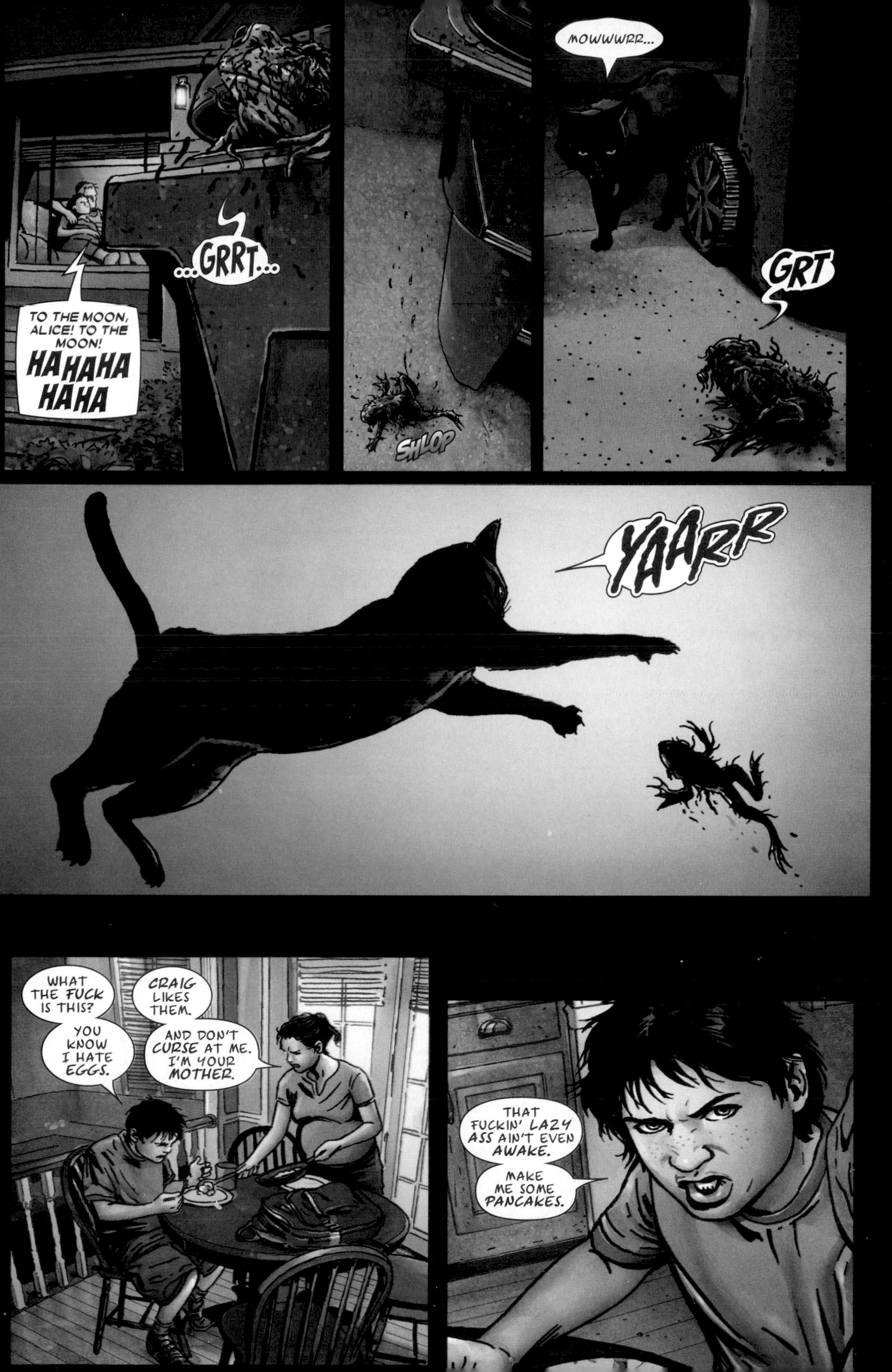
...GRRT...
TO THE MOON, ALICE! TO THE MOON! HAHAHA HAHA
SHLOP
MOWWWRR...
GRT
YAARR
WHAT THE FUCK IS THIS?
CRAIG LIKES THEM.
YOU KNOW I HATE EGGS.
AND DON'T CURSE AT ME. I'M YOUR MOTHER.
THAT FUCKIN' LAZY ASS AIN'T EVEN AWAKE.
MAKE ME SOME PANCAKES.

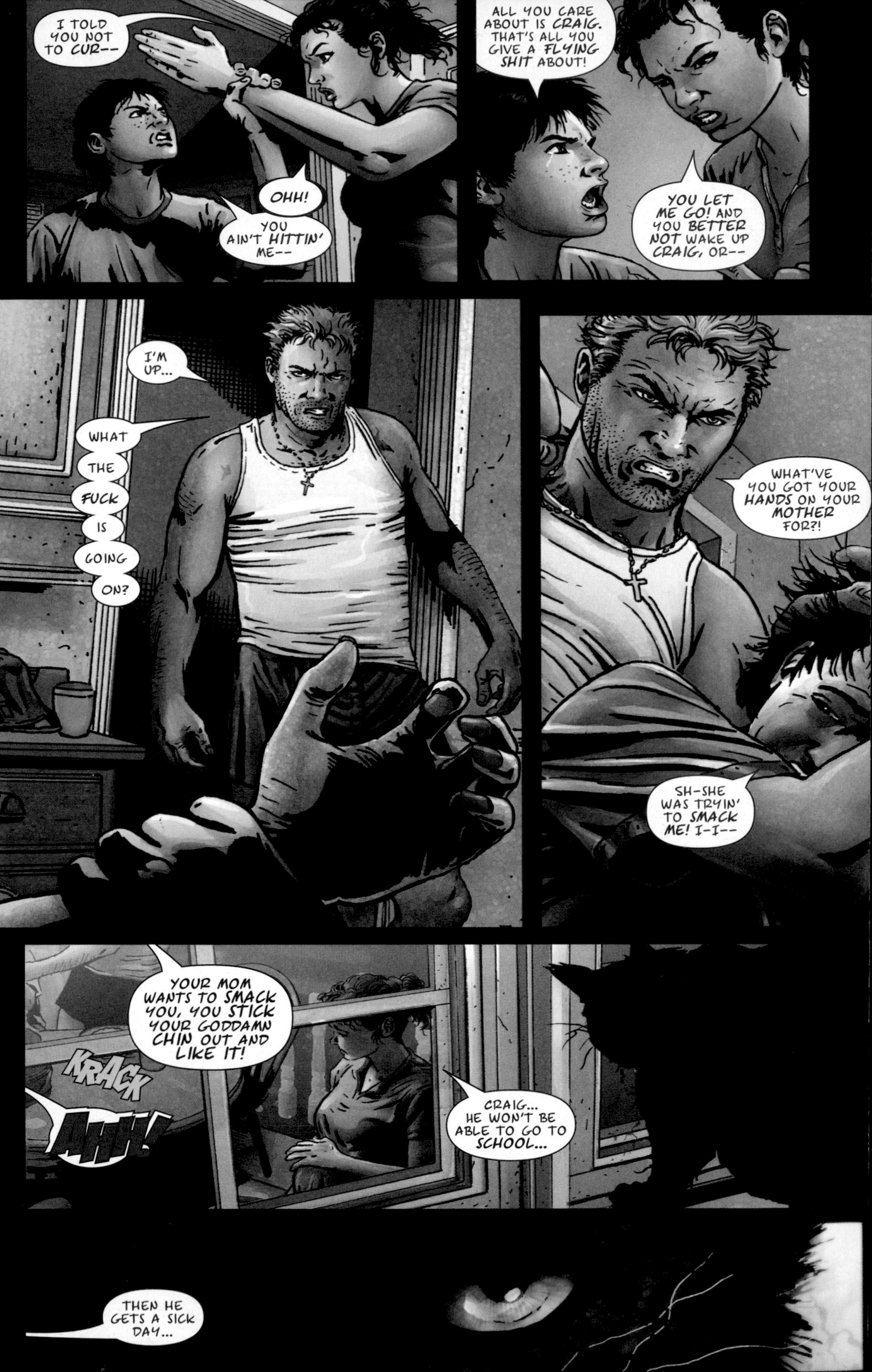
I TOLD YOU NOT TO CUR--
OHH!
YOU AIN'T HITTIN' ME--
ALL YOU CARE ABOUT IS CRAIG. THAT'S ALL YOU GIVE A FLYING SHIT ABOUT!
YOU LET ME GO! AND YOU BETTER NOT WAKE UP CRAIG, OR--
I'M UP...
WHAT THE FUCK IS GOING ON?
WHAT'VE YOU GOT YOUR HANDS ON YOUR MOTHER FOR?!
SH-SHE WAS TRYIN' TO SMACK ME! I-I--
YOUR MOM WANTS TO SMACK YOU, YOU STICK YOUR GODDAMN CHIN OUT AND LIKE IT!
KRACK
AHH!
CRAIG... HE WON'T BE ABLE TO GO TO SCHOOL...
THEN HE GETS A SICK DAY...

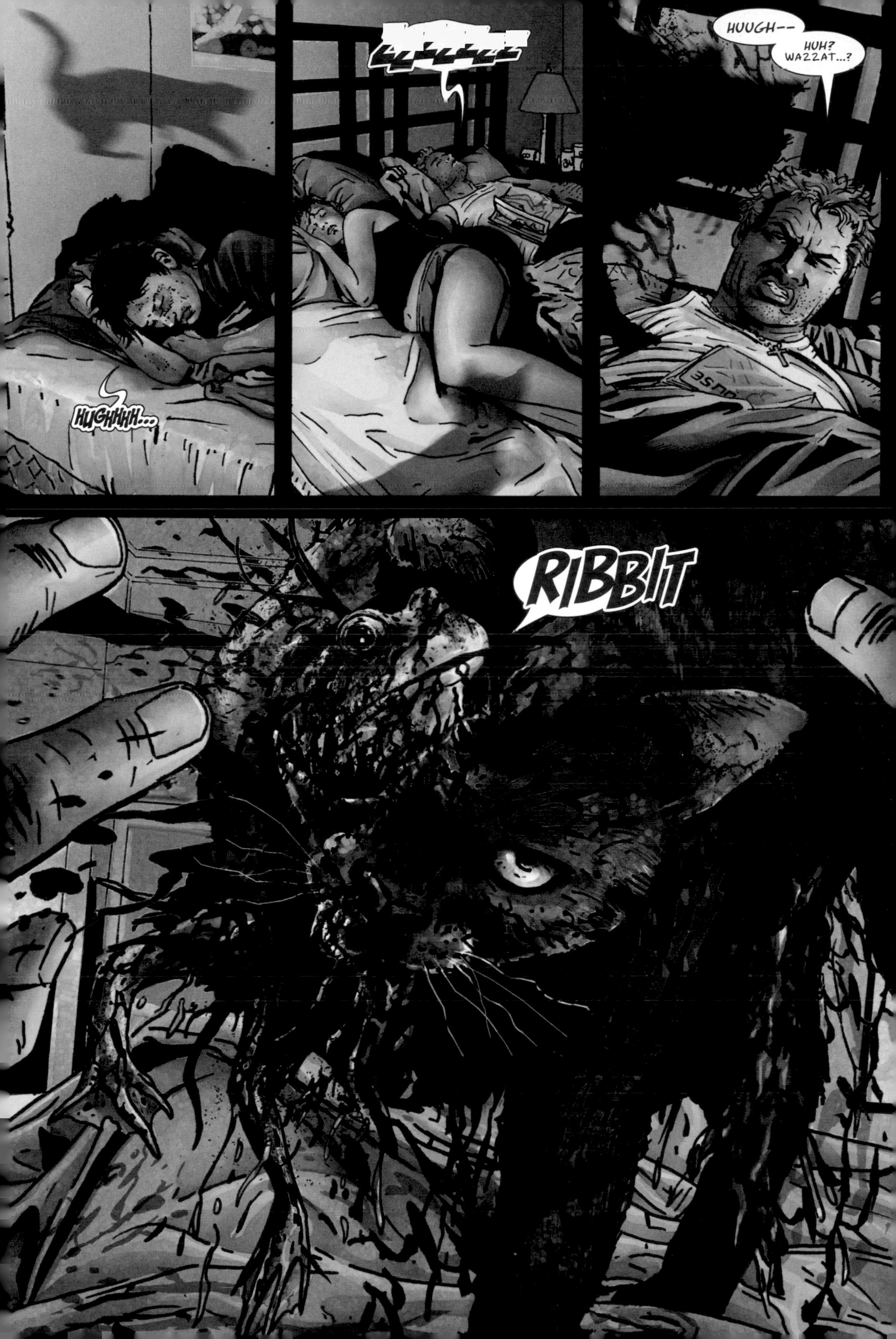
HUGHHHH...
HUUGH--
HUH? WAZZAT...?
RIBBIT

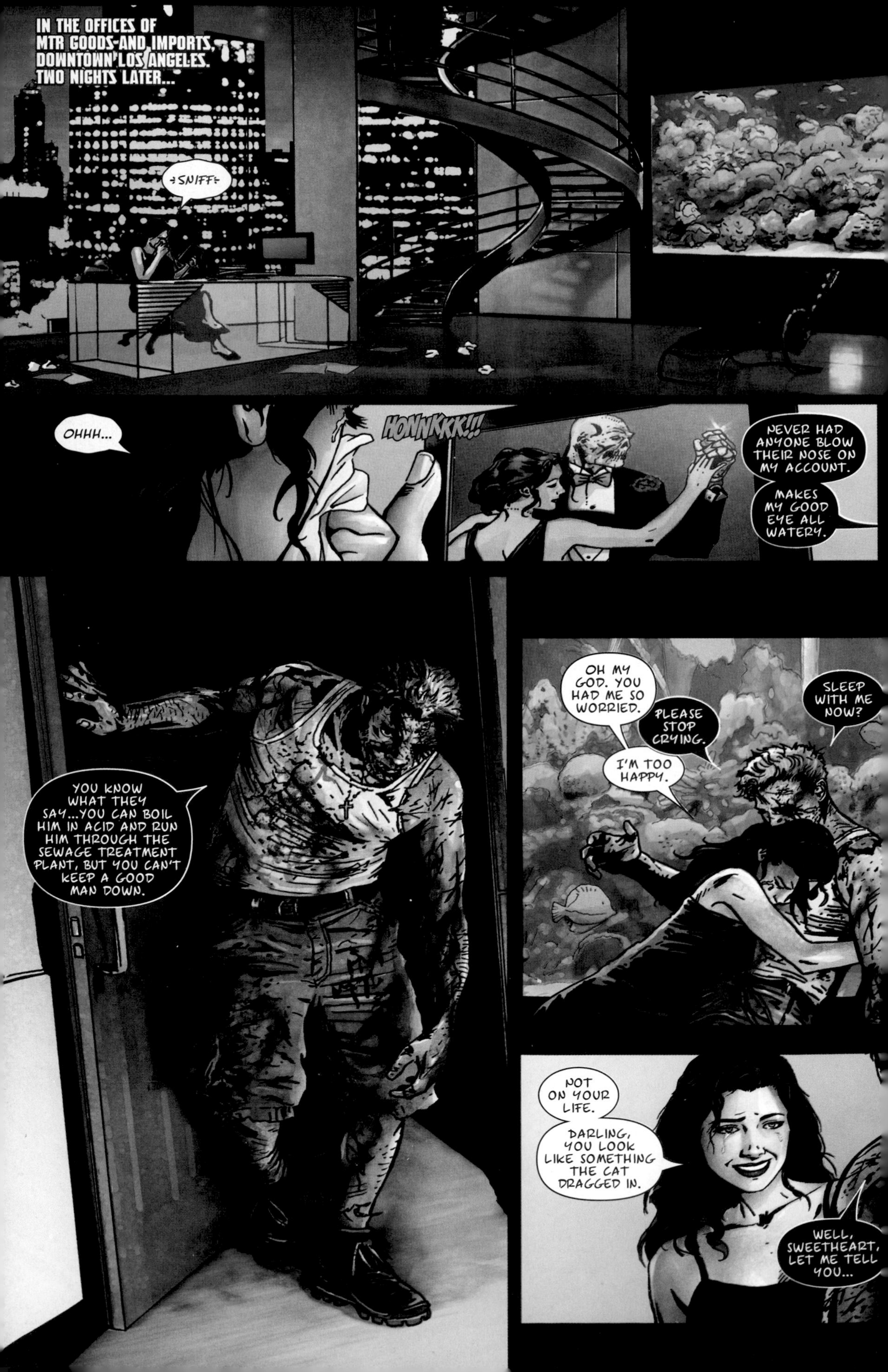

IN THE OFFICES OF MTR GOODS-AND IMPORTS, DOWNTOWN LOS ANGELES. TWO NIGHTS LATER...
SNIFF
OHHH...
HONNKKK!!!
NEVER HAD ANYONE BLOW THEIR NOSE ON MY ACCOUNT.
MAKES MY GOOD EYE ALL WATERY.
YOU KNOW WHAT THEY SAY...YOU CAN BOIL HIM IN ACID AND RUN HIM THROUGH THE SEWAGE TREATMENT PLANT, BUT YOU CAN'T KEEP A GOOD MAN DOWN.
OH MY GOD. YOU HAD ME SO WORRIED.
PLEASE STOP CRYING.
I'M TOO HAPPY.
SLEEP WITH ME NOW?
NOT ON YOUR LIFE.
DARLING, YOU LOOK LIKE SOMETHING THE CAT DRAGGED IN.
WELL, SWEETHEART, LET ME TELL YOU...

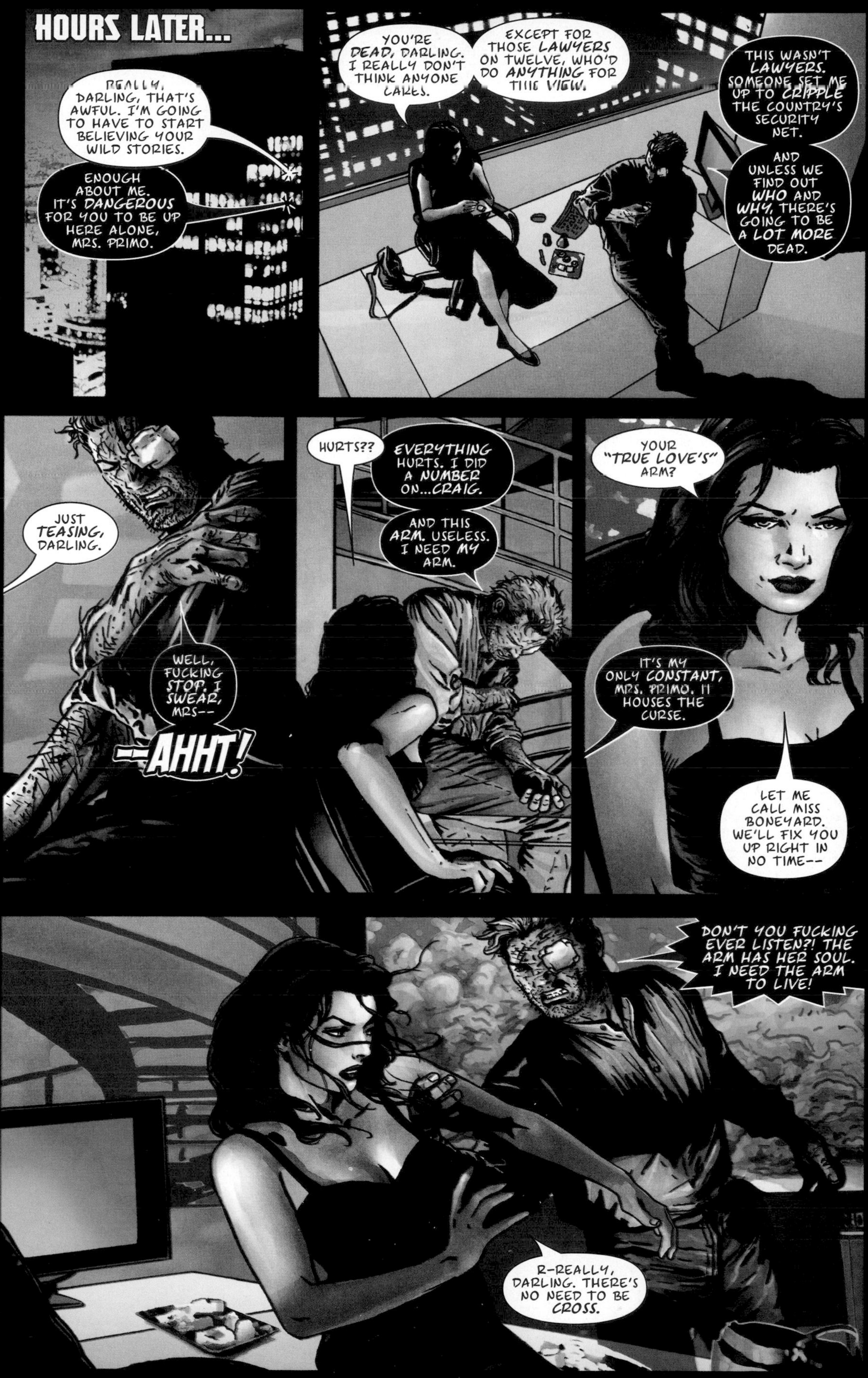
HOURS LATER...
REALLY, DARLING, THAT'S AWFUL. I'M GOING TO HAVE TO START BELIEVING YOUR WILD STORIES.
ENOUGH ABOUT ME. IT'S DANGEROUS FOR YOU TO BE UP HERE ALONE, MRS. PRIMO.
YOU'RE DEAD, DARLING. I REALLY DON'T THINK ANYONE CARES.
EXCEPT FOR THOSE LAWYERS ON TWELVE, WHO'D DO ANYTHING FOR THE VIEW.
THIS WASN'T LAWYERS. SOMEONE SET ME UP TO CRIPPLE THE COUNTRY'S SECURITY NET.
AND UNLESS WE FIND OUT WHO AND WHY, THERE'S GOING TO BE A LOT MORE DEAD.
JUST TEASING, DARLING.
WELL, FUCKING STOP, I SWEAR, MRS--
--AHHT!
HURTS??
EVERYTHING HURTS. I DID A NUMBER ON...CRAIG.
AND THIS ARM. USELESS. I NEED MY ARM.
YOUR "TRUE LOVE'S" ARM?
IT'S MY ONLY CONSTANT, MRS. PRIMO. IT HOUSES THE CURSE.
LET ME CALL MISS BONEYARD. WE'LL FIX YOU UP RIGHT IN NO TIME--
DON'T YOU FUCKING EVER LISTEN?! THE ARM HAS HER SOUL. I NEED THE ARM TO LIVE!
R-REALLY, DARLING. THERE'S NO NEED TO BE CROSS.

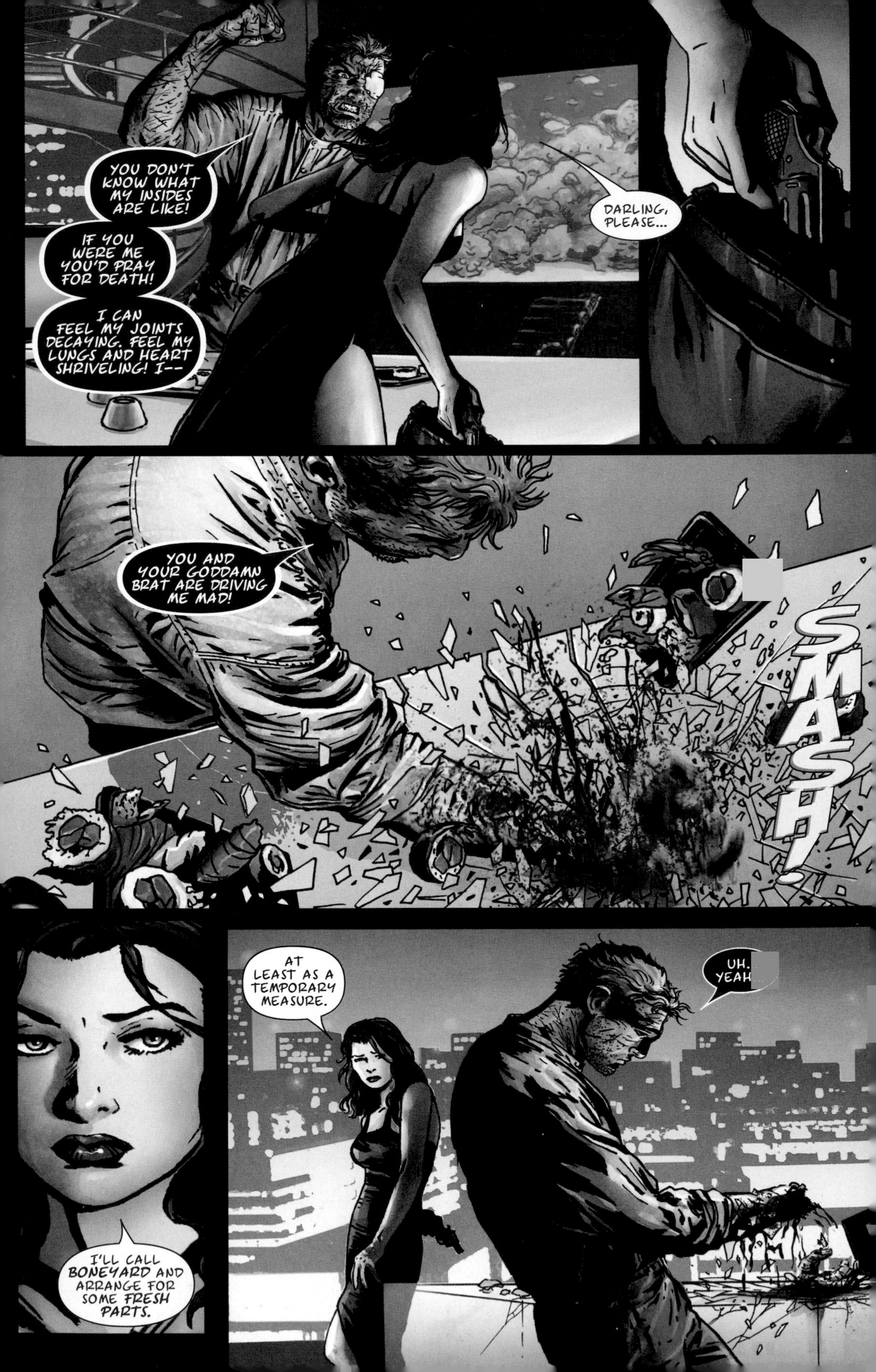

YOU DON'T KNOW WHAT MY INSIDES ARE LIKE!
IF YOU WERE ME YOU'D PRAY FOR DEATH!
I CAN FEEL MY JOINTS DECAYING. FEEL MY LUNGS AND HEART SHRIVELING! I--
DARLING, PLEASE...
YOU AND YOUR GODDAMN BRAT ARE DRIVING ME MAD!
SMASH!
I'LL CALL BONEYARD AND ARRANGE FOR SOME FRESH PARTS.
AT LEAST AS A TEMPORARY MEASURE.
UH. YEAH

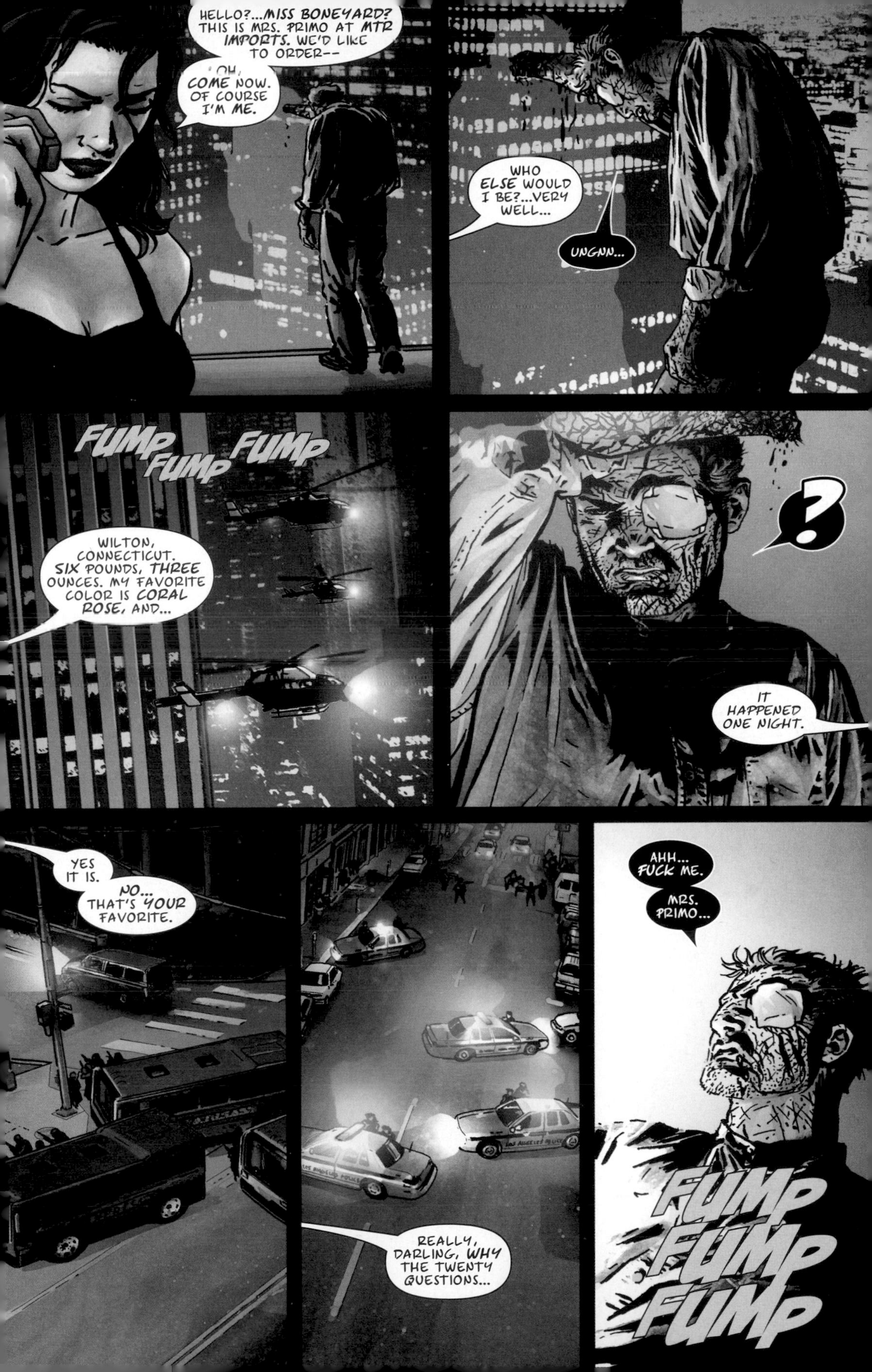
HELLO?...MISS BONEYARD? THIS IS MRS. PRIMO AT MTR IMPORTS. WE'D LIKE TO ORDER--
OH, COME NOW. OF COURSE I'M ME.
WHO ELSE WOULD I BE?...VERY WELL...
UNGNN...
FUMP FUMP FUMP
WILTON, CONNECTICUT. SIX POUNDS, THREE OUNCES. MY FAVORITE COLOR IS CORAL ROSE, AND...
?
IT HAPPENED ONE NIGHT.
YES IT IS.
NO... THAT'S YOUR FAVORITE.
REALLY, DARLING, WHY THE TWENTY QUESTIONS...
AHH... FUCK ME.
MRS. PRIMO...
FUMP FUMP FUMP

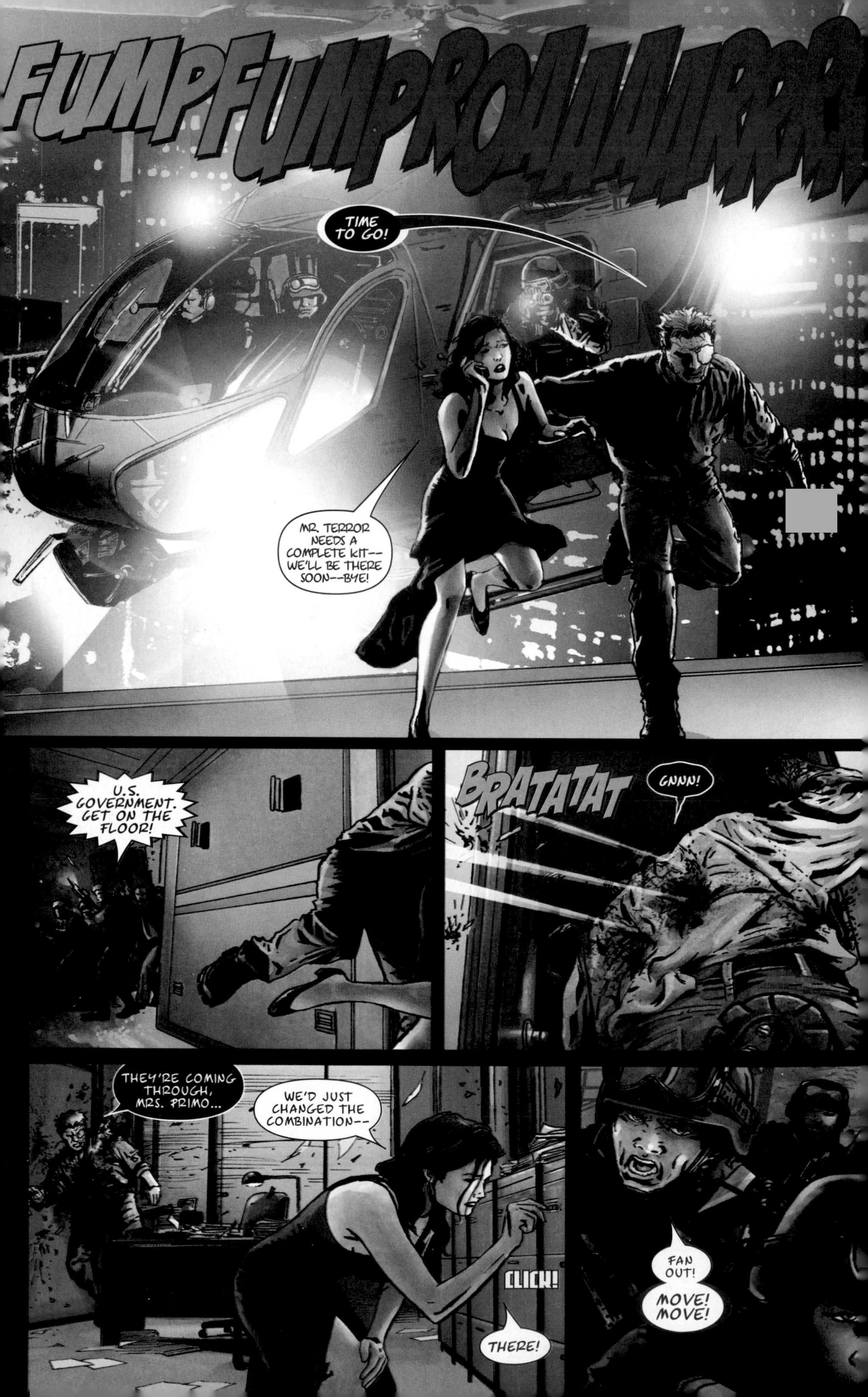
FUMPFUMPROAAARRR
TIME TO GO!
MR. TERROR NEEDS A COMPLETE KIT-- WE'LL BE THERE SOON--BYE!
U.S. GOVERNMENT. GET ON THE FLOOR!
BRATATAT
GNNN!
THEY'RE COMING THROUGH, MRS. PRIMO...
WE'D JUST CHANGED THE COMBINATION--
CLICK!
THERE!
FAN OUT!
MOVE! MOVE!

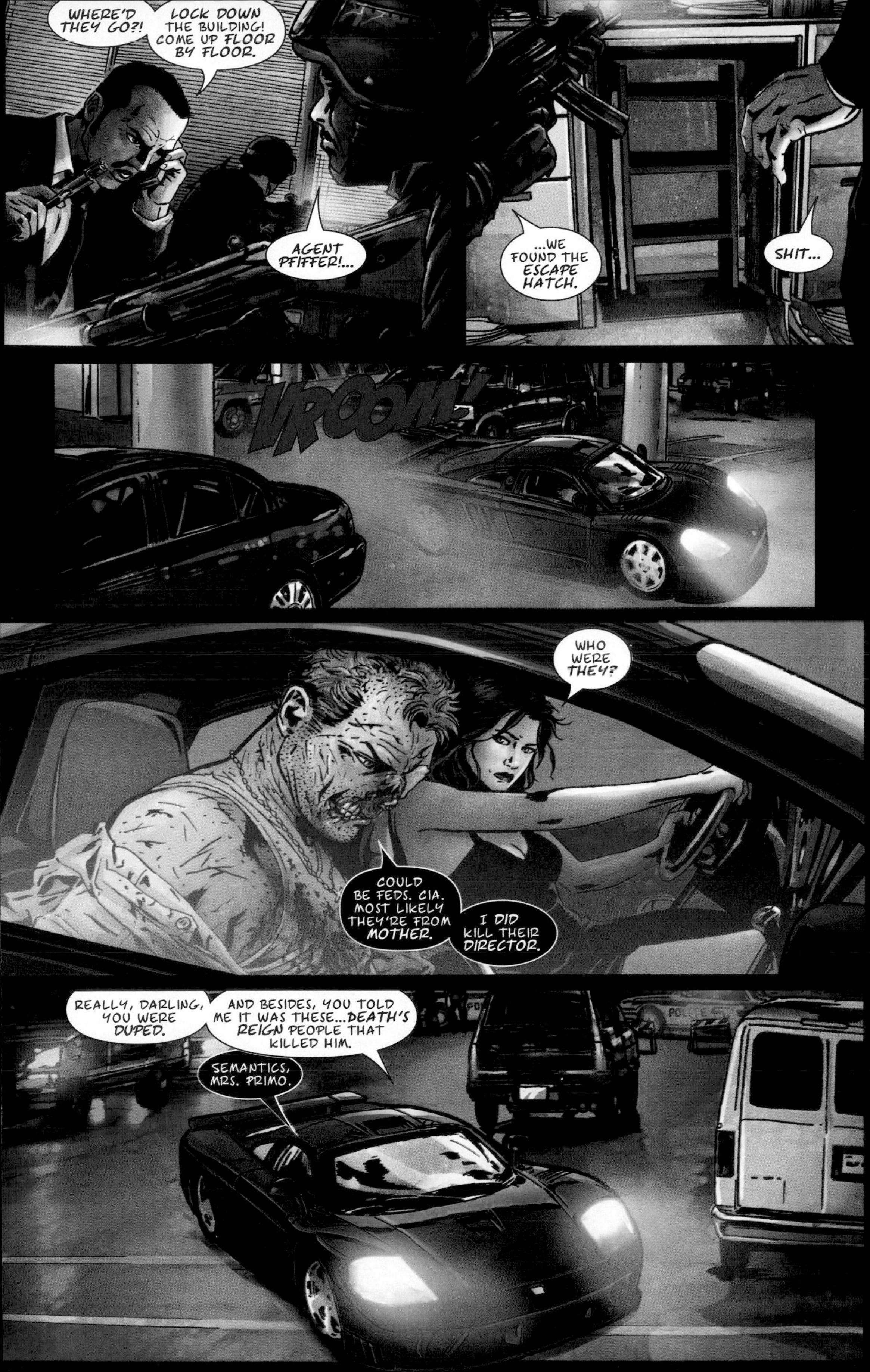
WHERE'D THEY GO?!
LOCK DOWN THE BUILDING! COME UP FLOOR BY FLOOR.
AGENT PFIFFER!...
...WE FOUND THE ESCAPE HATCH.
SHIT...
VROOM!
WHO WERE THEY?
COULD BE FEDS. CIA. MOST LIKELY THEY'RE FROM MOTHER.
I DID KILL THEIR DIRECTOR.
REALLY, DARLING, YOU WERE DUPED.
AND BESIDES, YOU TOLD ME IT WAS THESE...DEATH'S REIGN PEOPLE THAT KILLED HIM.
SEMANTICS, MRS. PRIMO.

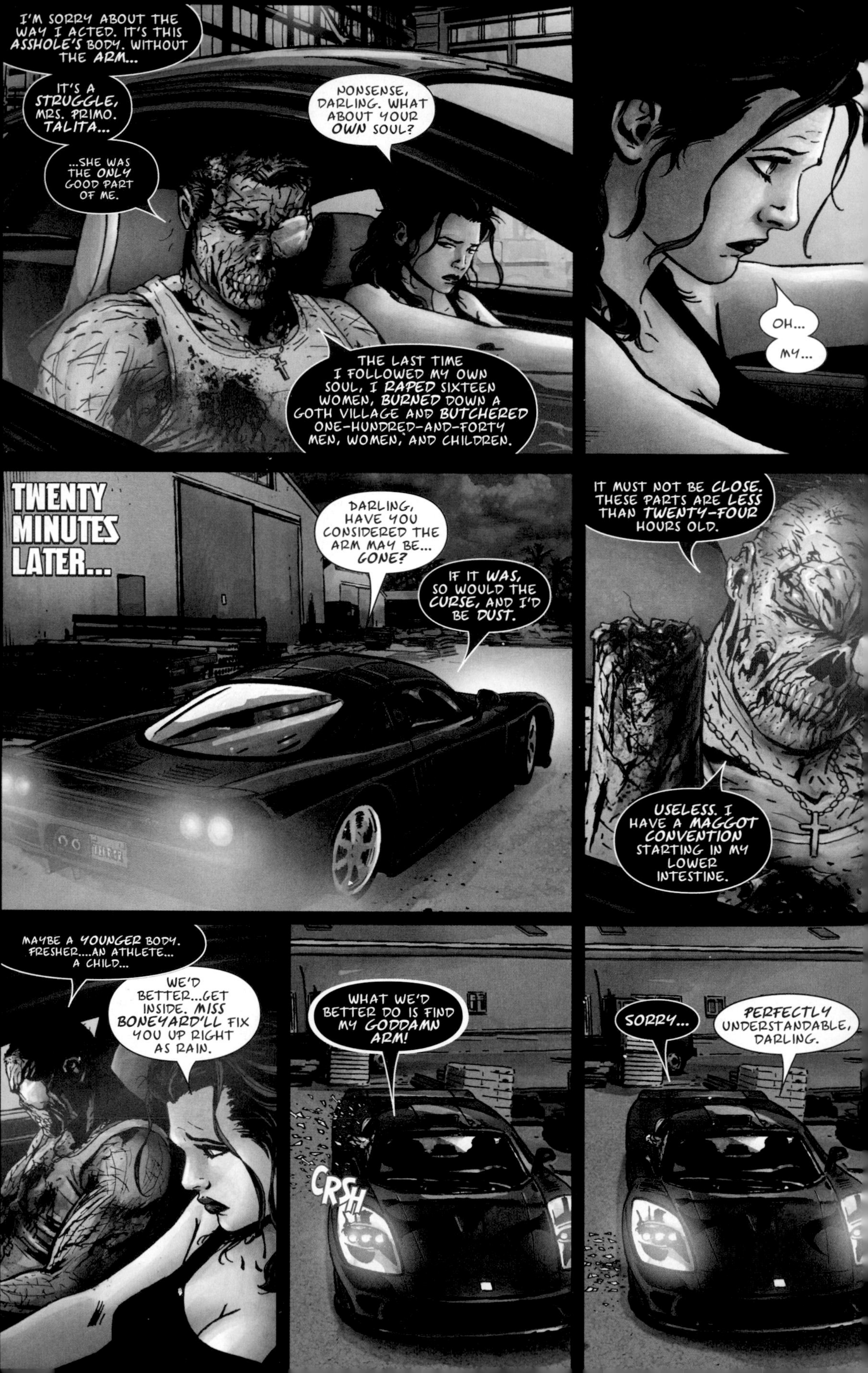

I'M SORRY ABOUT THE WAY I ACTED. IT'S THIS ASSHOLE'S BODY. WITHOUT THE ARM...
IT'S A STRUGGLE, MRS. PRIMO. TALITA...
...SHE WAS THE ONLY GOOD PART OF ME.
NONSENSE, DARLING. WHAT ABOUT YOUR OWN SOUL?
THE LAST TIME I FOLLOWED MY OWN SOUL, I RAPED SIXTEEN WOMEN, BURNED DOWN A GOTH VILLAGE AND BUTCHERED ONE-HUNDRED-AND-FORTY MEN, WOMEN, AND CHILDREN.
OH...
MY...
TWENTY MINUTES LATER...
DARLING, HAVE YOU CONSIDERED THE ARM MAY BE... GONE?
IF IT WAS, SO WOULD THE CURSE, AND I'D BE DUST.
IT MUST NOT BE CLOSE. THESE PARTS ARE LESS THAN TWENTY-FOUR HOURS OLD.
USELESS. I HAVE A MAGGOT CONVENTION STARTING IN MY LOWER INTESTINE.
MAYBE A YOUNGER BODY. FRESHER....AN ATHLETE... A CHILD...
WE'D BETTER...GET INSIDE. MISS BONEYARD'LL FIX YOU UP RIGHT AS RAIN.
WHAT WE'D BETTER DO IS FIND MY GODDAMN ARM!
CRSH
SORRY...
PERFECTLY UNDERSTANDABLE, DARLING.

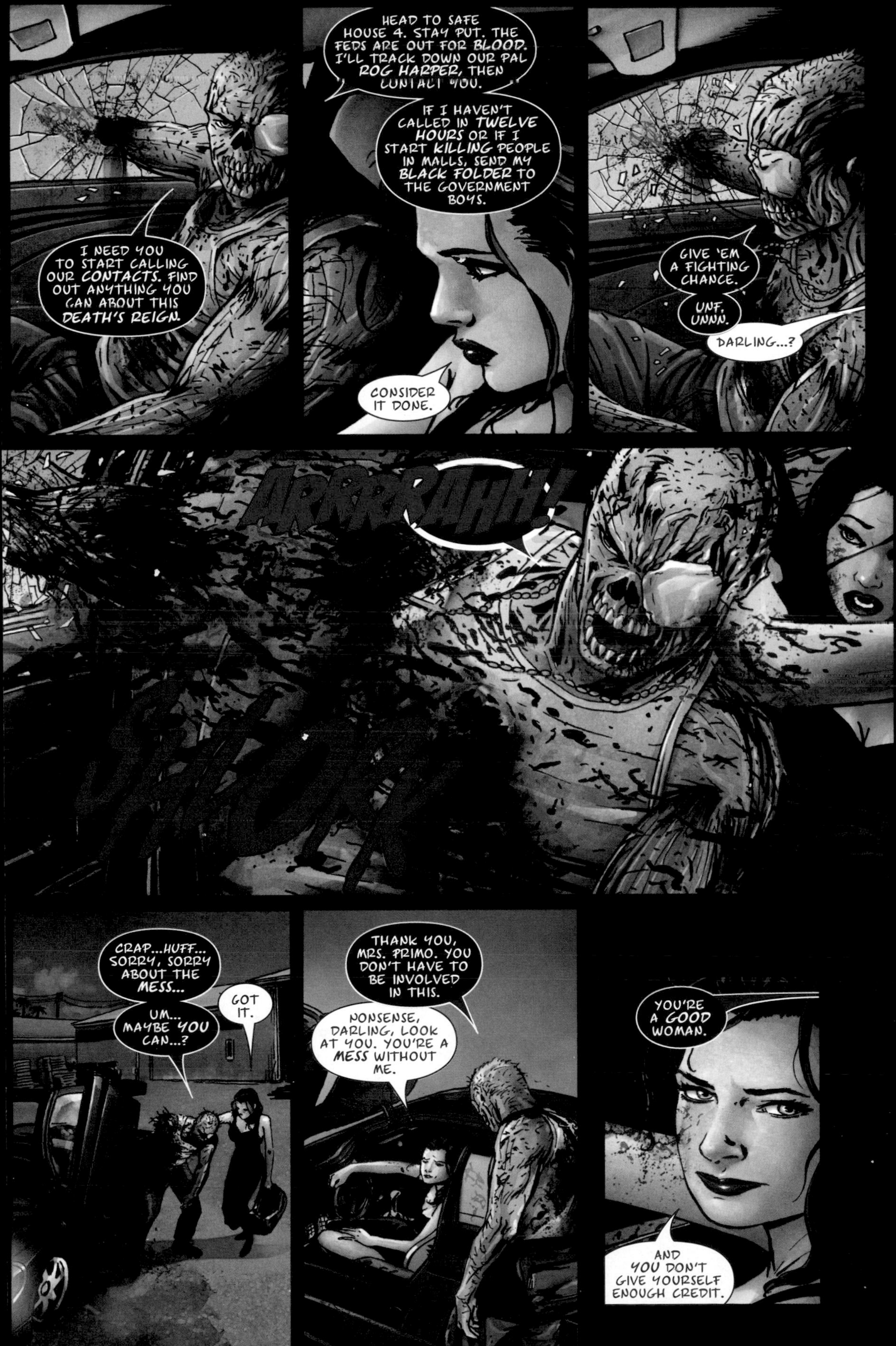
I NEED YOU TO START CALLING OUR CONTACTS. FIND OUT ANYTHING YOU CAN ABOUT THIS DEATH'S REIGN.
HEAD TO SAFE HOUSE 4. STAY PUT. THE FEDS ARE OUT FOR BLOOD. I'LL TRACK DOWN OUR PAL ROG HARPER, THEN CONTACT YOU.
IF I HAVEN'T CALLED IN TWELVE HOURS OR IF I START KILLING PEOPLE IN MALLS, SEND MY BLACK FOLDER TO THE GOVERNMENT BOYS.
CONSIDER IT DONE.
GIVE 'EM A FIGHTING CHANCE.
UNF. UNNN.
DARLING...?
ARRRRAHH!
CRAP...HUFF... SORRY, SORRY ABOUT THE MESS...
UM... MAYBE YOU CAN...?
GOT IT.
THANK YOU, MRS. PRIMO. YOU DON'T HAVE TO BE INVOLVED IN THIS.
NONSENSE, DARLING, LOOK AT YOU. YOU'RE A MESS WITHOUT ME.
YOU'RE A GOOD WOMAN.
AND YOU DON'T GIVE YOURSELF ENOUGH CREDIT.

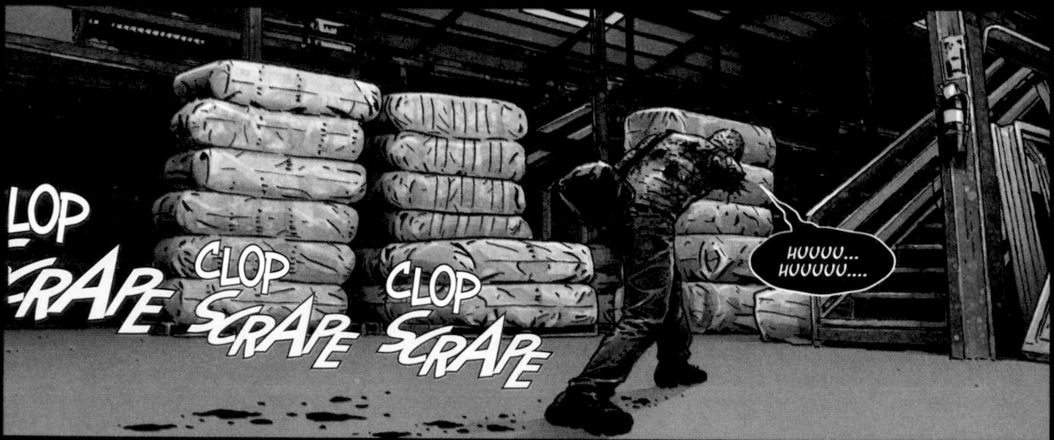
CLOP
SCRAPE
CLOP
SCRAPE
CLOP
SCRAPE
HUUUU...
HUUUUU....
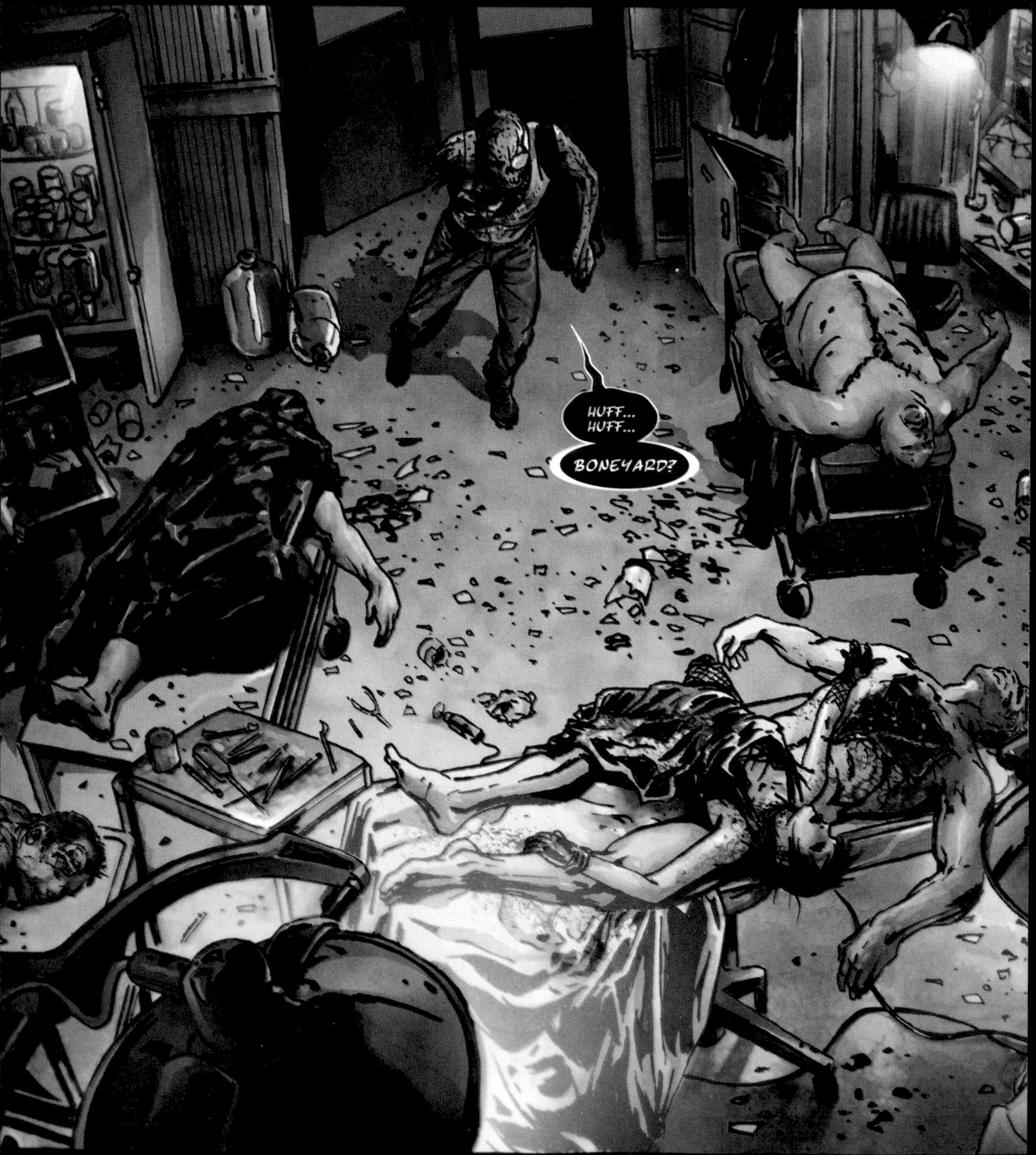
HUFF...
HUFF...
BONEYARD?

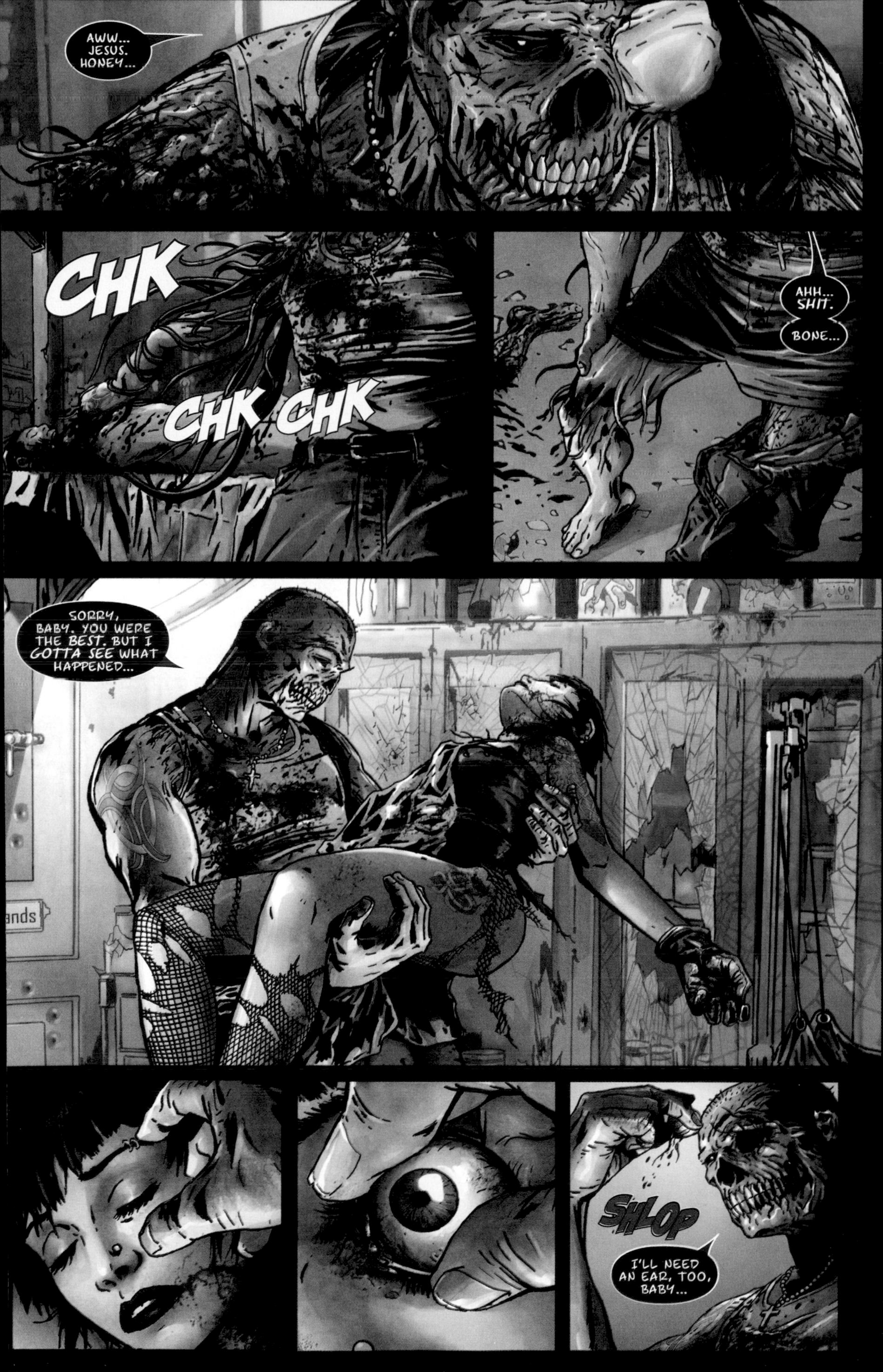
AWW... JESUS. HONEY...
CHK
CHK CHK
AHH... SHIT.
BONE...
SORRY, BABY. YOU WERE THE BEST. BUT I GOTTA SEE WHAT HAPPENED...
ands
SHLOP
I'LL NEED AN EAR, TOO, BABY...

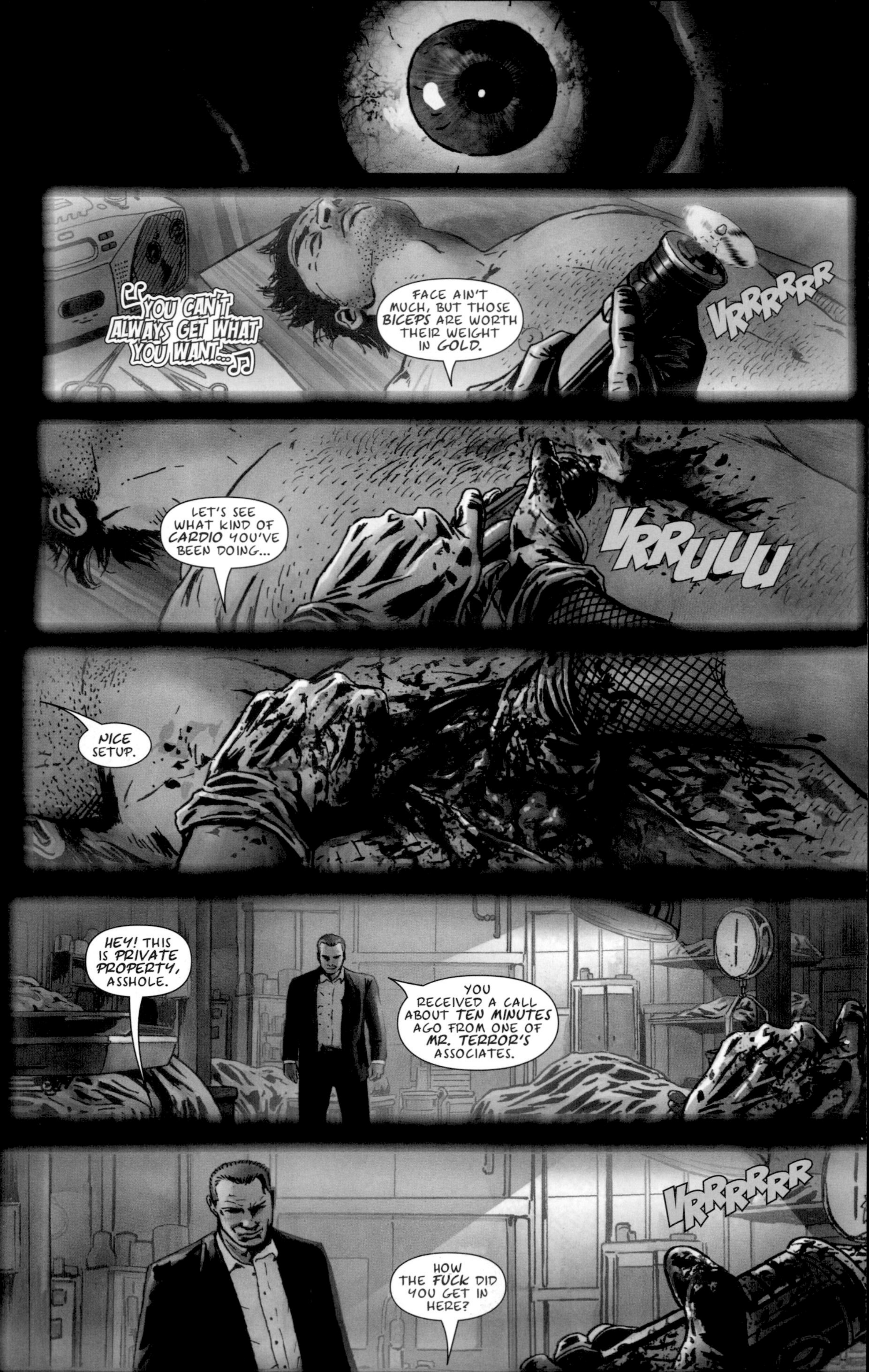

YOU CAN'T ALWAYS GET WHAT YOU WANT...
FACE AIN'T MUCH, BUT THOSE BICEPS ARE WORTH THEIR WEIGHT IN GOLD.
VRRRRRR
LET'S SEE WHAT KIND OF CARDIO YOU'VE BEEN DOING...
VRRUUU
NICE SETUP.
HEY! THIS IS PRIVATE PROPERTY, ASSHOLE.
YOU RECEIVED A CALL ABOUT TEN MINUTES AGO FROM ONE OF MR. TERROR'S ASSOCIATES.
VRRRRRR
HOW THE FUCK DID YOU GET IN HERE?

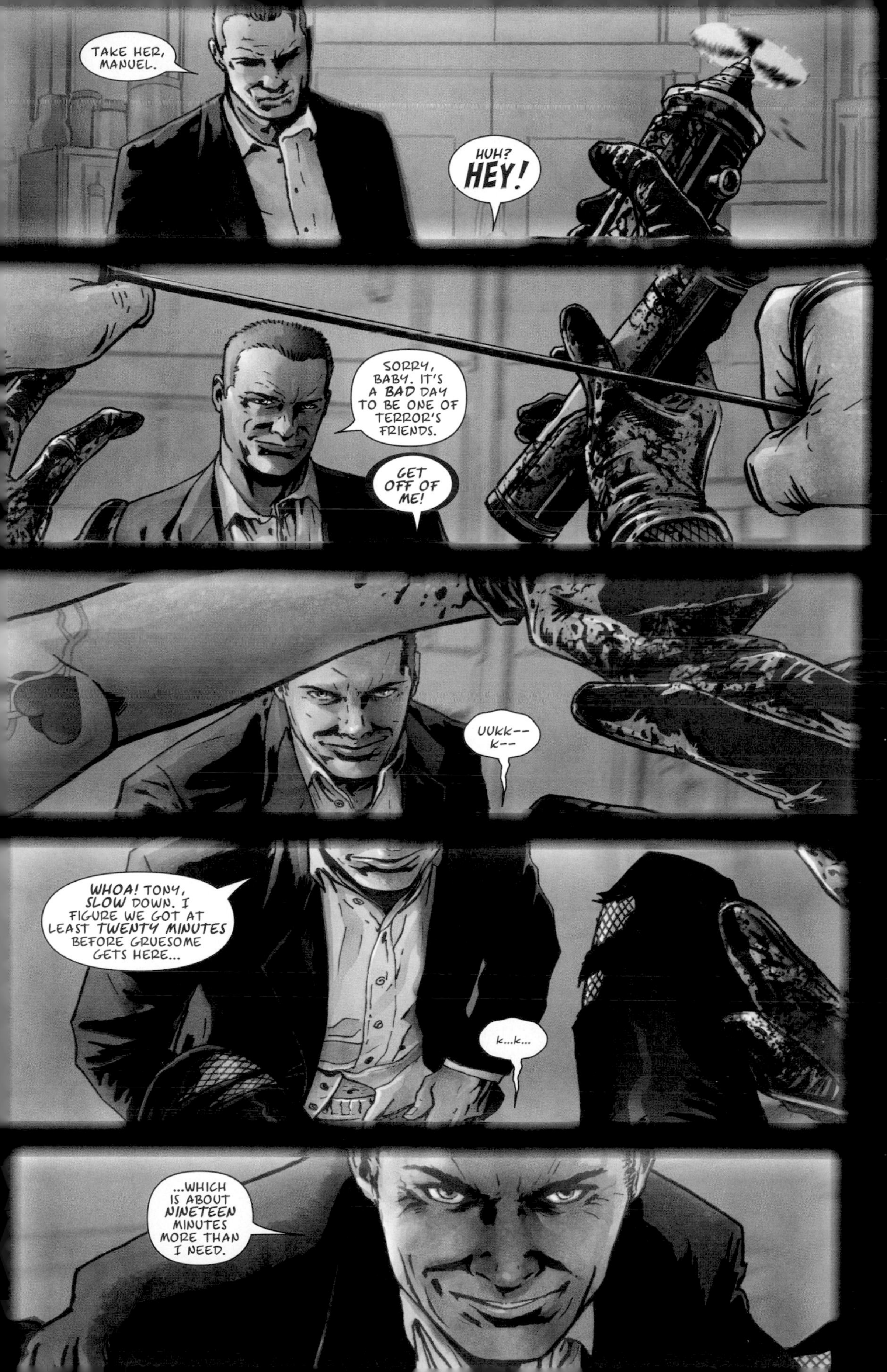
TAKE HER, MANUEL.
HUH? HEY!
SORRY, BABY. IT'S A BAD DAY TO BE ONE OF TERROR'S FRIENDS.
GET OFF OF ME!
UUKK-- K--
WHOA! TONY, SLOW DOWN. I FIGURE WE GOT AT LEAST TWENTY MINUTES BEFORE GRUESOME GETS HERE...
K...K...
...WHICH IS ABOUT NINETEEN MINUTES MORE THAN I NEED.

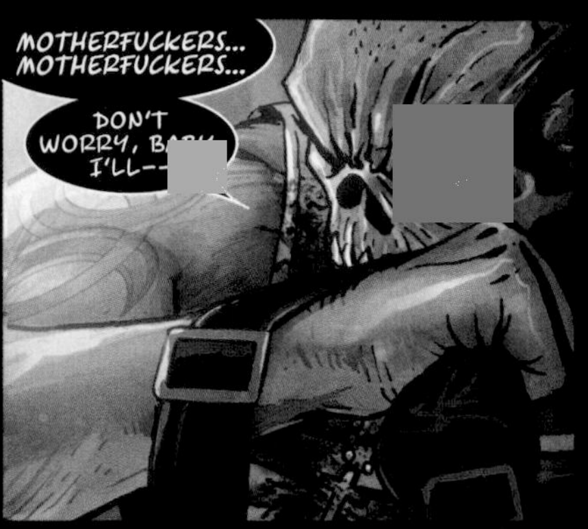
MOTHERFUCKERS... MOTHERFUCKERS...
DON'T WORRY, BA
I'LL--

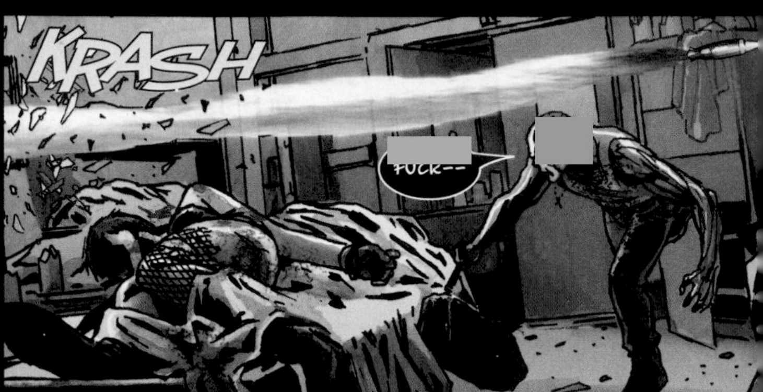
KRASH
FUCK--

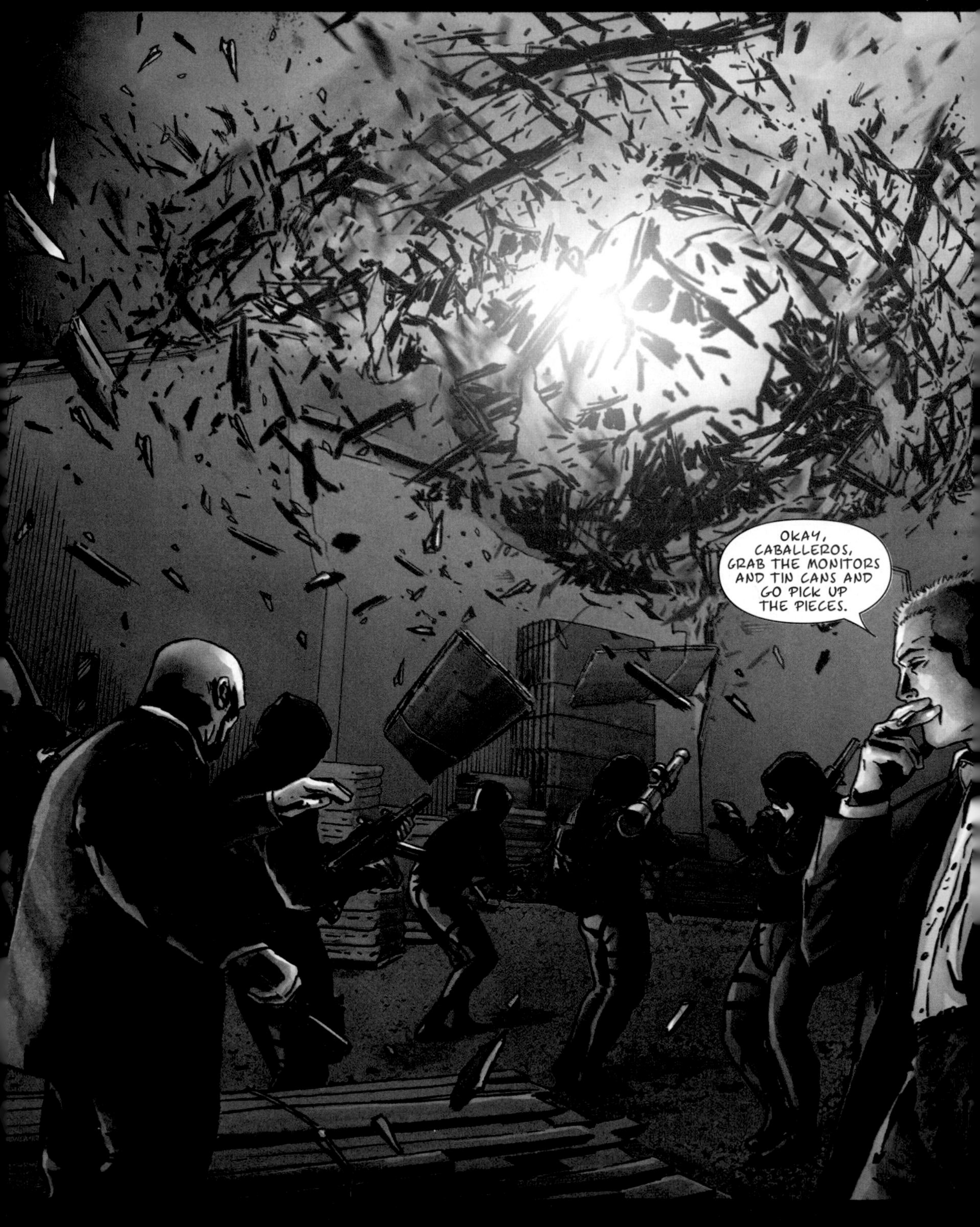
OKAY, CABALLEROS, GRAB THE MONITORS AND TIN CANS AND GO PICK UP THE PIECES.

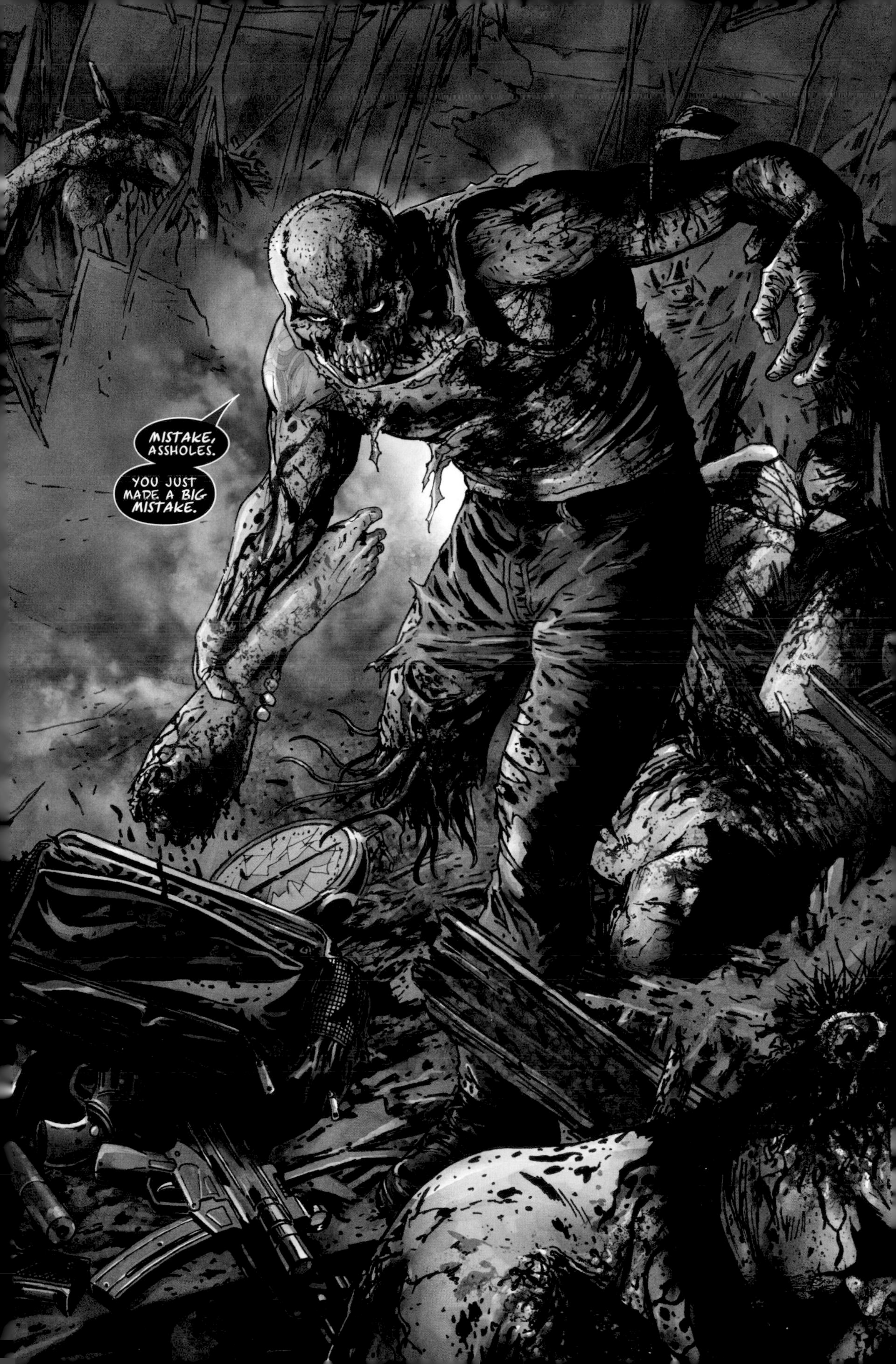
MISTAKE, ASSHOLES.
YOU JUST MADE A BIG MISTAKE.

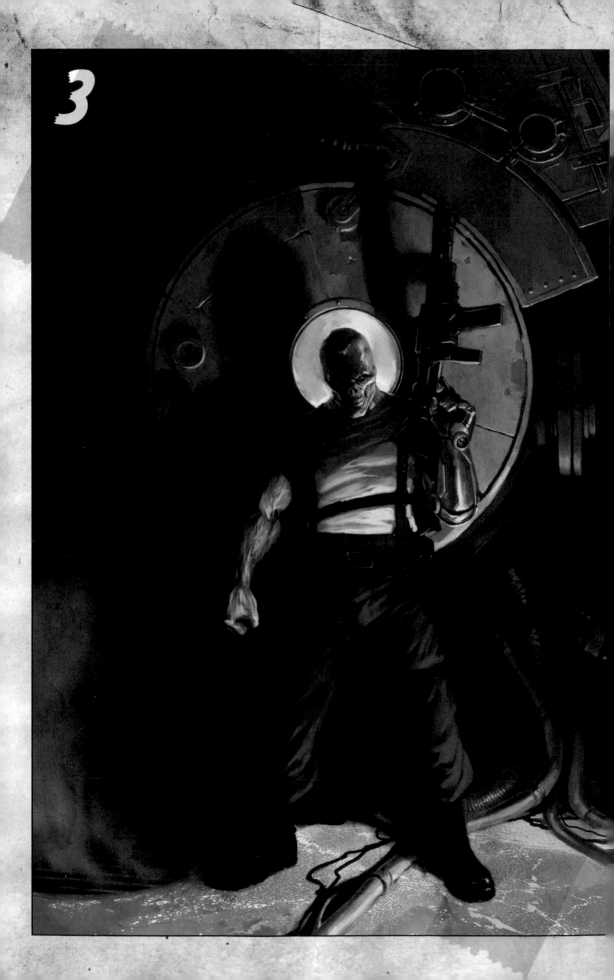

A Bit Of You, A Bit Of Me (But A Bit More Of You)

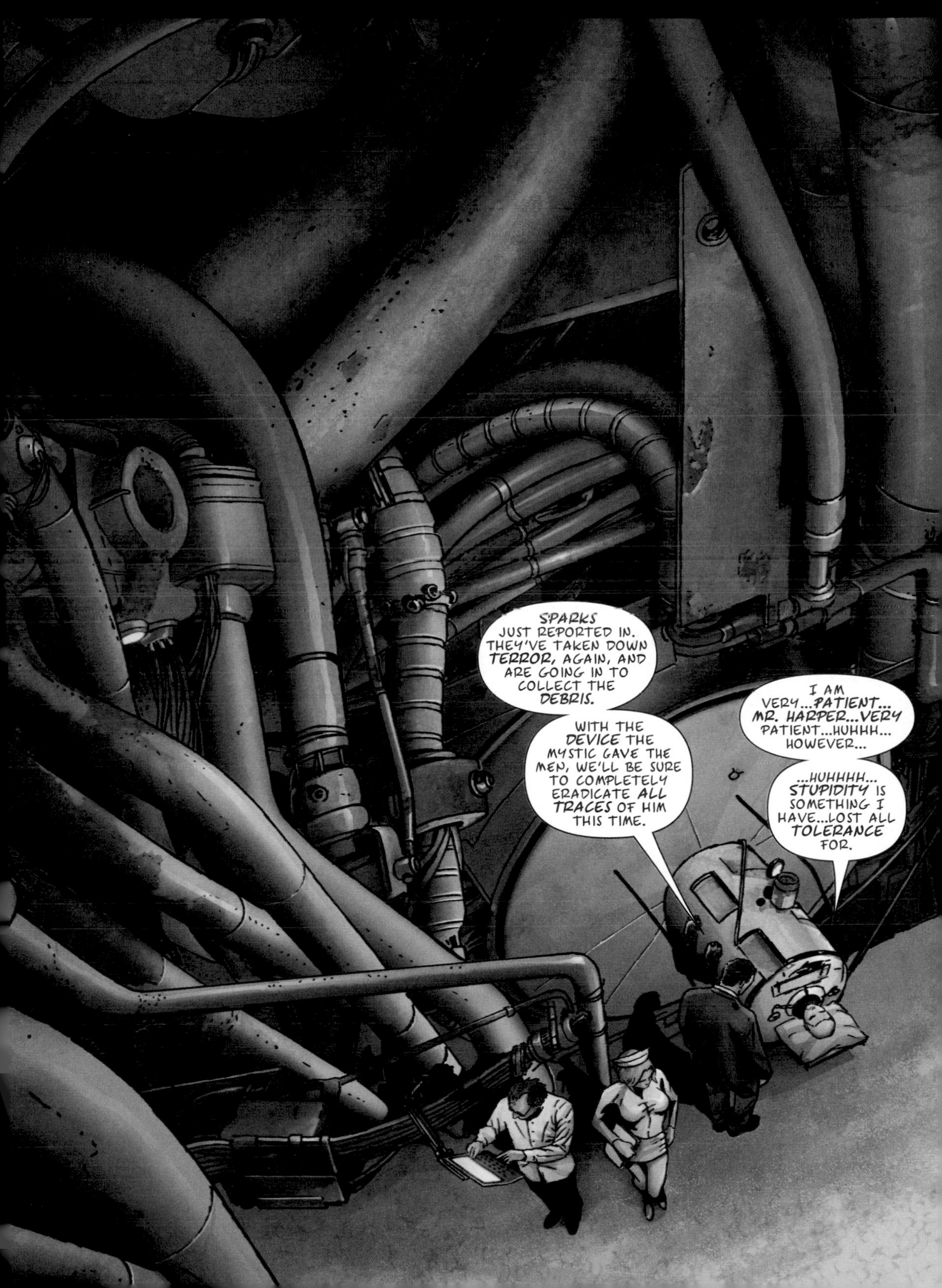
SPARKS JUST REPORTED IN. THEY'VE TAKEN DOWN TERROR, AGAIN, AND ARE GOING IN TO COLLECT THE DEBRIS.
WITH THE DEVICE THE MYSTIC GAVE THE MEN, WE'LL BE SURE TO COMPLETELY ERADICATE ALL TRACES OF HIM THIS TIME.
I AM VERY...PATIENT... MR. HARPER...VERY PATIENT...HUHHH... HOWEVER...
...HUHHHH... STUPIDITY IS SOMETHING I HAVE...LOST ALL TOLERANCE FOR.

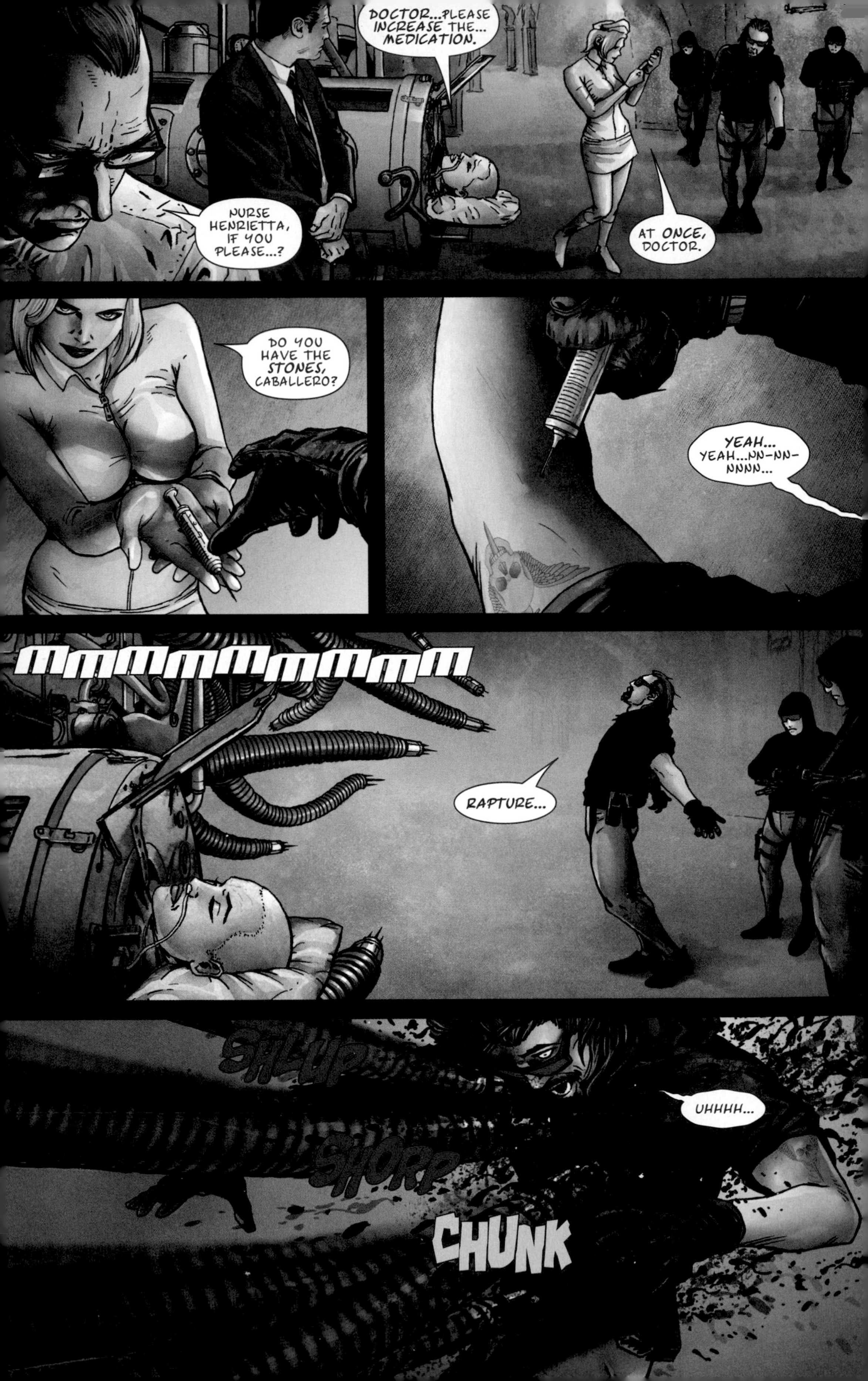
DOCTOR...PLEASE INCREASE THE... MEDICATION.
NURSE HENRIETTA, IF YOU PLEASE...?
AT ONCE, DOCTOR.
DO YOU HAVE THE STONES, CABALLERO?
YEAH... YEAH...NN-NN-NNNN...
MMMMMMMMMMM
RAPTURE...
SHLUP
UHHHH...
SHORP
CHUNK

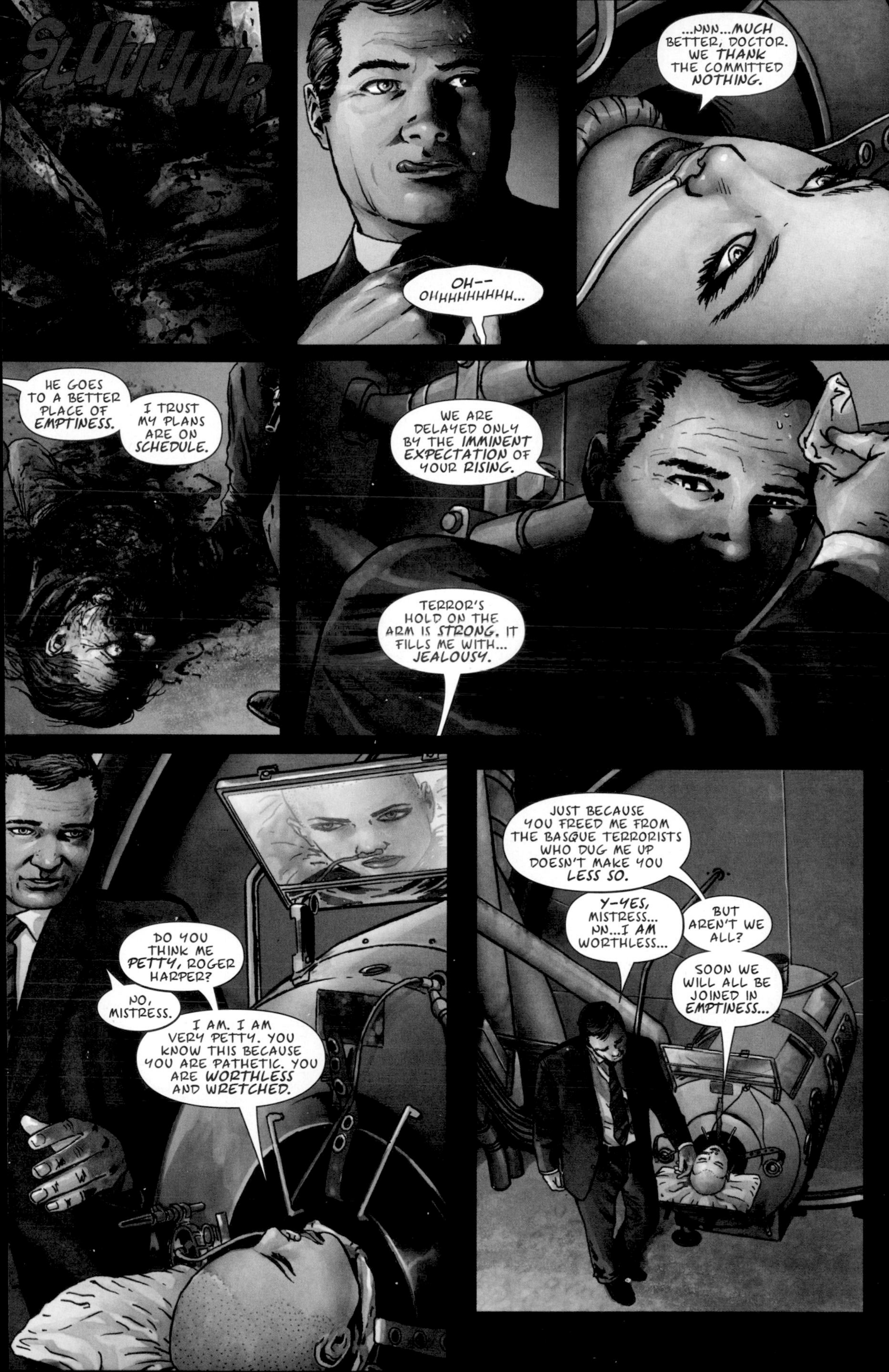
SLUUUUUUP
OH-- OHHHHHHHHH...
...NNN...MUCH BETTER, DOCTOR. WE THANK THE COMMITTED NOTHING.
HE GOES TO A BETTER PLACE OF EMPTINESS.
I TRUST MY PLANS ARE ON SCHEDULE.
WE ARE DELAYED ONLY BY THE IMMINENT EXPECTATION OF YOUR RISING.
TERROR'S HOLD ON THE ARM IS STRONG. IT FILLS ME WITH... JEALOUSY.
DO YOU THINK ME PETTY, ROGER HARPER?
NO, MISTRESS.
I AM. I AM VERY PETTY. YOU KNOW THIS BECAUSE YOU ARE PATHETIC. YOU ARE WORTHLESS AND WRETCHED.
JUST BECAUSE YOU FREED ME FROM THE BASQUE TERRORISTS WHO DUG ME UP DOESN'T MAKE YOU LESS SO.
Y-YES, MISTRESS... NN...I AM WORTHLESS...
BUT AREN'T WE ALL?
SOON WE WILL ALL BE JOINED IN EMPTINESS...

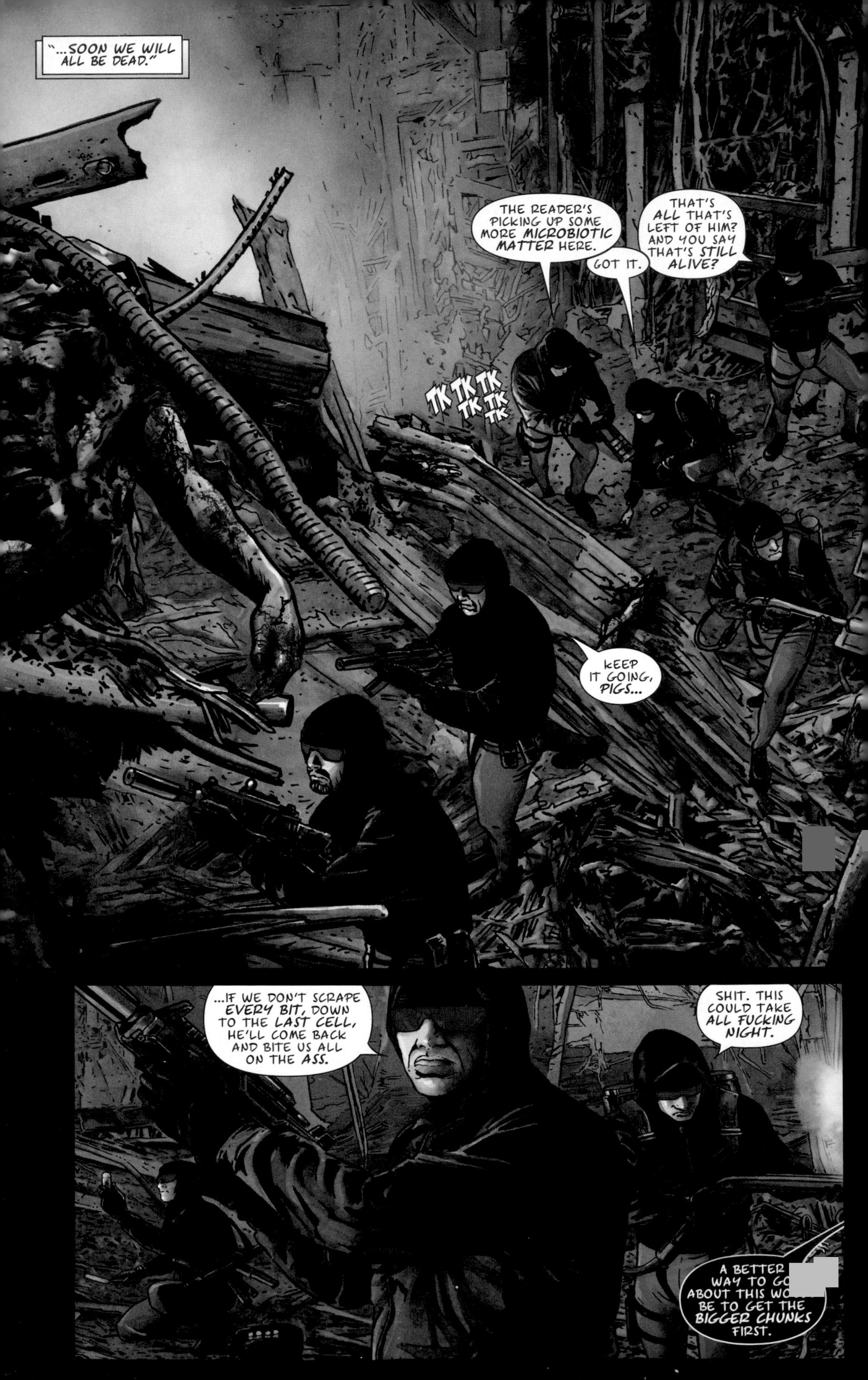
"...SOON WE WILL ALL BE DEAD."
THE READER'S PICKING UP SOME MORE MICROBIOTIC MATTER HERE.
GOT IT.
THAT'S ALL THAT'S LEFT OF HIM? AND YOU SAY THAT'S STILL ALIVE?
TK TK TK TK TK TK
KEEP IT GOING, PIGS...
...IF WE DON'T SCRAPE EVERY BIT, DOWN TO THE LAST CELL, HE'LL COME BACK AND BITE US ALL ON THE ASS.
SHIT. THIS COULD TAKE ALL FUCKING NIGHT.
A BETTER WAY TO GO ABOUT THIS WO BE TO GET THE BIGGER CHUNKS FIRST.

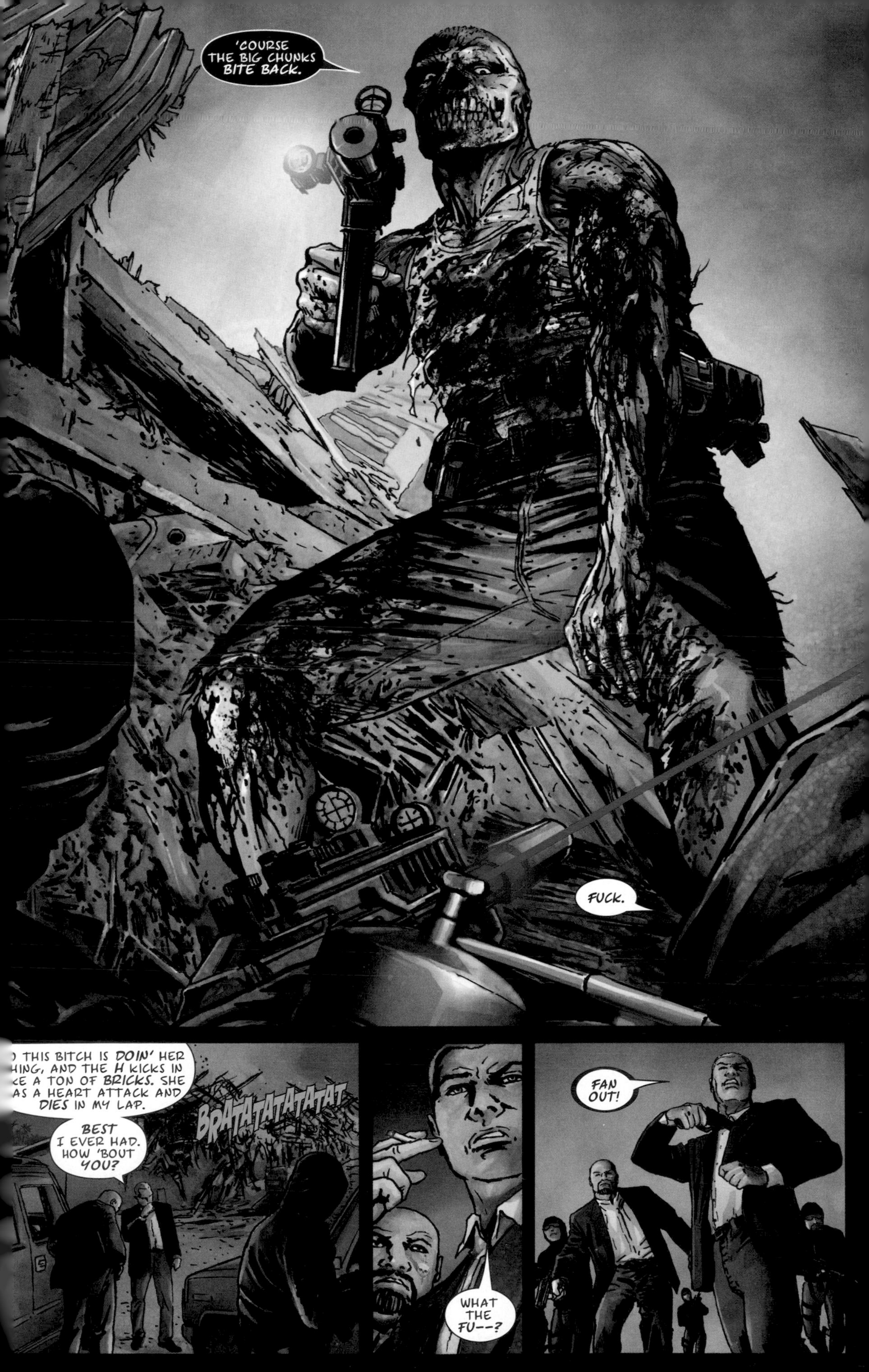
'COURSE THE BIG CHUNKS BITE BACK.
FUCK.
O THIS BITCH IS DOIN' HER HING, AND THE H KICKS IN KE A TON OF BRICKS. SHE AS A HEART ATTACK AND DIES IN MY LAP.
BEST I EVER HAD. HOW 'BOUT YOU?
BRATATATATATAT
WHAT THE FU--?
FAN OUT!

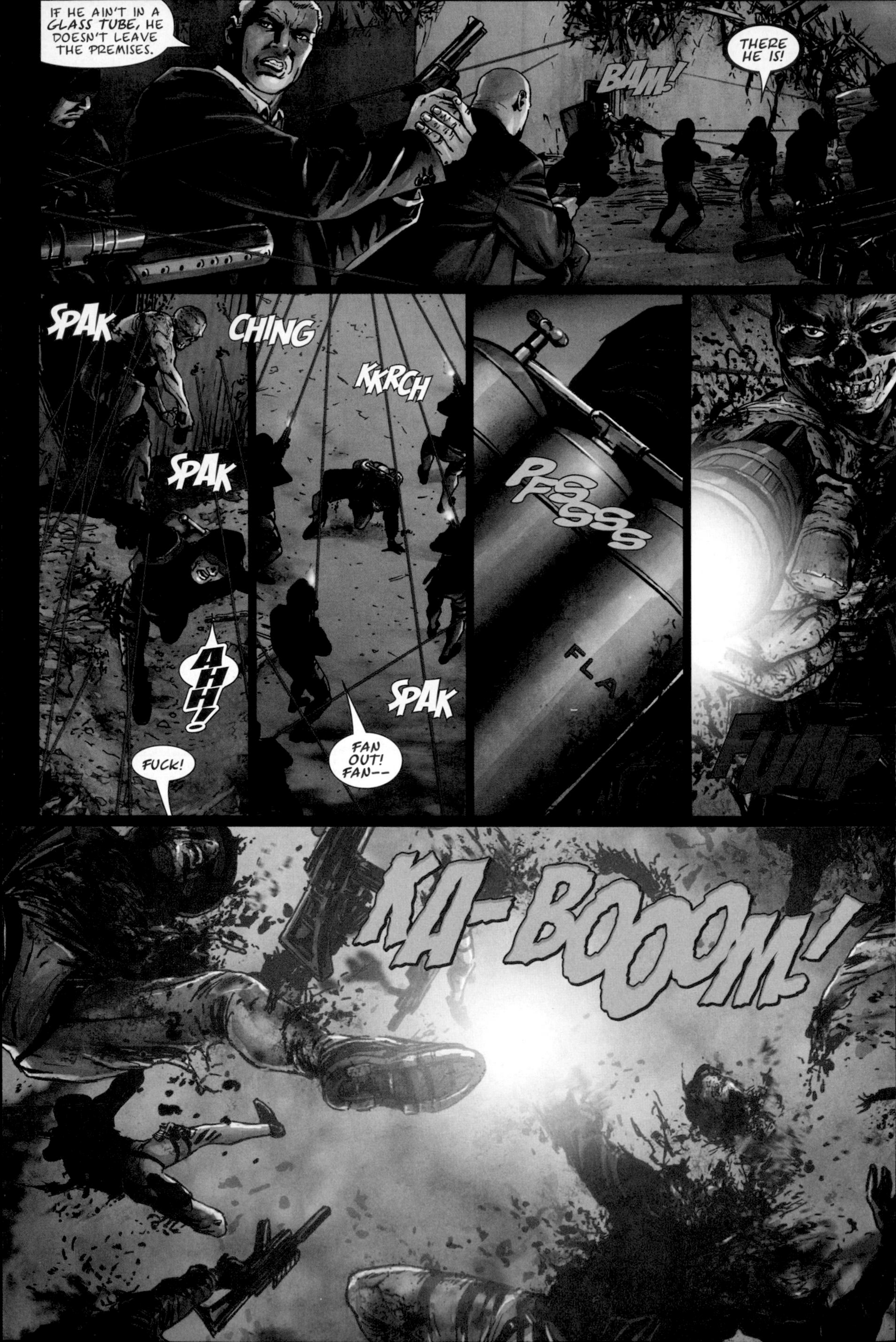
IF HE AIN'T IN A GLASS TUBE, HE DOESN'T LEAVE THE PREMISES.
BAM!
THERE HE IS!
SPAK
CHING
SPAK
AHHH!
FUCK!
KKRCH
SPAK
FAN OUT! FAN--
PFSSSSS
FLA
KA-BOOOM!

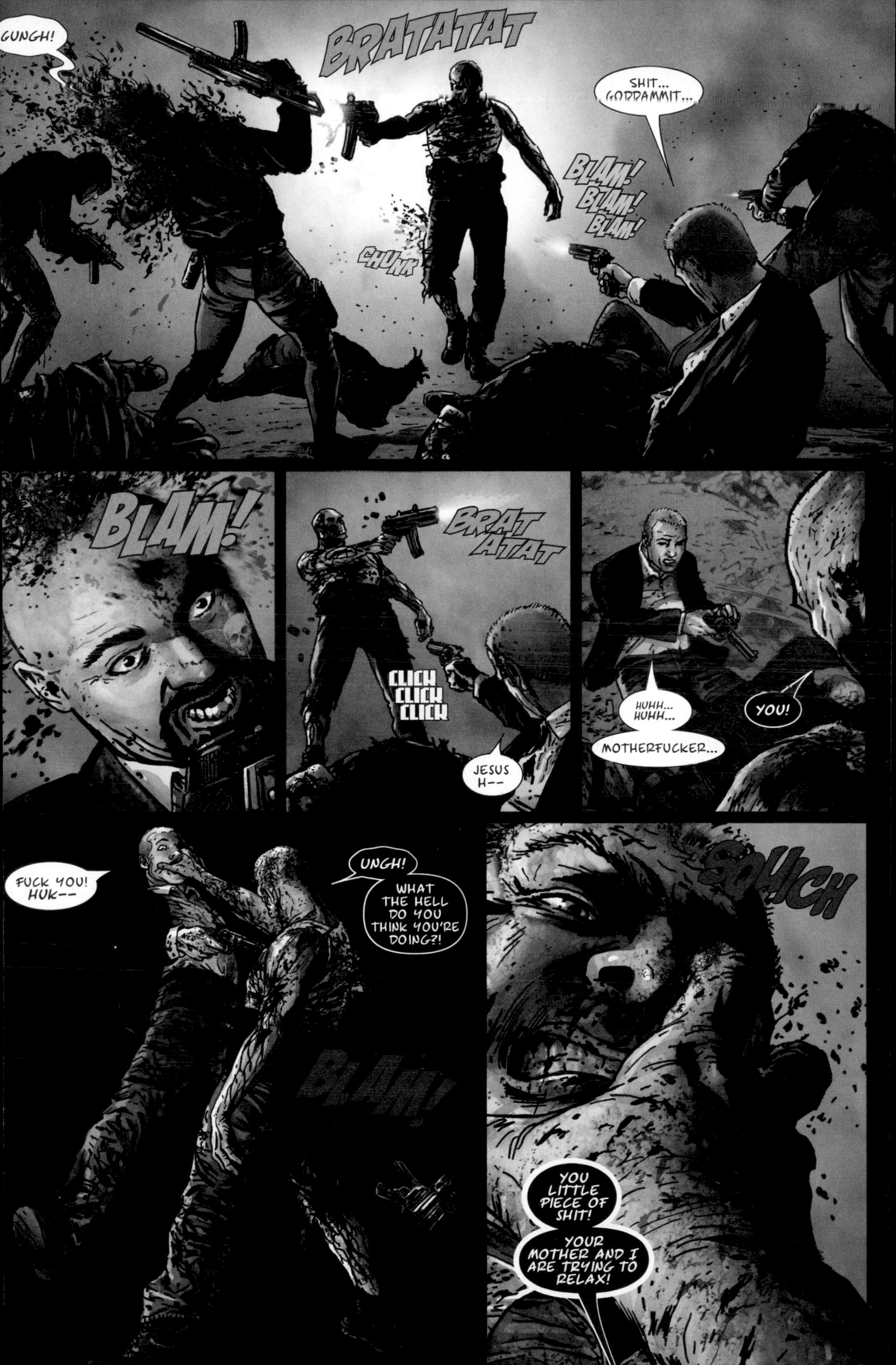
GUNGH!
BRATATAT
SHIT... GODDAMMIT...
BLAM! BLAM! BLAM!
CHUNK
BLAM!
BRAT ATAT
CLICK CLICK CLICK
JESUS H--
HUHH... HUHH...
MOTHERFUCKER...
YOU!
FUCK YOU! HUK--
UNGH!
WHAT THE HELL DO YOU THINK YOU'RE DOING?!
BLAM!
SQUICH
YOU LITTLE PIECE OF SHIT!
YOUR MOTHER AND I ARE TRYING TO RELAX!

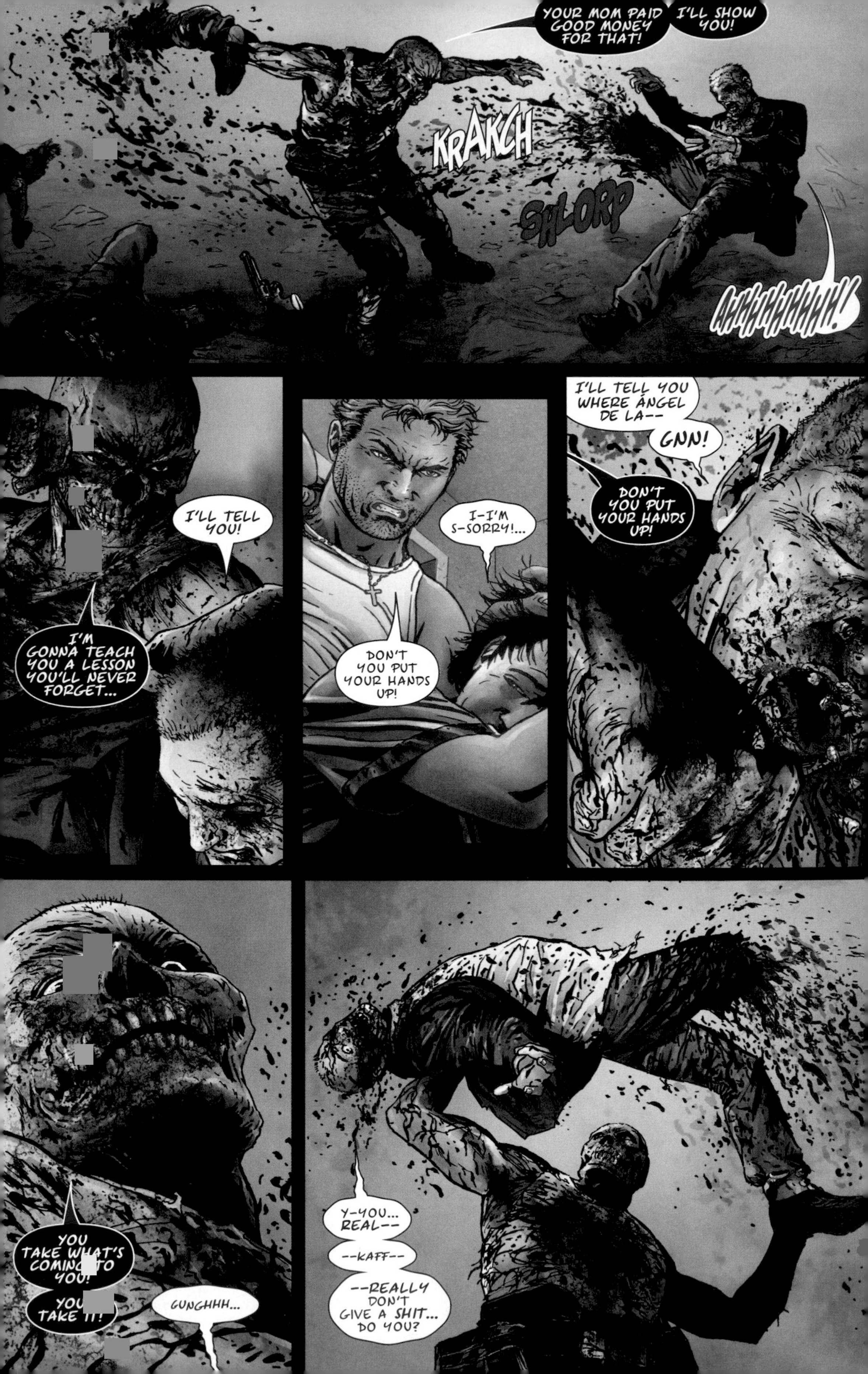
YOUR MOM PAID GOOD MONEY FOR THAT!
I'LL SHOW YOU!
KRAKCH
SHLORP
AHHHHHHHHH!
I'LL TELL YOU!
I'M GONNA TEACH YOU A LESSON YOU'LL NEVER FORGET...
I-I'M S-SORRY!...
DON'T YOU PUT YOUR HANDS UP!
I'LL TELL YOU WHERE ÁNGEL DE LA--
GNN!
DON'T YOU PUT YOUR HANDS UP!
YOU TAKE WHAT'S COMING TO YOU!
YOU TAKE IT!
GUNGHHH...
Y-YOU... REAL--
--KAFF--
--REALLY DON'T GIVE A SHIT... DO YOU?

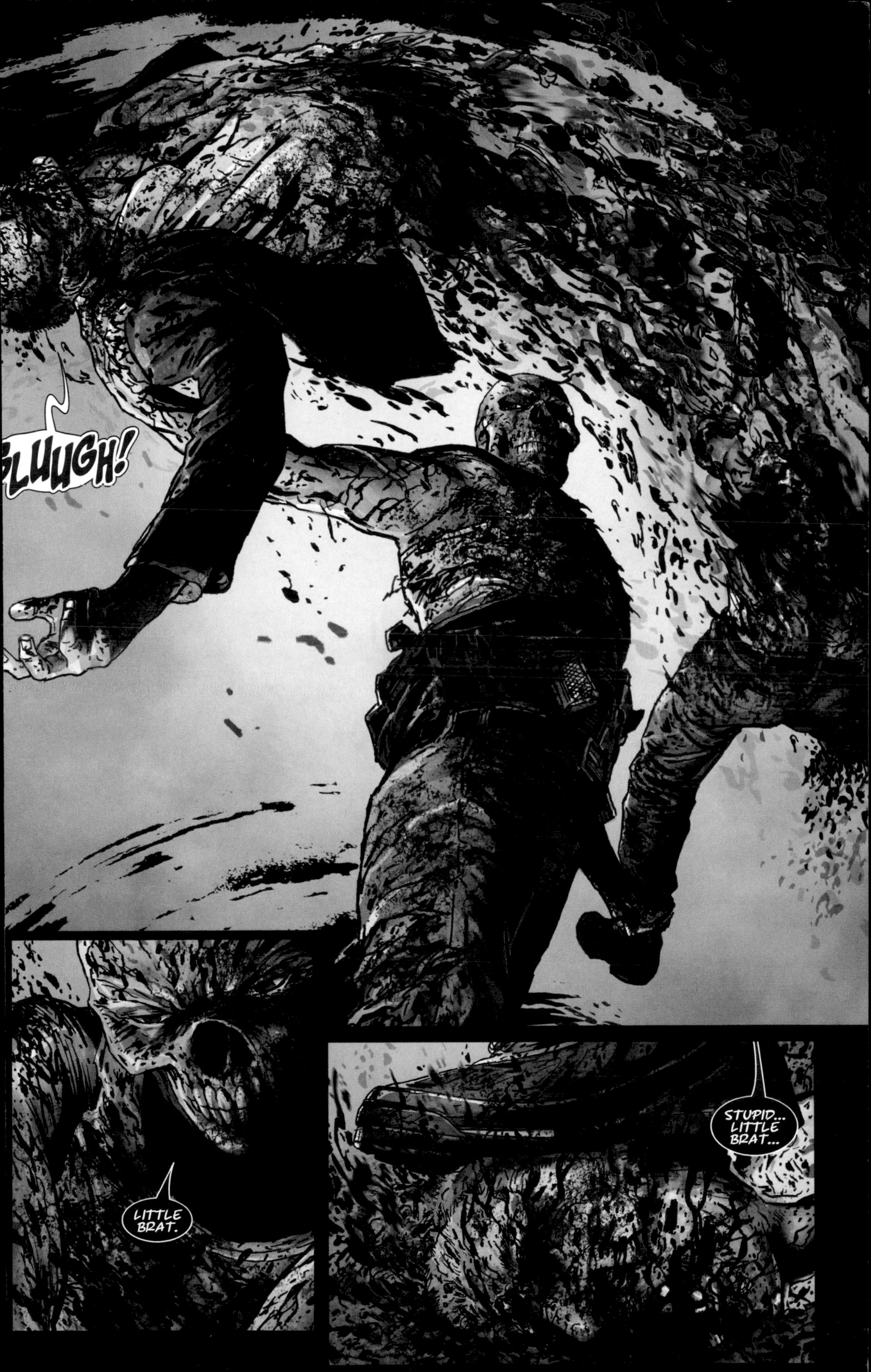
SLUUGH!
LITTLE BRAT.
STUPID... LITTLE BRAT...

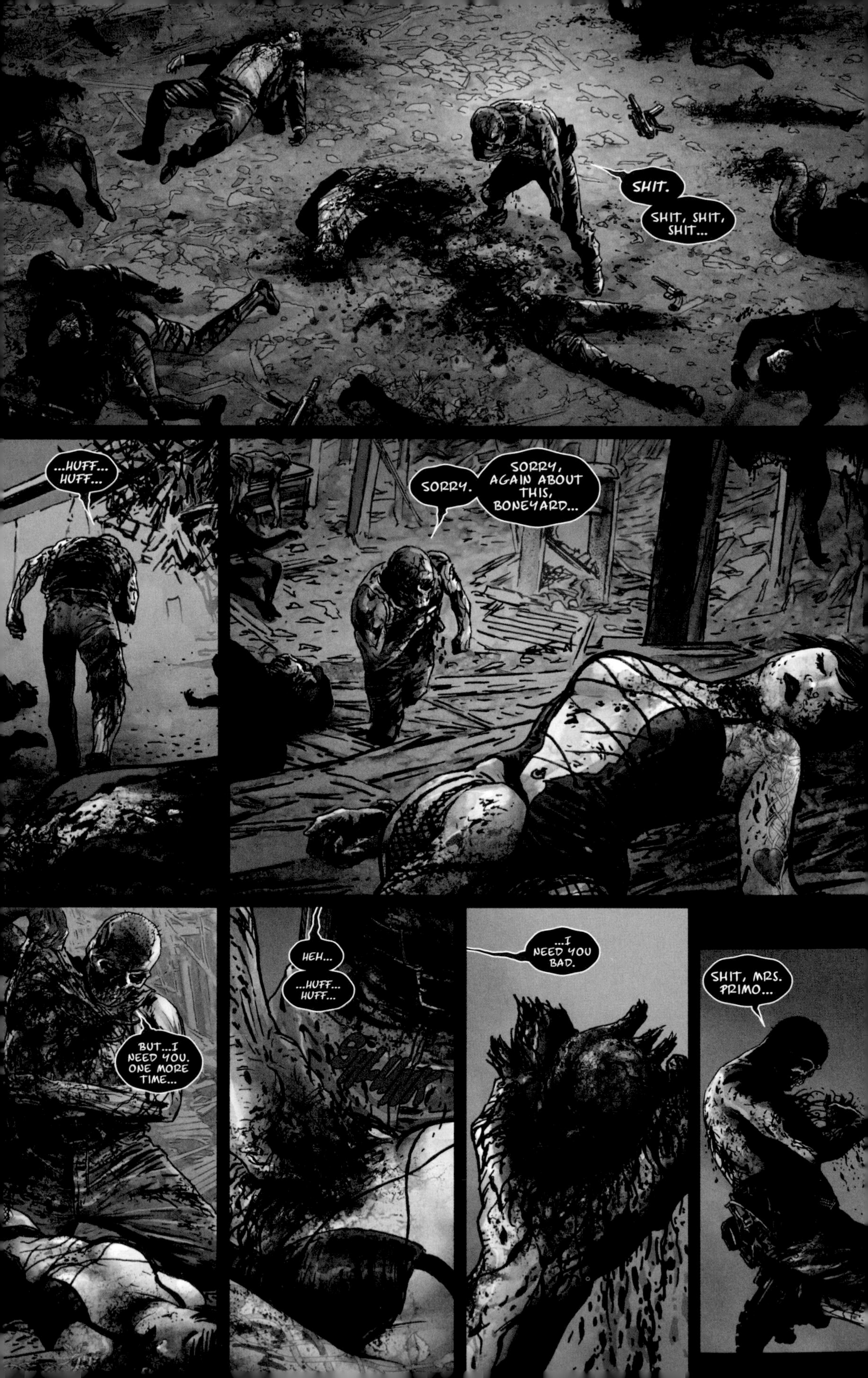
SHIT.
SHIT, SHIT, SHIT...
...HUFF... HUFF...
SORRY.
SORRY, AGAIN ABOUT THIS, BONEYARD...
BUT...I NEED YOU. ONE MORE TIME...
HEH...
...HUFF... HUFF...
...I NEED YOU BAD.
SHIT, MRS. PRIMO...

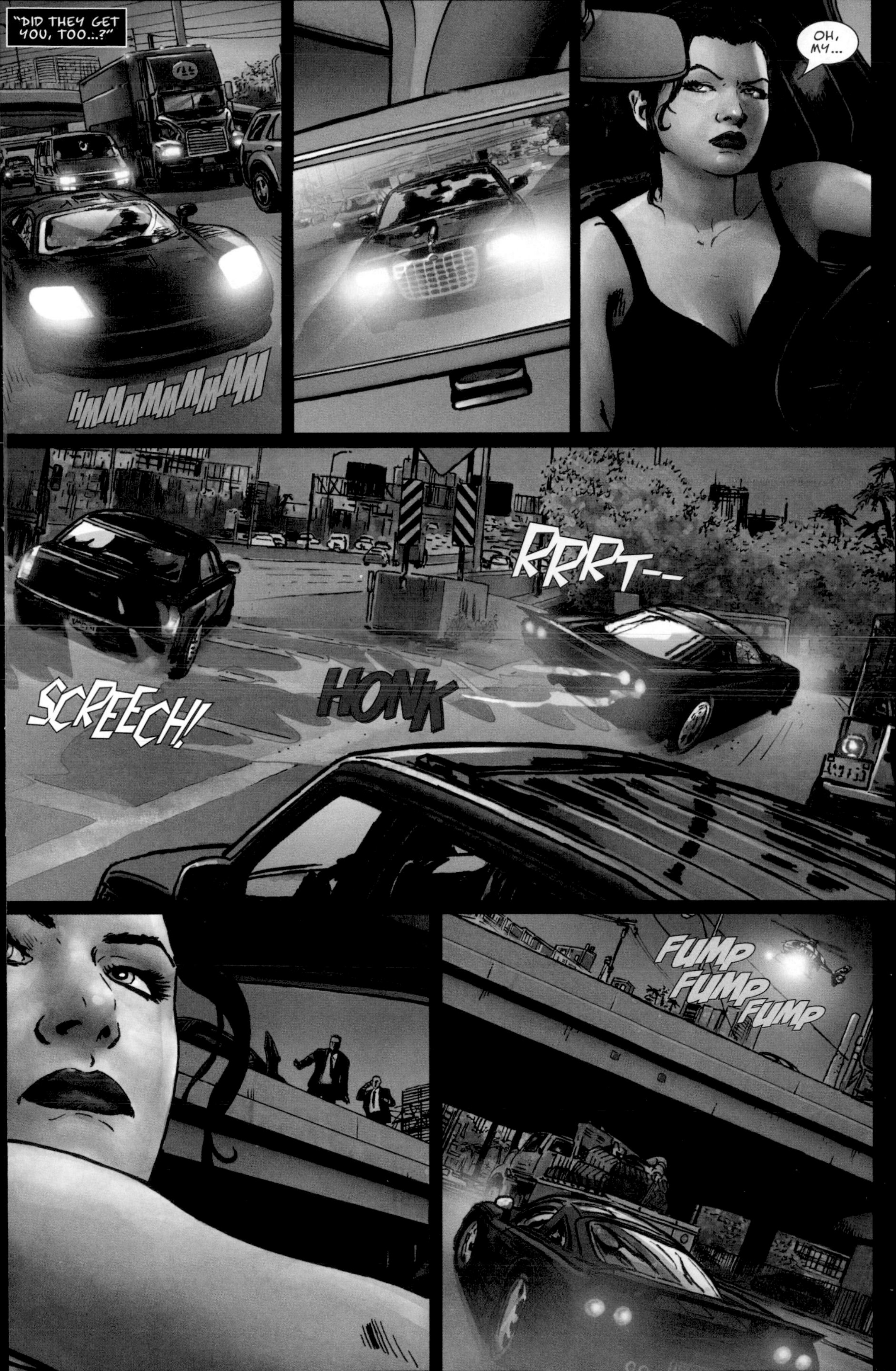
"DID THEY GET YOU, TOO...?"
HMMMMMMMMMM
OH, MY...
RRRT--
SCREECH!
HONK
FUMP FUMP FUMP

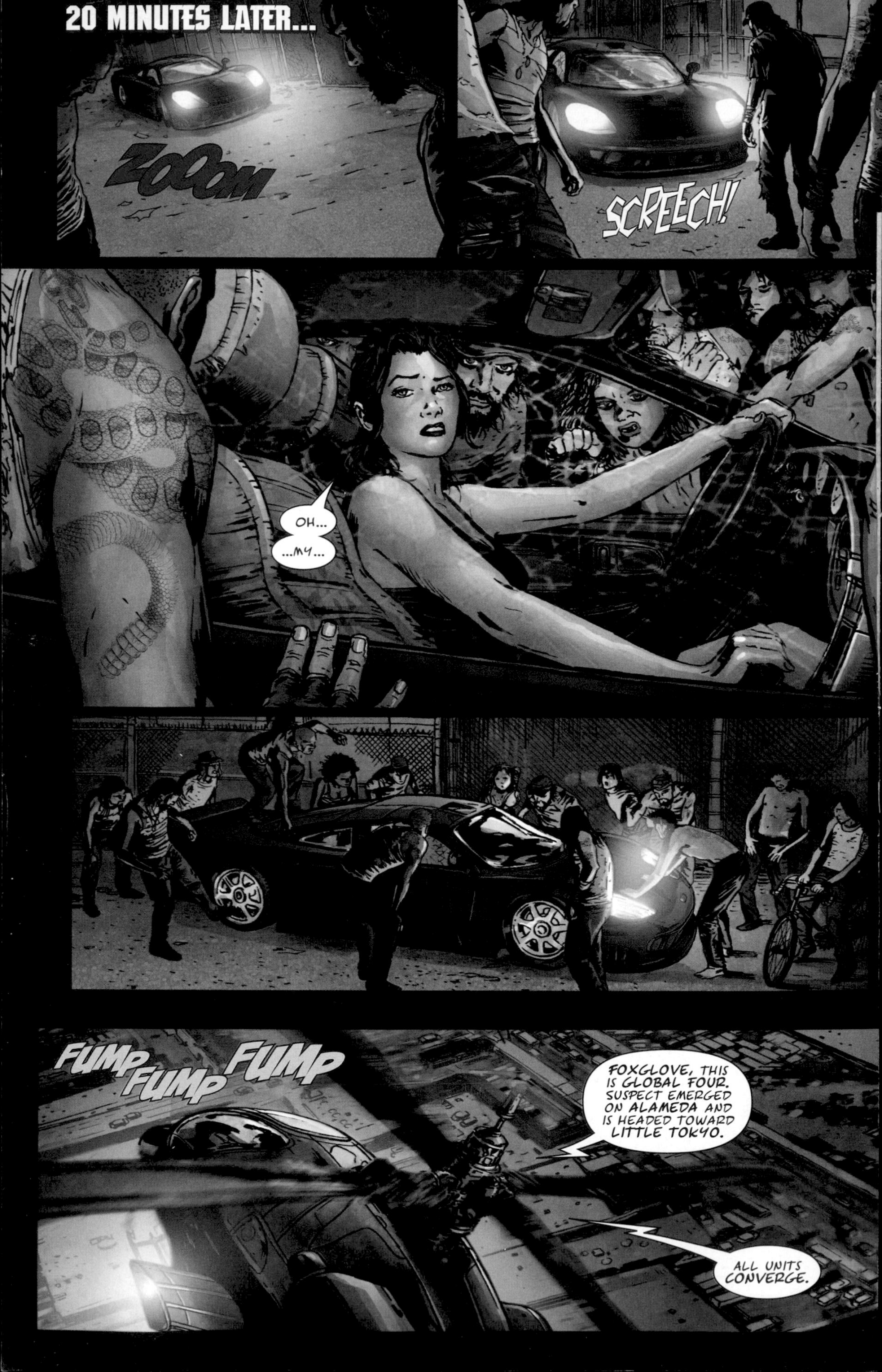
20 MINUTES LATER...
ZOOOM
SCREECH!
OH...
...MY...
FUMP FUMP FUMP
FOXGLOVE, THIS IS GLOBAL FOUR. SUSPECT EMERGED ON ALAMEDA AND IS HEADED TOWARD LITTLE TOKYO.
ALL UNITS CONVERGE.

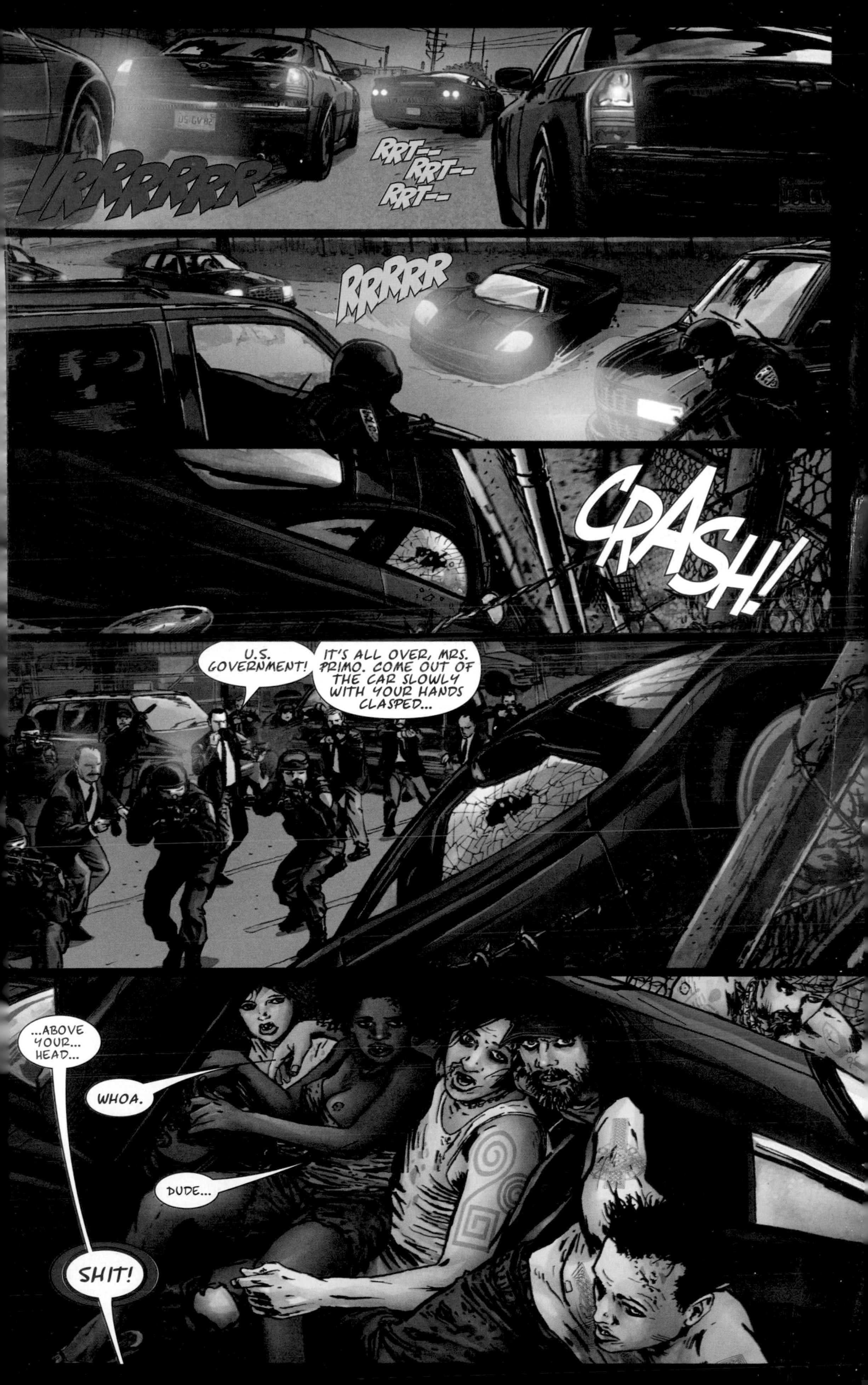
VRRRRRR
RRT-- RRT-- RRT--
RRRRR
CRASH!
U.S. GOVERNMENT!
IT'S ALL OVER, MRS. PRIMO. COME OUT OF THE CAR SLOWLY WITH YOUR HANDS CLASPED...
...ABOVE YOUR... HEAD...
WHOA.
DUDE...
SHIT!

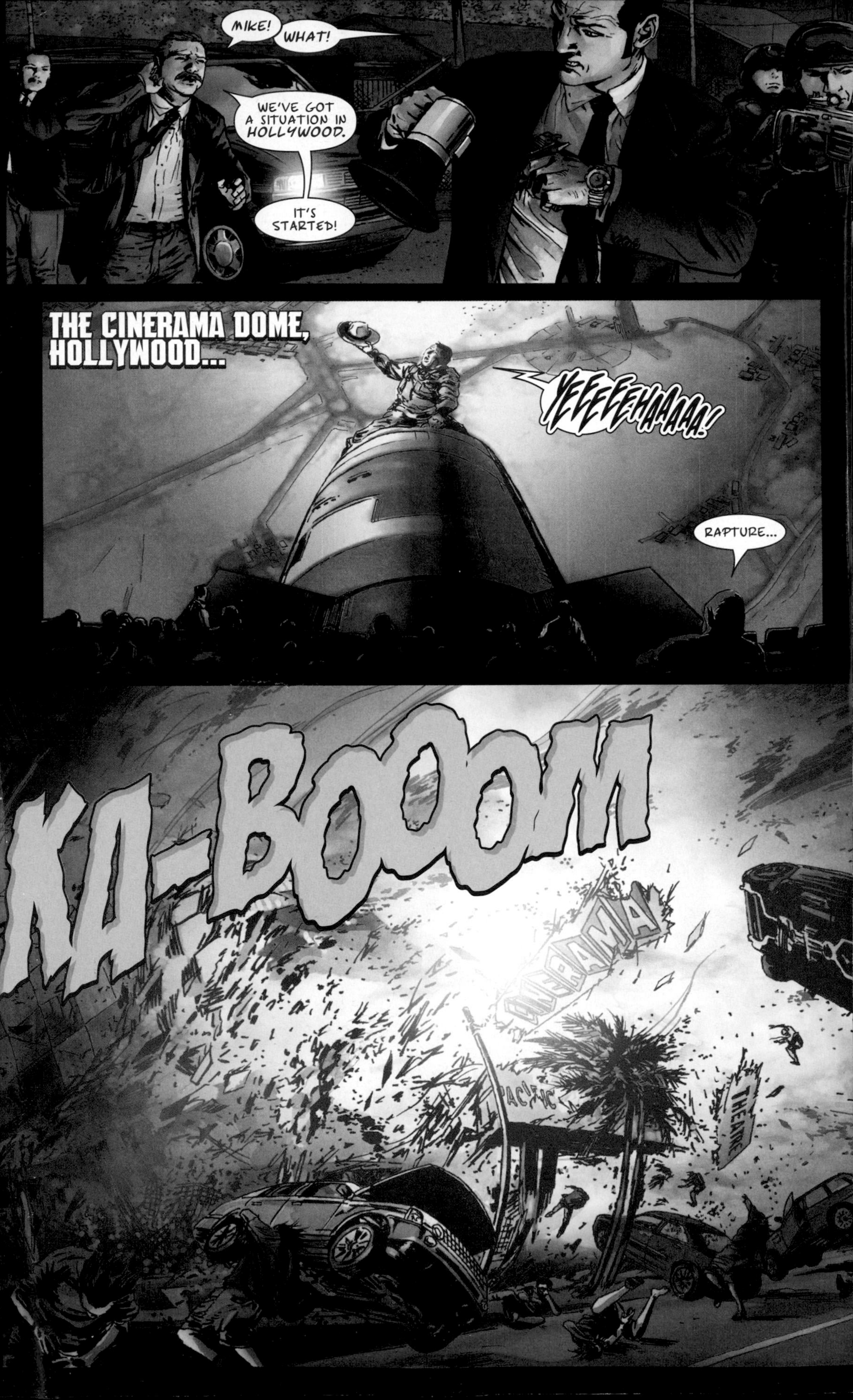
MIKE!
WHAT!
WE'VE GOT A SITUATION IN HOLLYWOOD.
IT'S STARTED!
THE CINERAMA DOME, HOLLYWOOD...
YEEEEEHAAAAA!
RAPTURE...
KA-BOOOM
CINERAMA
PACIFIC
THEATRE

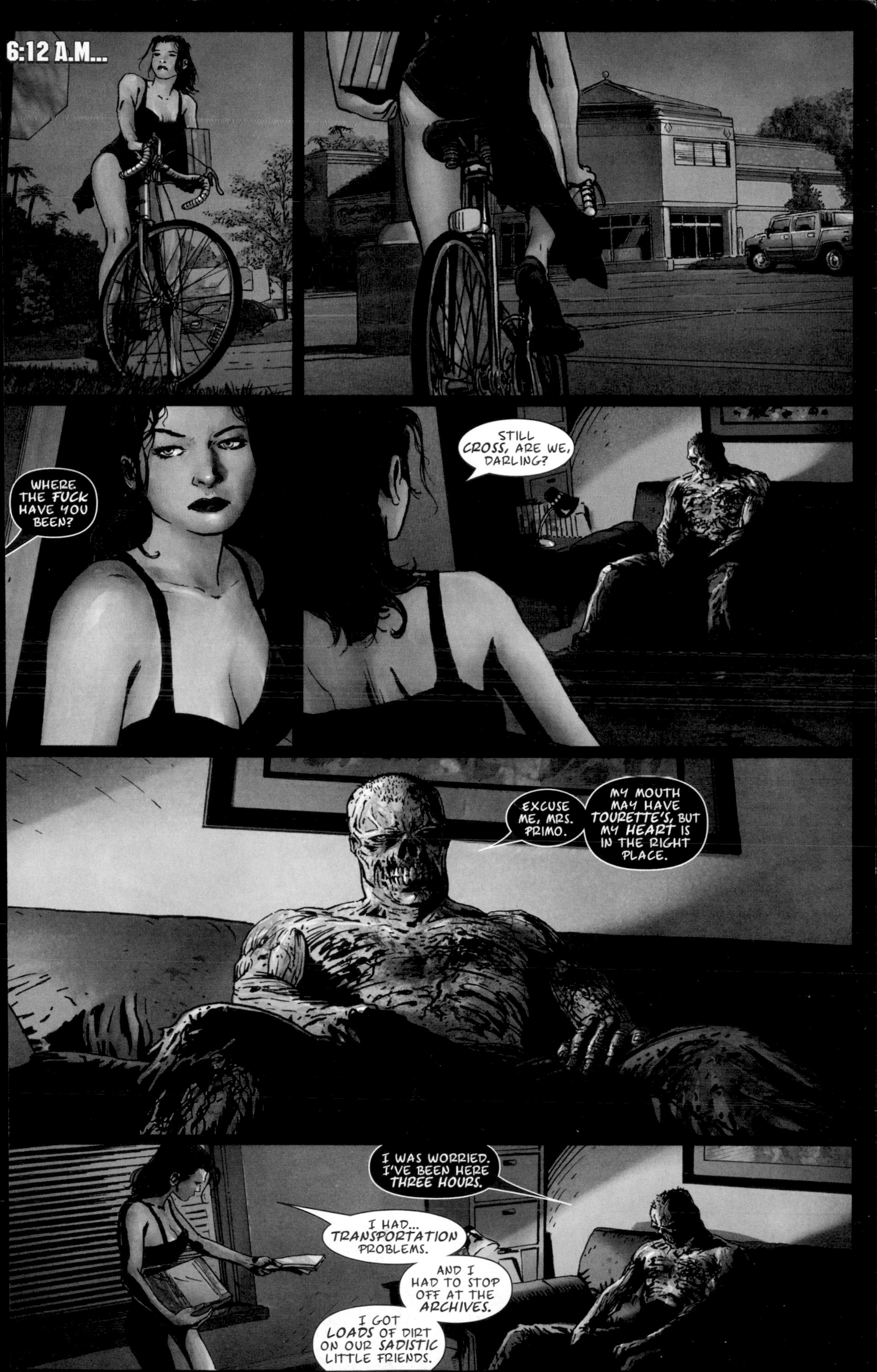
6:12 A.M...
WHERE THE FUCK HAVE YOU BEEN?
STILL CROSS, ARE WE, DARLING?
EXCUSE ME, MRS. PRIMO.
MY MOUTH MAY HAVE TOURETTE'S, BUT MY HEART IS IN THE RIGHT PLACE.
I WAS WORRIED. I'VE BEEN HERE THREE HOURS.
I HAD... TRANSPORTATION PROBLEMS.
AND I HAD TO STOP OFF AT THE ARCHIVES.
I GOT LOADS OF DIRT ON OUR SADISTIC LITTLE FRIENDS.

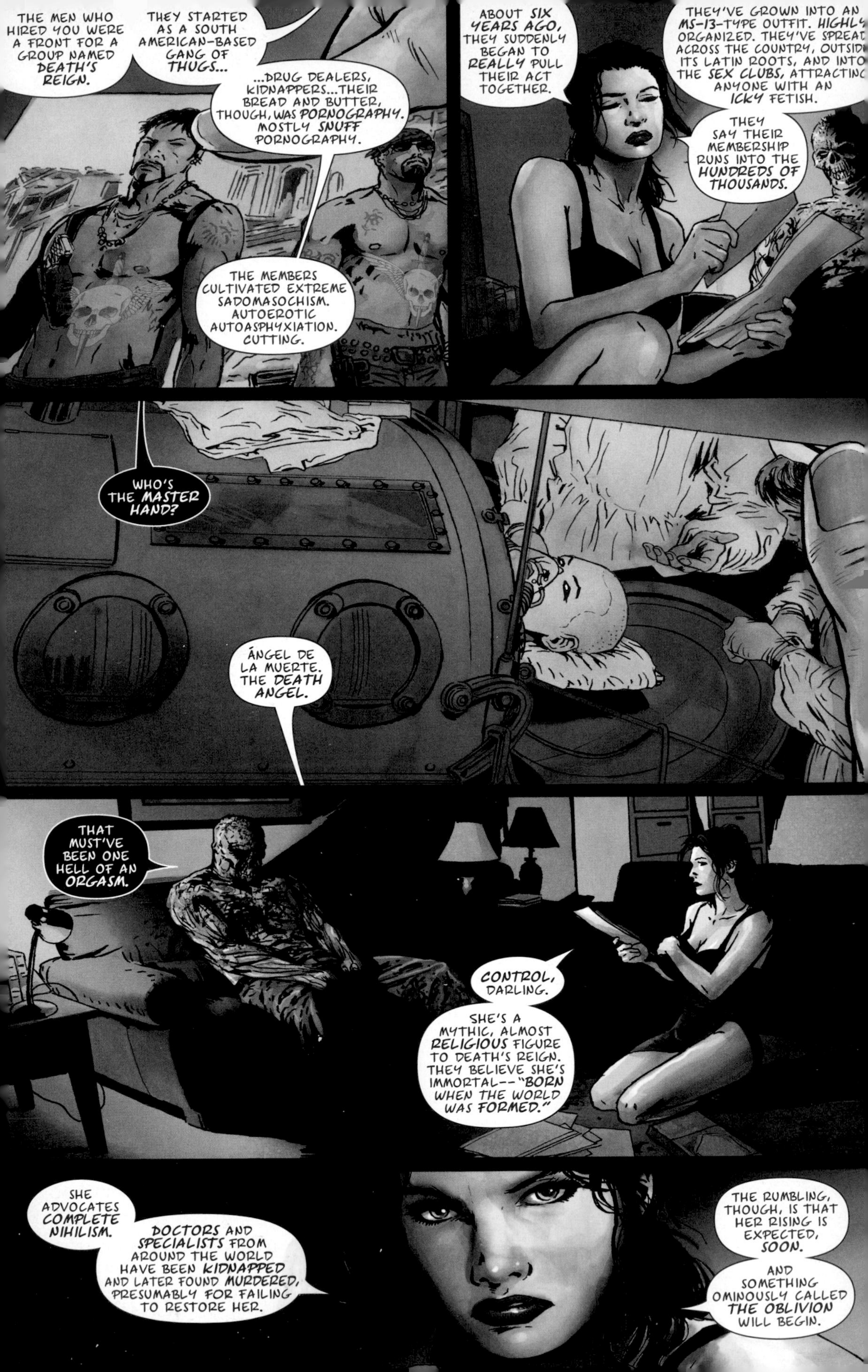
THE MEN WHO HIRED YOU WERE A FRONT FOR A GROUP NAMED DEATH'S REIGN.
THEY STARTED AS A SOUTH AMERICAN-BASED GANG OF THUGS...
...DRUG DEALERS, KIDNAPPERS...THEIR BREAD AND BUTTER, THOUGH, WAS PORNOGRAPHY. MOSTLY SNUFF PORNOGRAPHY.
THE MEMBERS CULTIVATED EXTREME SADOMASOCHISM. AUTOEROTIC AUTOASPHYXIATION. CUTTING.
ABOUT SIX YEARS AGO, THEY SUDDENLY BEGAN TO REALLY PULL THEIR ACT TOGETHER.
THEY'VE GROWN INTO AN MS-13-TYPE OUTFIT. HIGHLY ORGANIZED. THEY'VE SPREAD ACROSS THE COUNTRY, OUTSIDE ITS LATIN ROOTS, AND INTO THE SEX CLUBS, ATTRACTING ANYONE WITH AN ICKY FETISH.
THEY SAY THEIR MEMBERSHIP RUNS INTO THE HUNDREDS OF THOUSANDS.
WHO'S THE MASTER HAND?
ÁNGEL DE LA MUERTE. THE DEATH ANGEL.
THAT MUST'VE BEEN ONE HELL OF AN ORGASM.
CONTROL, DARLING.
SHE'S A MYTHIC, ALMOST RELIGIOUS FIGURE TO DEATH'S REIGN. THEY BELIEVE SHE'S IMMORTAL--"BORN WHEN THE WORLD WAS FORMED."
SHE ADVOCATES COMPLETE NIHILISM.
DOCTORS AND SPECIALISTS FROM AROUND THE WORLD HAVE BEEN KIDNAPPED AND LATER FOUND MURDERED, PRESUMABLY FOR FAILING TO RESTORE HER.
THE RUMBLING, THOUGH, IS THAT HER RISING IS EXPECTED, SOON.
AND SOMETHING OMINOUSLY CALLED THE OBLIVION WILL BEGIN.

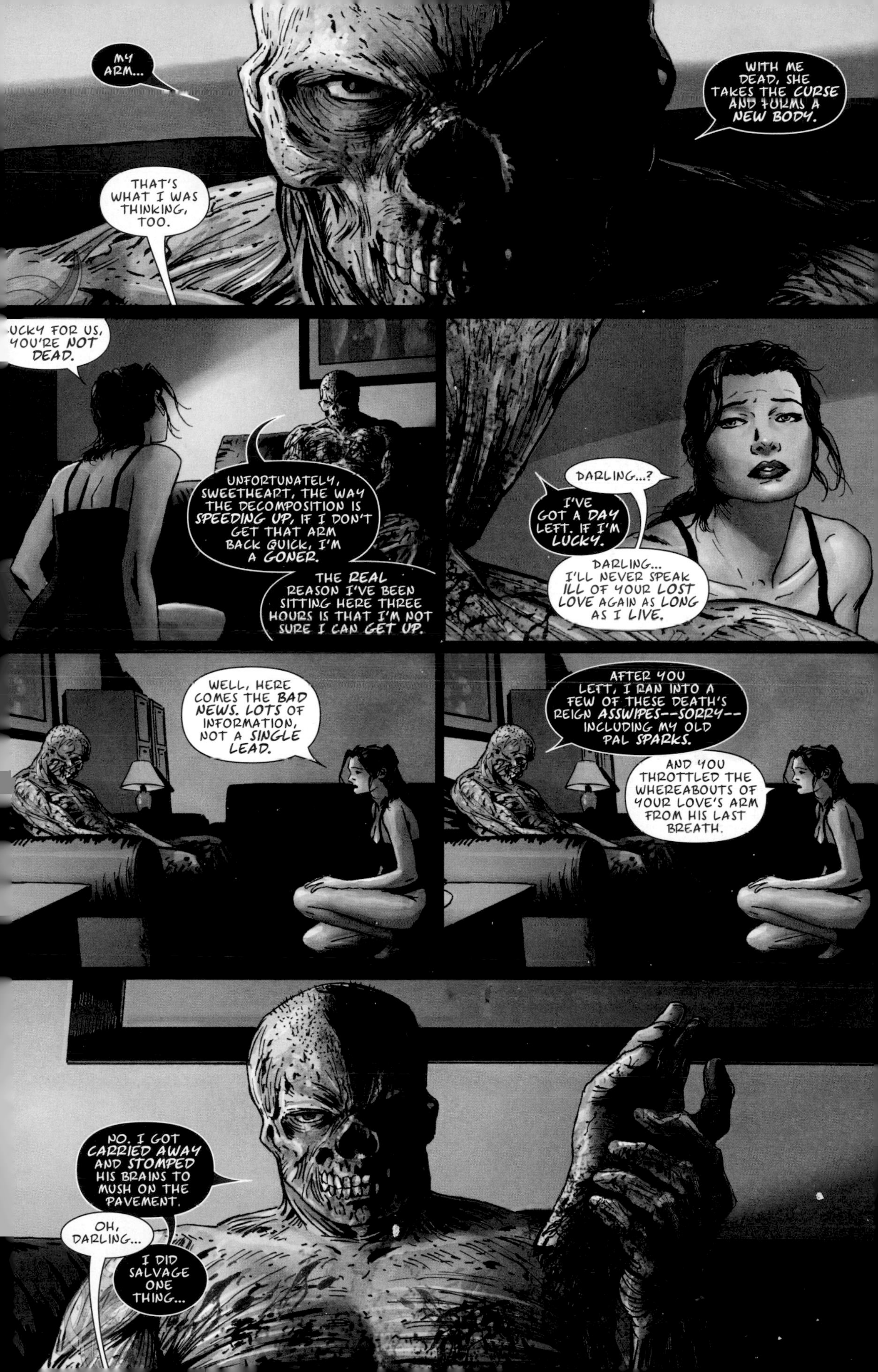
MY ARM...
THAT'S WHAT I WAS THINKING, TOO.
WITH ME DEAD, SHE TAKES THE CURSE AND FORMS A NEW BODY.
LUCKY FOR US, YOU'RE NOT DEAD.
UNFORTUNATELY, SWEETHEART, THE WAY THE DECOMPOSITION IS SPEEDING UP, IF I DON'T GET THAT ARM BACK QUICK, I'M A GONER.
THE REAL REASON I'VE BEEN SITTING HERE THREE HOURS IS THAT I'M NOT SURE I CAN GET UP.
DARLING...?
I'VE GOT A DAY LEFT. IF I'M LUCKY.
DARLING... I'LL NEVER SPEAK ILL OF YOUR LOST LOVE AGAIN AS LONG AS I LIVE.
WELL, HERE COMES THE BAD NEWS. LOTS OF INFORMATION, NOT A SINGLE LEAD.
AFTER YOU LEFT, I RAN INTO A FEW OF THESE DEATH'S REIGN ASSWIPES--SORRY--INCLUDING MY OLD PAL SPARKS.
AND YOU THROTTLED THE WHEREABOUTS OF YOUR LOVE'S ARM FROM HIS LAST BREATH.
NO. I GOT CARRIED AWAY AND STOMPED HIS BRAINS TO MUSH ON THE PAVEMENT.
OH, DARLING...
I DID SALVAGE ONE THING...

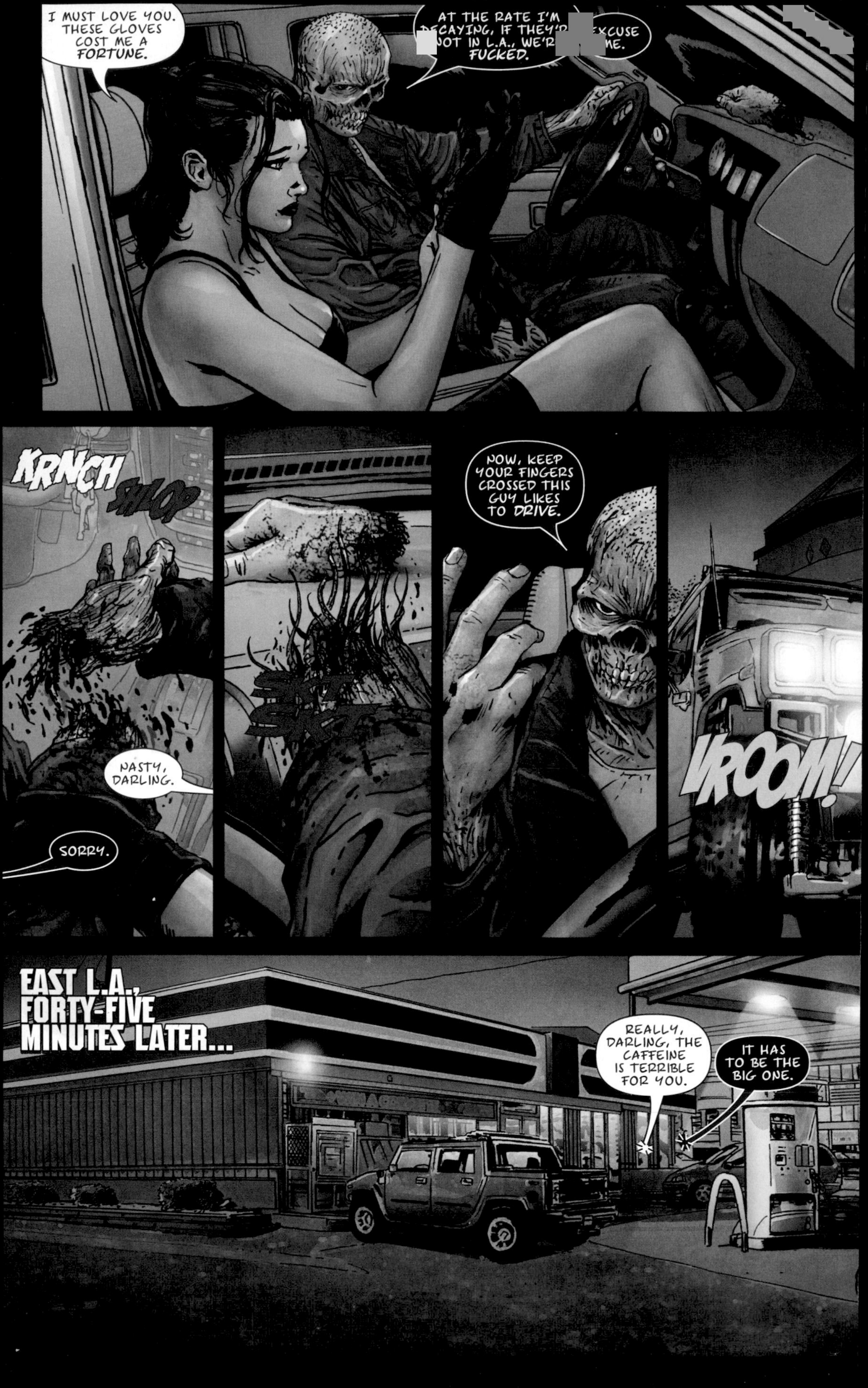
I MUST LOVE YOU. THESE GLOVES COST ME A FORTUNE.
AT THE RATE I'M DECAYING, IF THEY'R OT IN L.A., WE'R FUCKED.
XCUSE ME.
KRNCH
SHLOP
NASTY, DARLING.
SORRY.
NOW, KEEP YOUR FINGERS CROSSED THIS GUY LIKES TO DRIVE.
VROOM!
EAST L.A., FORTY-FIVE MINUTES LATER...
REALLY, DARLING, THE CAFFEINE IS TERRIBLE FOR YOU.
IT HAS TO BE THE BIG ONE.

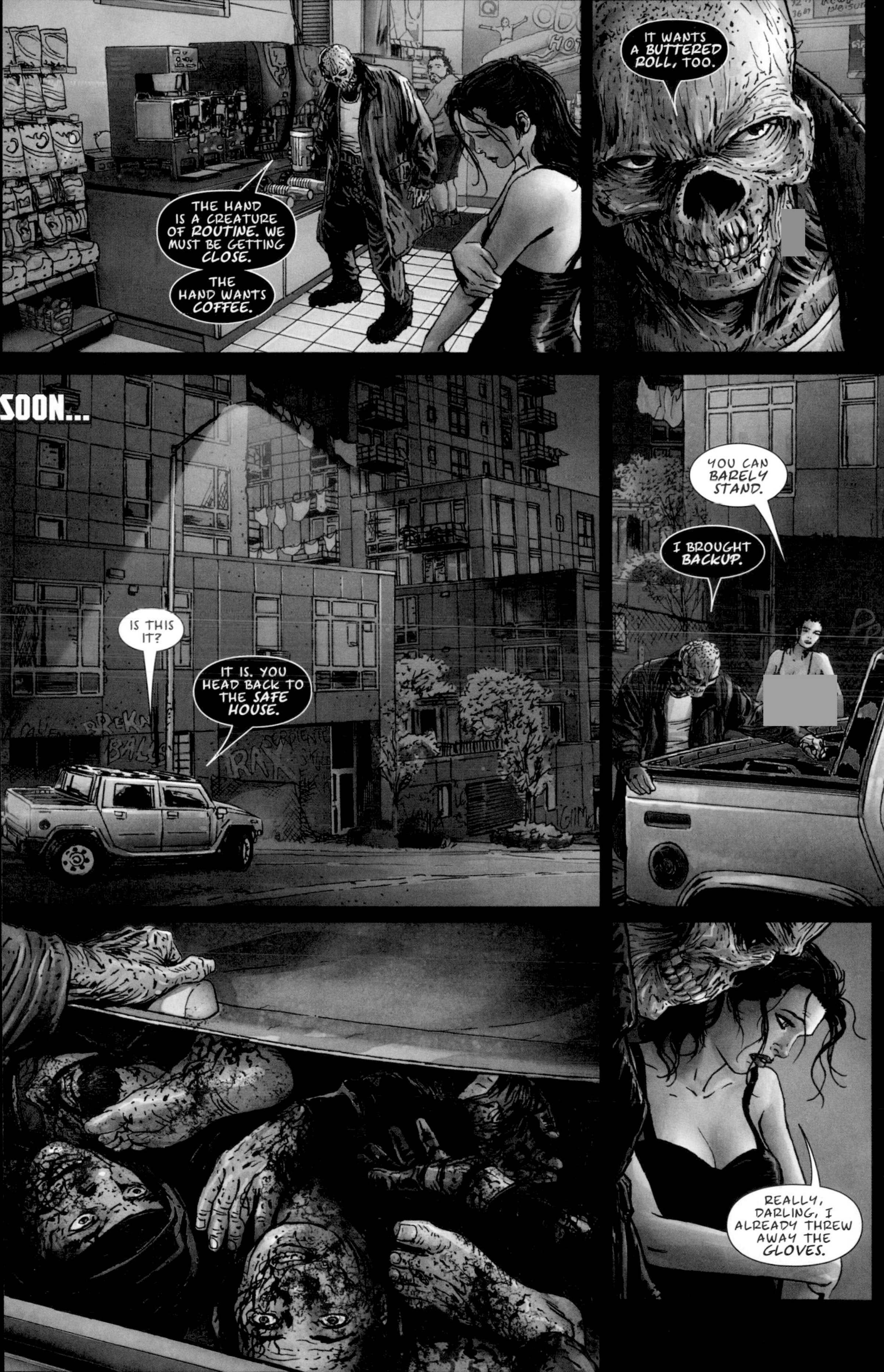
THE HAND IS A CREATURE OF ROUTINE. WE MUST BE GETTING CLOSE.
THE HAND WANTS COFFEE.
IT WANTS A BUTTERED ROLL, TOO.
SOON...
IS THIS IT?
IT IS. YOU HEAD BACK TO THE SAFE HOUSE.
YOU CAN BARELY STAND.
I BROUGHT BACKUP.
REALLY, DARLING, I ALREADY THREW AWAY THE GLOVES.

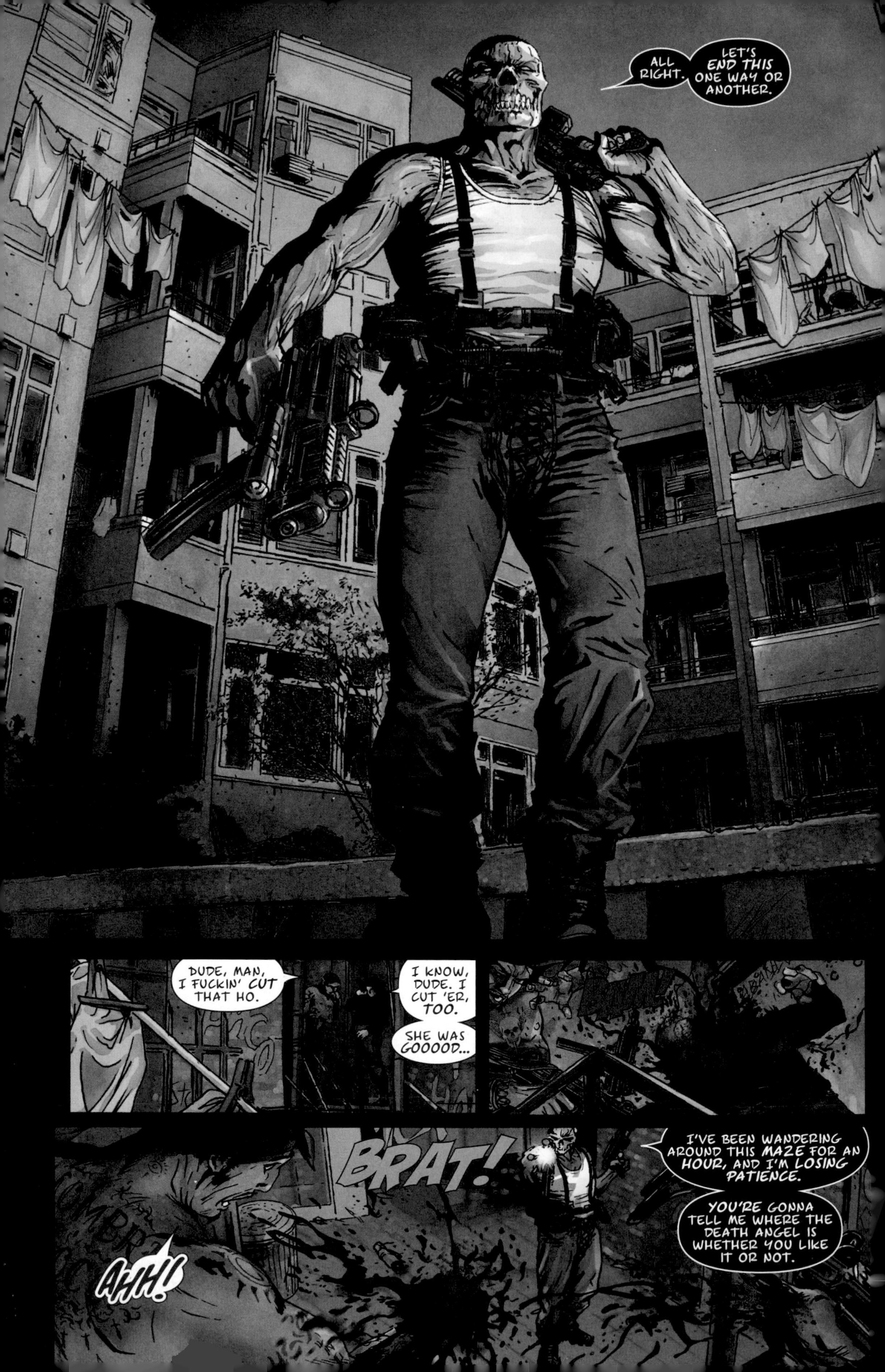
ALL RIGHT.
LET'S END THIS ONE WAY OR ANOTHER.
DUDE, MAN, I FUCKIN' CUT THAT HO.
I KNOW, DUDE. I CUT 'ER, TOO.
SHE WAS GOOOOD...
BRAT!
AHH!
I'VE BEEN WANDERING AROUND THIS MAZE FOR AN HOUR, AND I'M LOSING PATIENCE.
YOU'RE GONNA TELL ME WHERE THE DEATH ANGEL IS WHETHER YOU LIKE IT OR NOT.

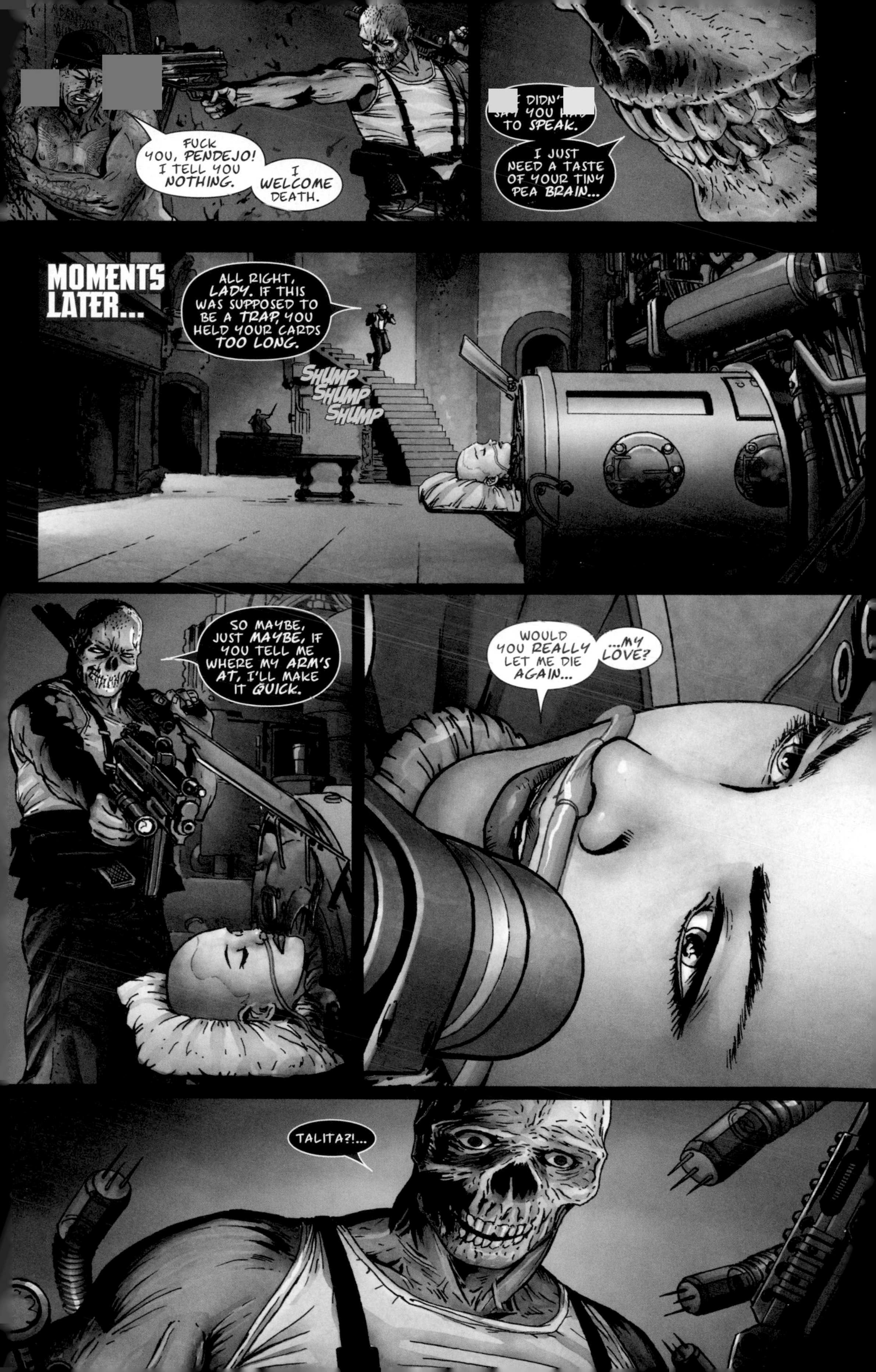
[redacted]
FUCK YOU, PENDEJO! I TELL YOU NOTHING.
I WELCOME DEATH.
[redacted] DIDN'T SAY YOU HA[redacted] TO SPEAK.
I JUST NEED A TASTE OF YOUR TINY PEA BRAIN...
MOMENTS LATER...
ALL RIGHT, LADY. IF THIS WAS SUPPOSED TO BE A TRAP, YOU HELD YOUR CARDS TOO LONG.
SHUMP SHUMP SHUMP
SO MAYBE, JUST MAYBE, IF YOU TELL ME WHERE MY ARM'S AT, I'LL MAKE IT QUICK.
WOULD YOU REALLY LET ME DIE AGAIN...
...MY LOVE?
TALITA?!...

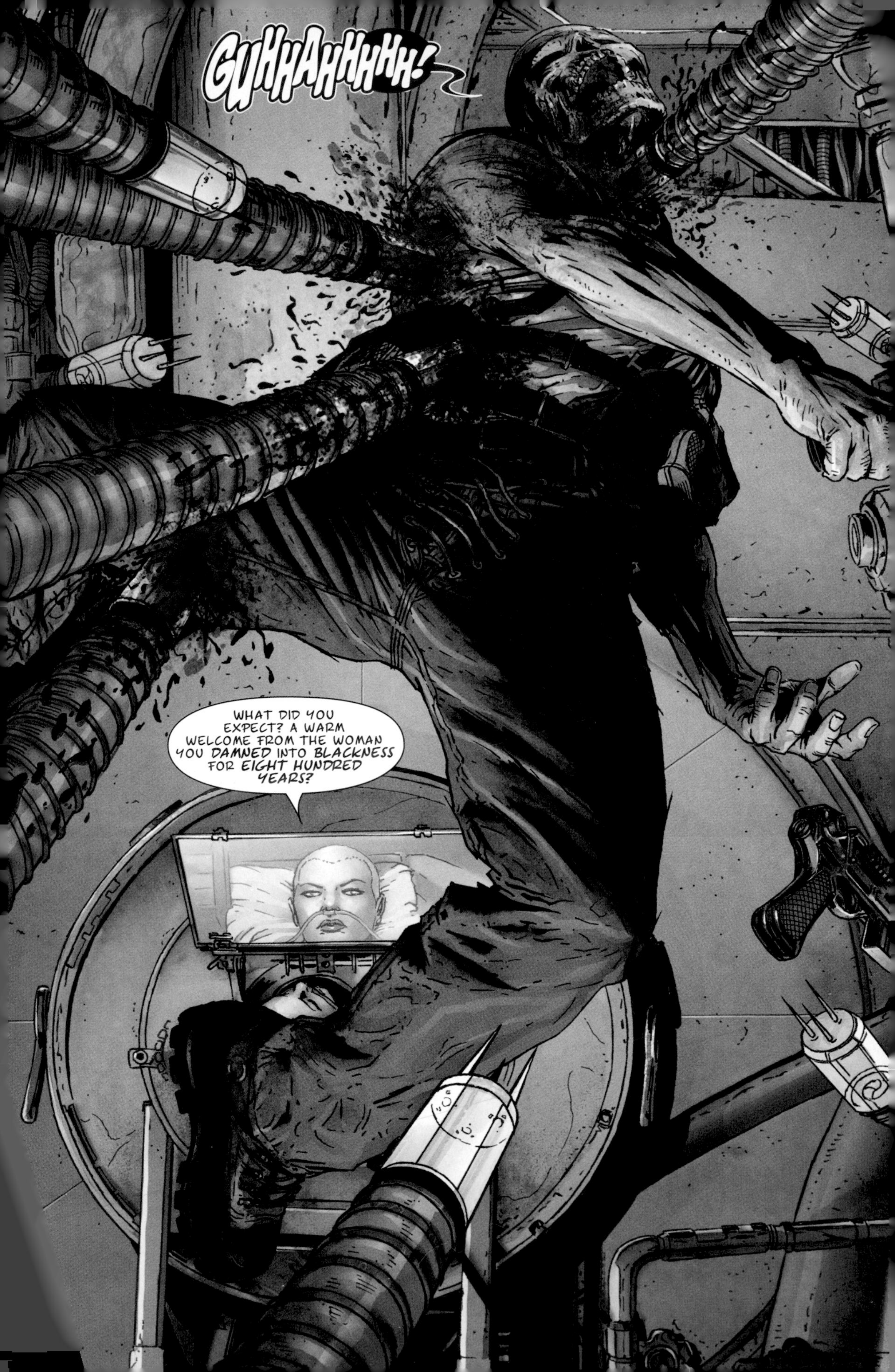
GUHHAHHHHH!
WHAT DID YOU EXPECT? A WARM WELCOME FROM THE WOMAN YOU DAMNED INTO BLACKNESS FOR EIGHT HUNDRED YEARS?

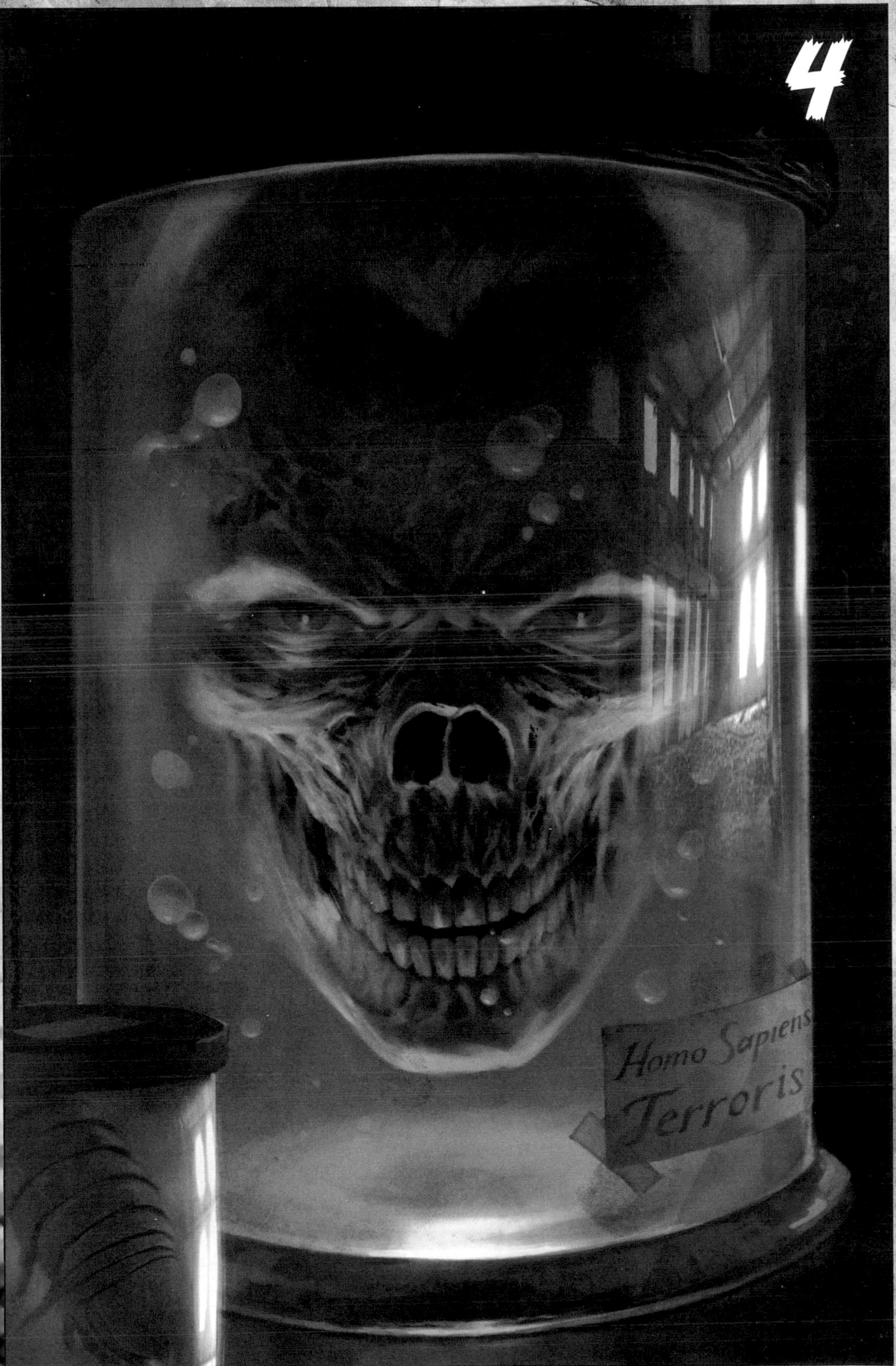
4
Homo Sapiens
Terroris

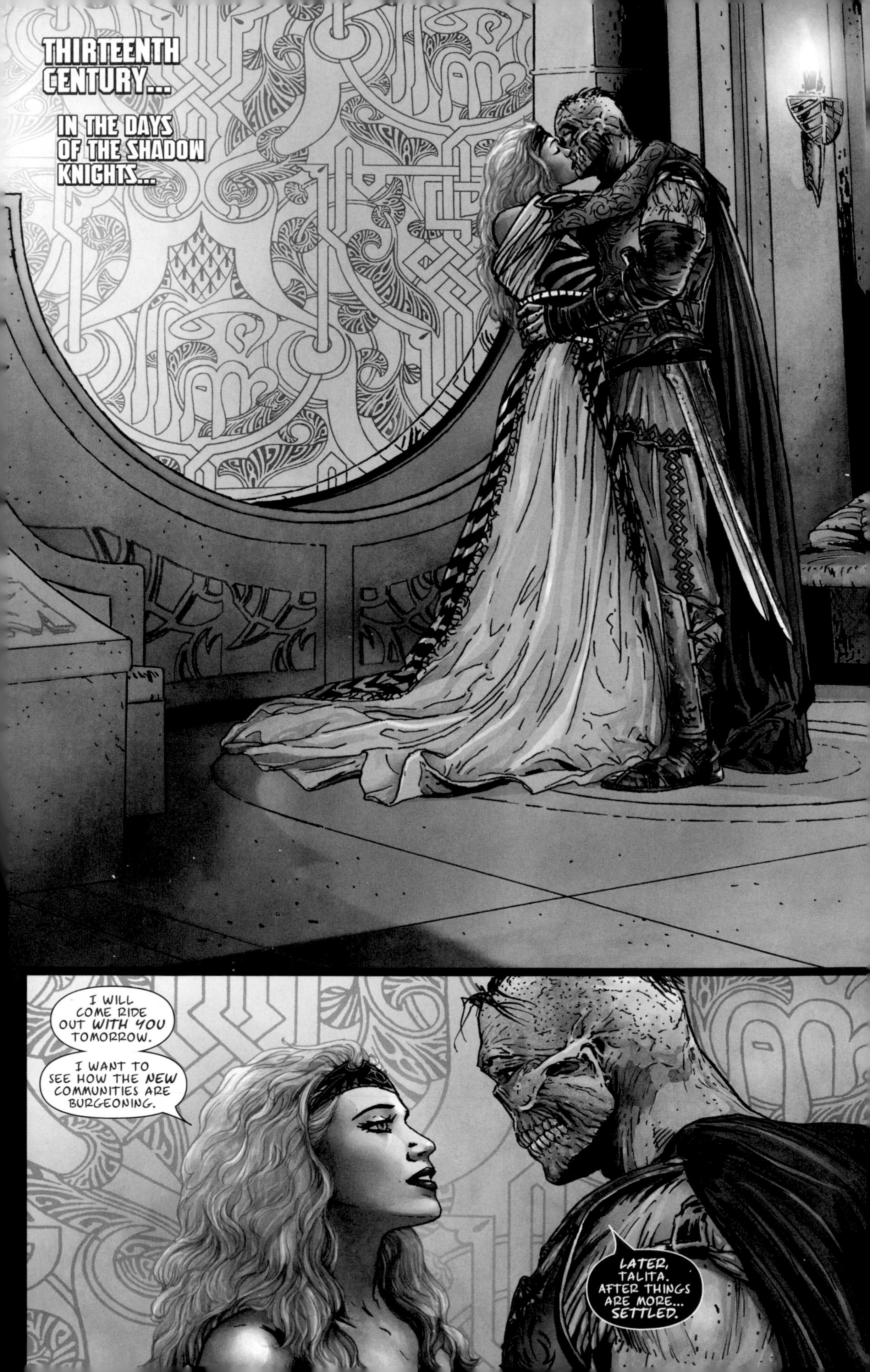
THIRTEENTH CENTURY...
IN THE DAYS OF THE SHADOW KNIGHTS...
I WILL COME RIDE OUT WITH YOU TOMORROW.
I WANT TO SEE HOW THE NEW COMMUNITIES ARE BURGEONING.
LATER, TALITA. AFTER THINGS ARE MORE... SETTLED.

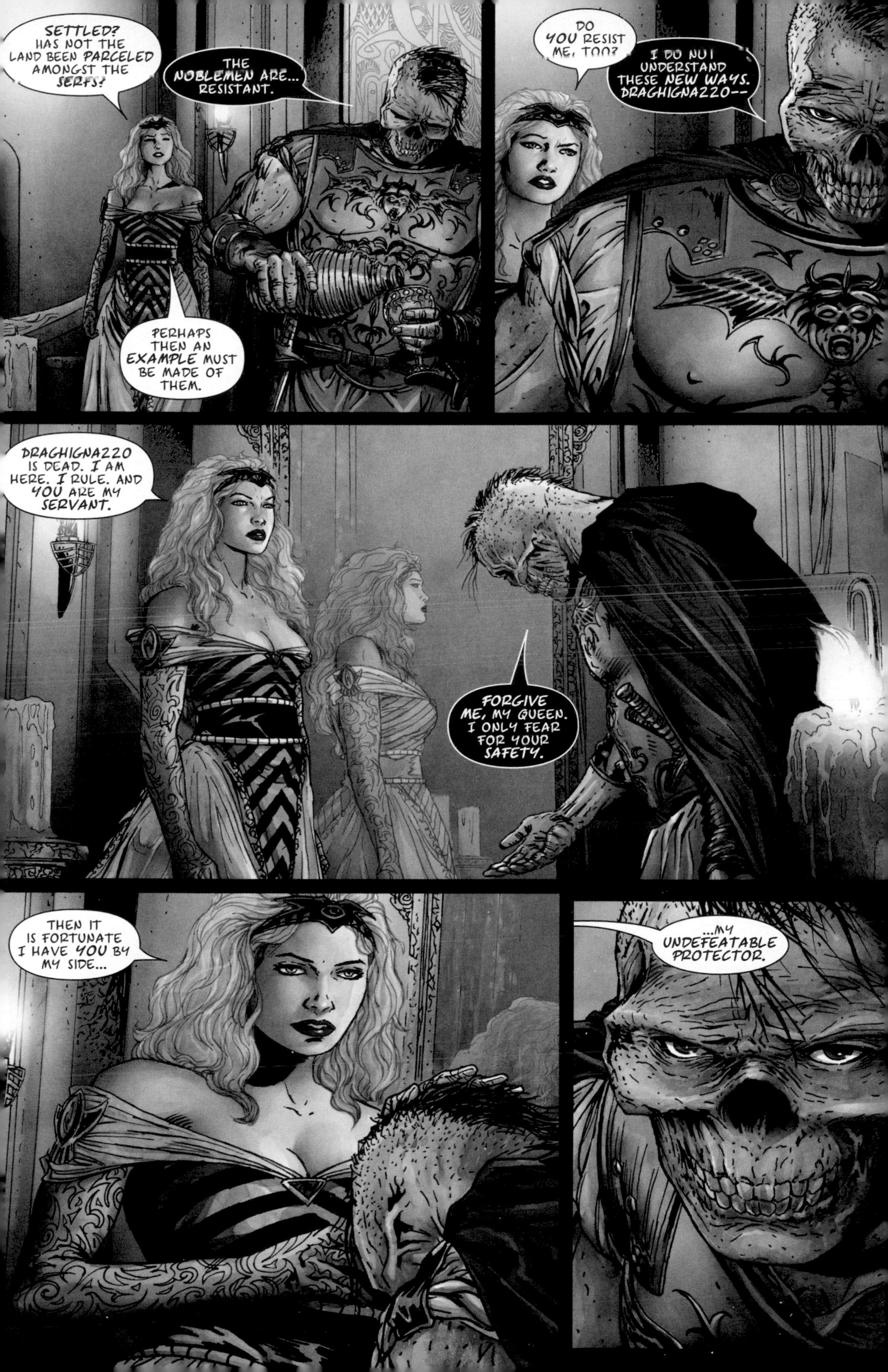
SETTLED? HAS NOT THE LAND BEEN PARCELED AMONGST THE SERFS?
THE NOBLEMEN ARE... RESISTANT.
PERHAPS THEN AN EXAMPLE MUST BE MADE OF THEM.
DO YOU RESIST ME, TOO?
I DO NOT UNDERSTAND THESE NEW WAYS. DRAGHIGNAZZO--
DRAGHIGNAZZO IS DEAD. I AM HERE. I RULE. AND YOU ARE MY SERVANT.
FORGIVE ME, MY QUEEN. I ONLY FEAR FOR YOUR SAFETY.
THEN IT IS FORTUNATE I HAVE YOU BY MY SIDE...
...MY UNDEFEATABLE PROTECTOR.

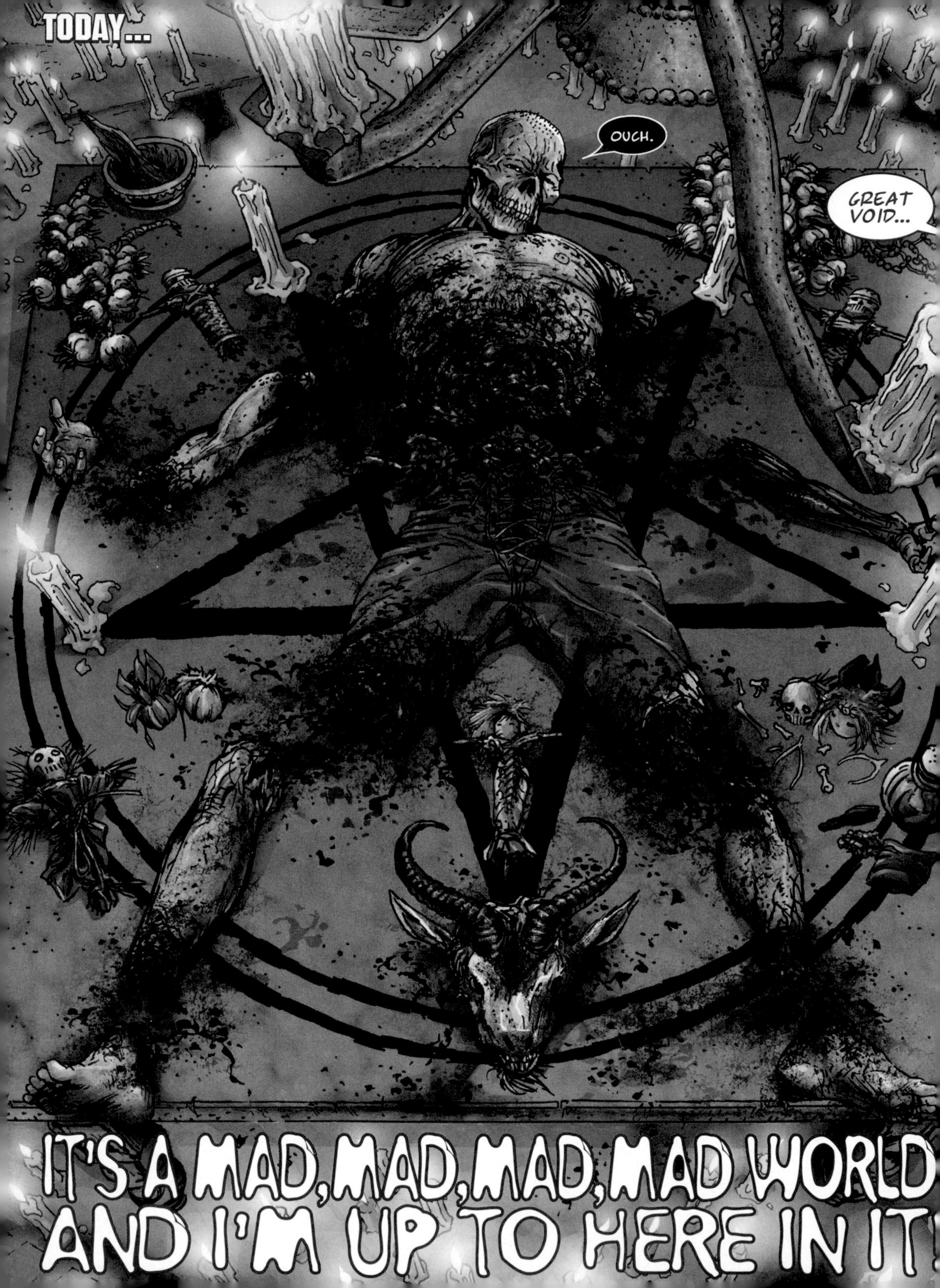
TODAY...
OUCH.
GREAT VOID...
IT'S A MAD, MAD, MAD, MAD WORLD AND I'M UP TO HERE IN IT!

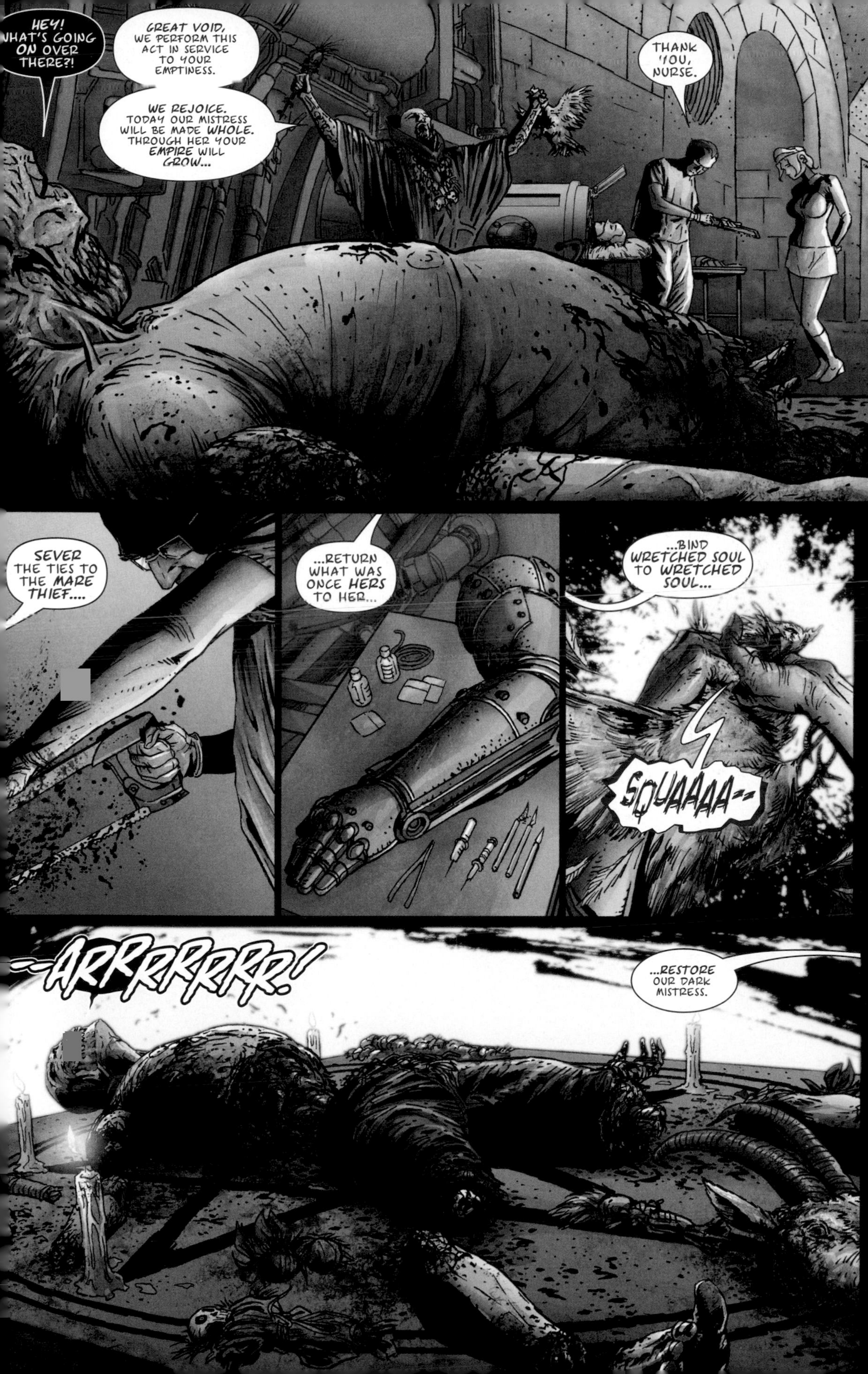
HEY! WHAT'S GOING ON OVER THERE?!
GREAT VOID, WE PERFORM THIS ACT IN SERVICE TO YOUR EMPTINESS.
WE REJOICE. TODAY OUR MISTRESS WILL BE MADE WHOLE. THROUGH HER YOUR EMPIRE WILL GROW...
THANK YOU, NURSE.
SEVER THE TIES TO THE MARE THIEF....
...RETURN WHAT WAS ONCE HERS TO HER...
...BIND WRETCHED SOUL TO WRETCHED SOUL...
SQUAAAA--
--ARRRRRRR!
...RESTORE OUR DARK MISTRESS.

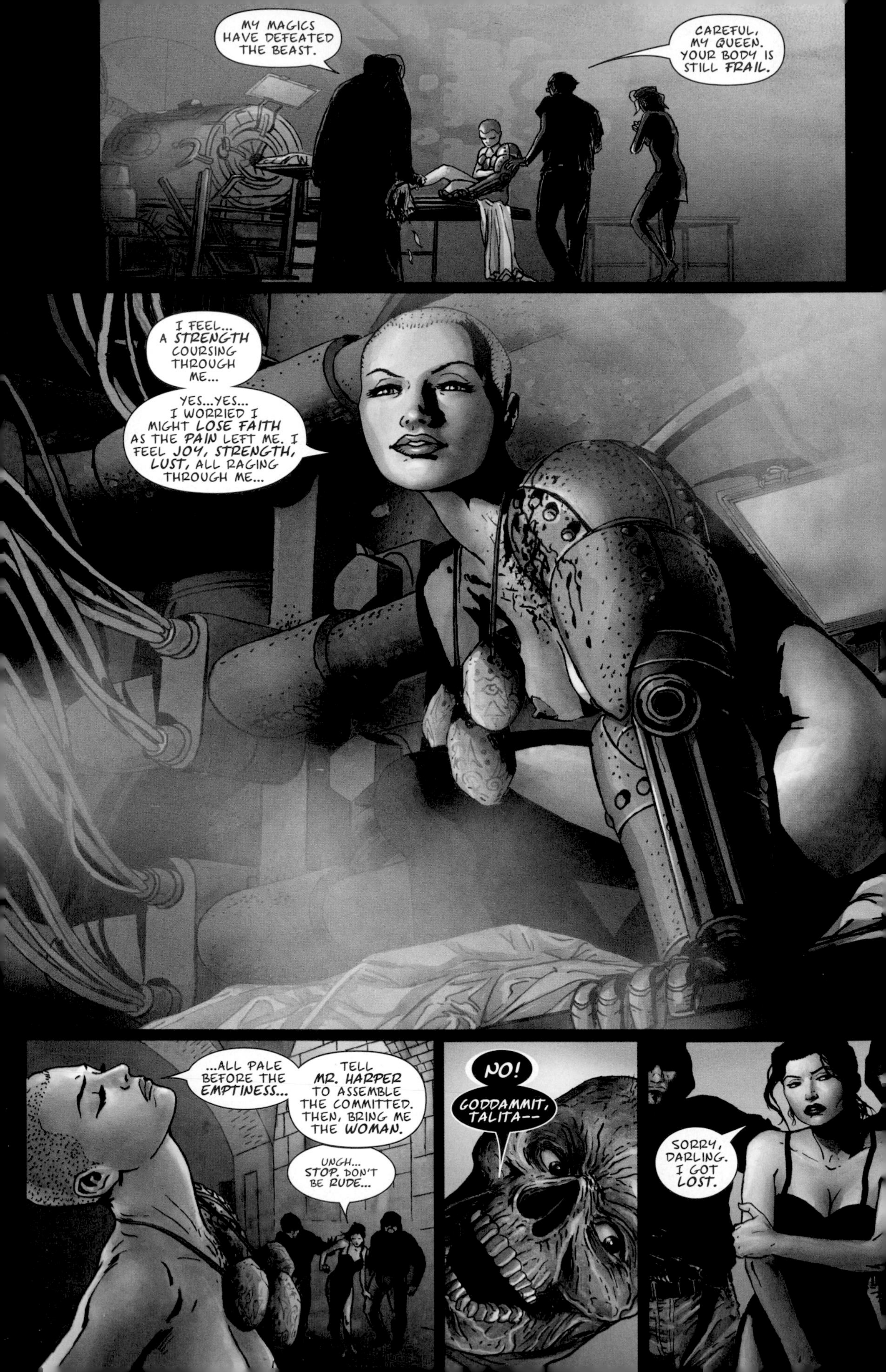
MY MAGICS HAVE DEFEATED THE BEAST.
CAREFUL, MY QUEEN. YOUR BODY IS STILL FRAIL.
I FEEL... A STRENGTH COURSING THROUGH ME...
YES...YES... I WORRIED I MIGHT LOSE FAITH AS THE PAIN LEFT ME. I FEEL JOY, STRENGTH, LUST, ALL RAGING THROUGH ME...
...ALL PALE BEFORE THE EMPTINESS...
TELL MR. HARPER TO ASSEMBLE THE COMMITTED. THEN, BRING ME THE WOMAN.
UNGH... STOP. DON'T BE RUDE...
NO!
GODDAMMIT, TALITA--
SORRY, DARLING. I GOT LOST.

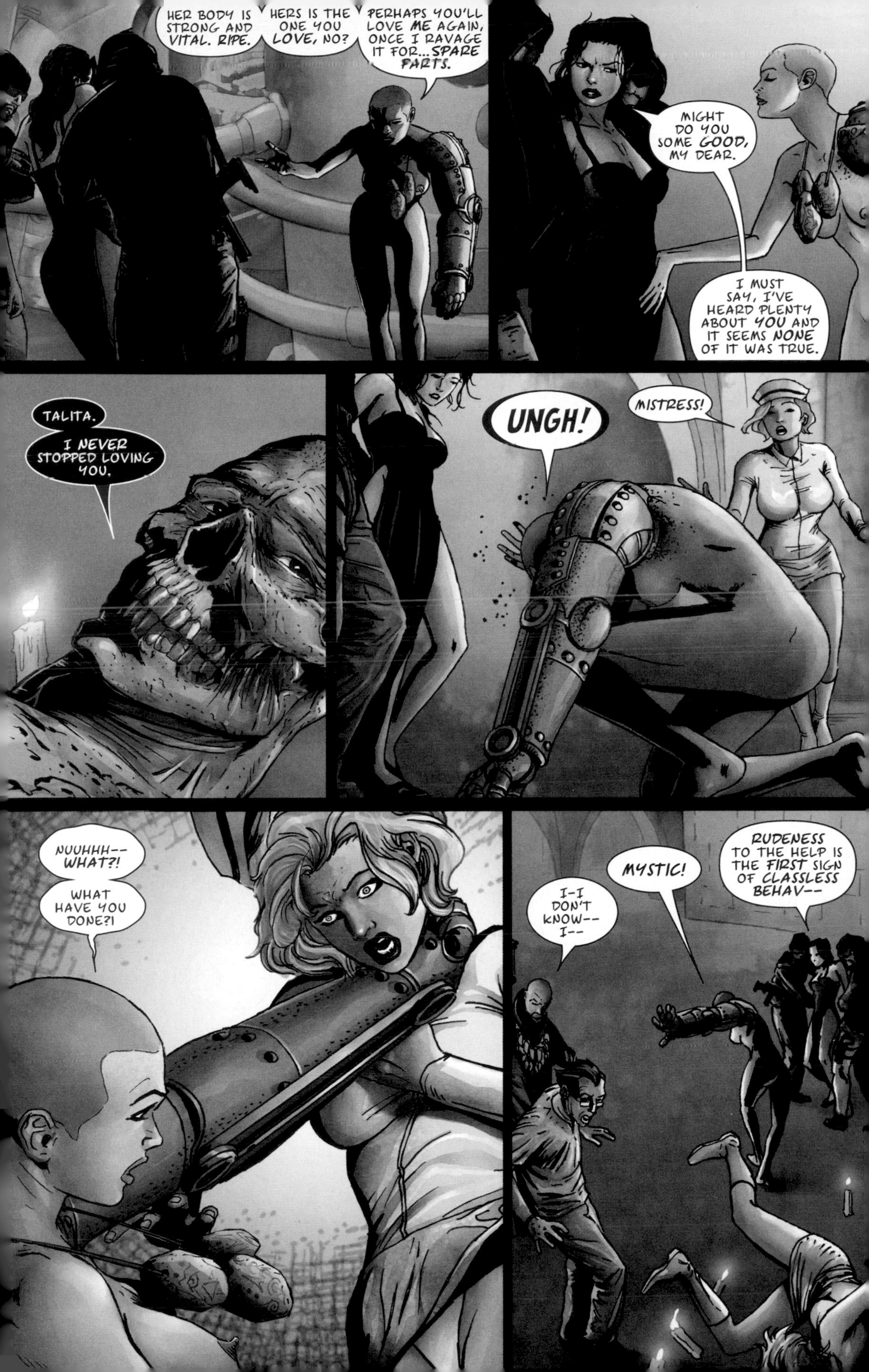
HER BODY IS STRONG AND VITAL. RIPE.
HERS IS THE ONE YOU LOVE, NO?
PERHAPS YOU'LL LOVE ME AGAIN, ONCE I RAVAGE IT FOR... SPARE PARTS.
MIGHT DO YOU SOME GOOD, MY DEAR.
I MUST SAY, I'VE HEARD PLENTY ABOUT YOU AND IT SEEMS NONE OF IT WAS TRUE.
TALITA.
I NEVER STOPPED LOVING YOU.
UNGH!
MISTRESS!
NUUHHH-- WHAT?!
WHAT HAVE YOU DONE?!
I-I DON'T KNOW-- I--
MYSTIC!
RUDENESS TO THE HELP IS THE FIRST SIGN OF CLASSLESS BEHAV--

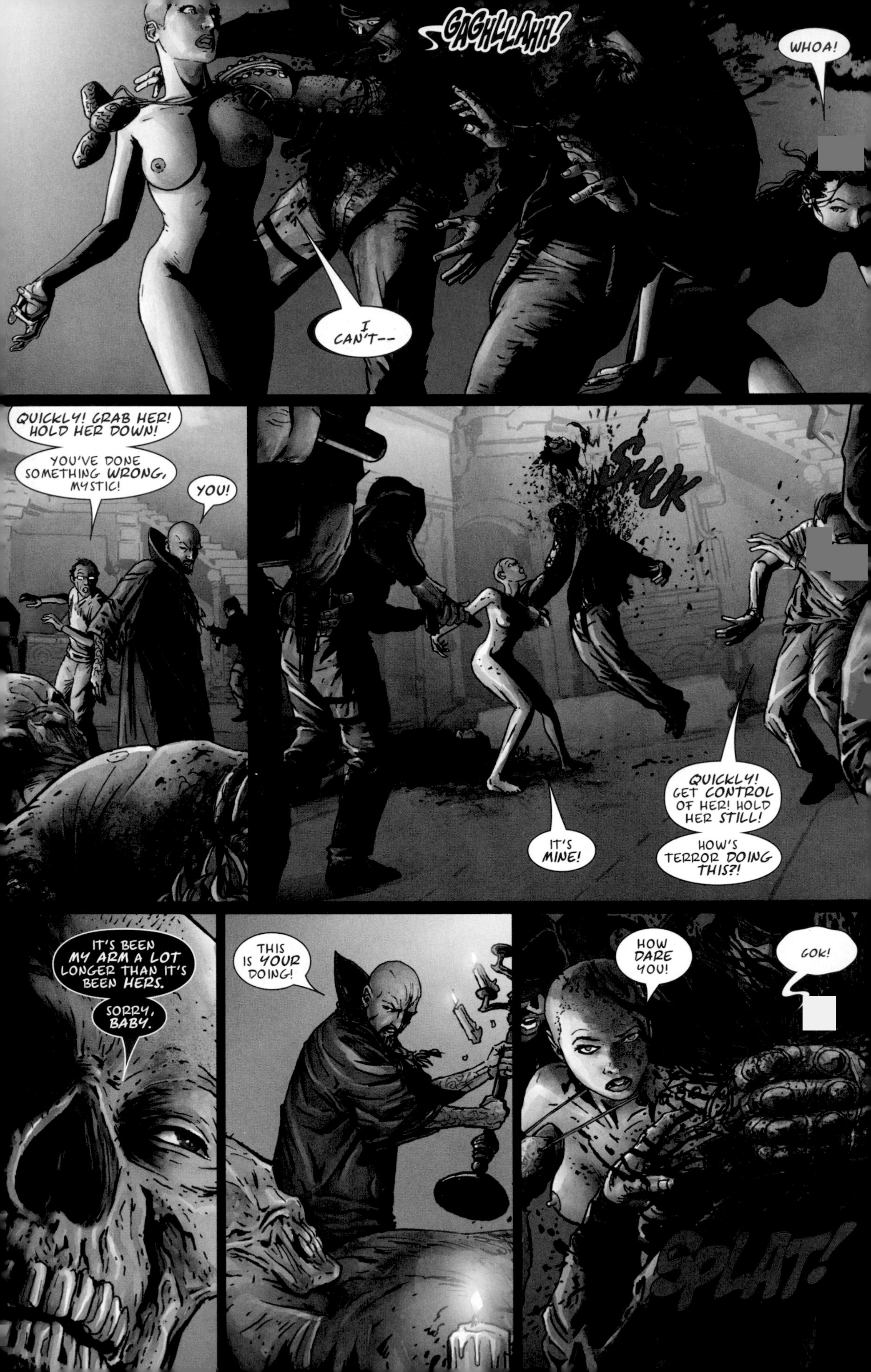
GAGHLLAHH!
WHOA!
I CAN'T--
QUICKLY! GRAB HER! HOLD HER DOWN!
YOU'VE DONE SOMETHING WRONG, MYSTIC!
YOU!
SHUK
IT'S MINE!
QUICKLY! GET CONTROL OF HER! HOLD HER STILL!
HOW'S TERROR DOING THIS?!
IT'S BEEN MY ARM A LOT LONGER THAN IT'S BEEN HERS.
SORRY, BABY.
THIS IS YOUR DOING!
HOW DARE YOU!
GOK!
SPLAT!

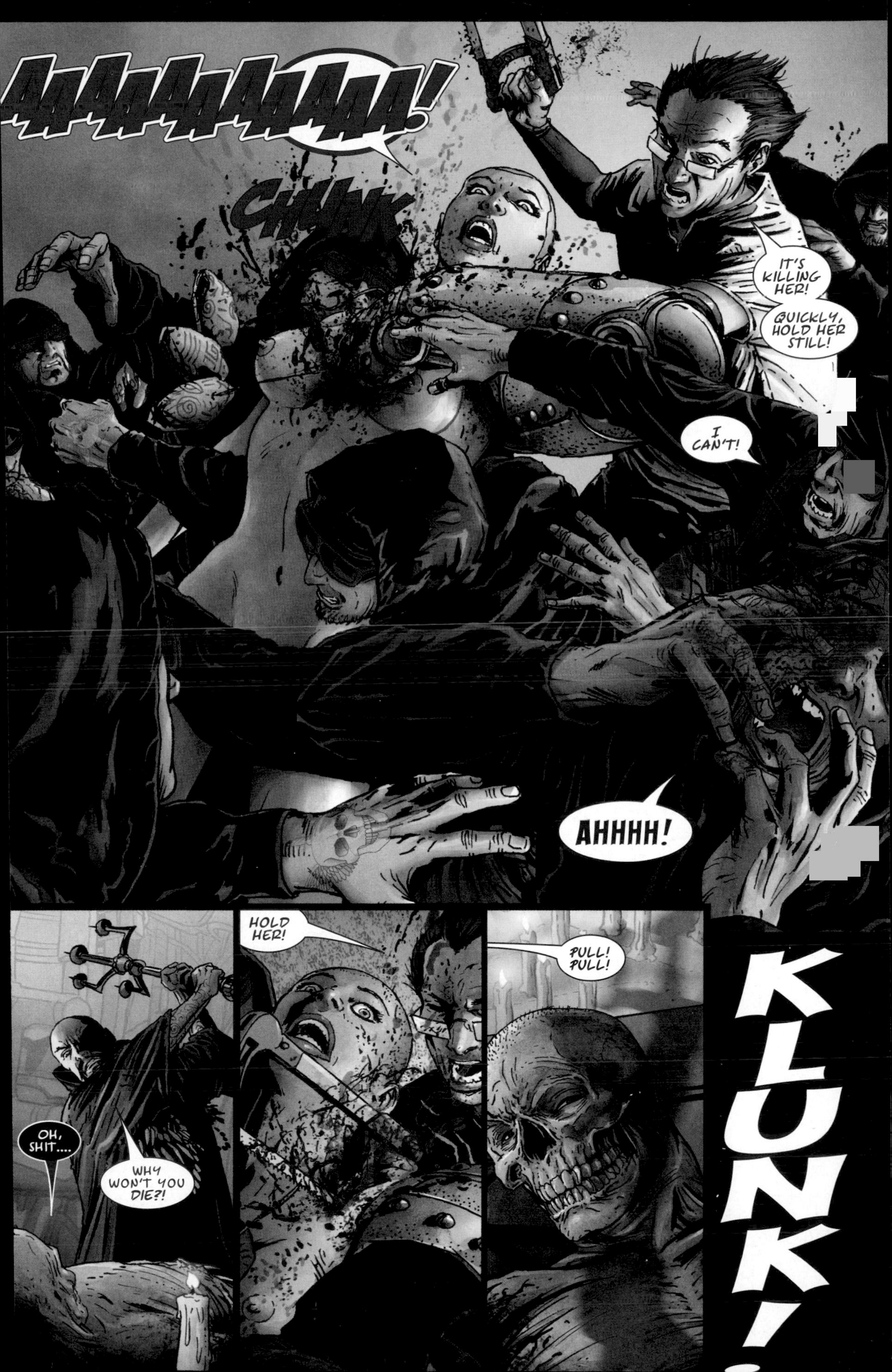
AAAAAAAAAA!
CHUNK
IT'S KILLING HER!
QUICKLY, HOLD HER STILL!
I CAN'T!
AHHHH!
OH, SHIT....
WHY WON'T YOU DIE?!
HOLD HER!
PULL! PULL!
KLUNK!

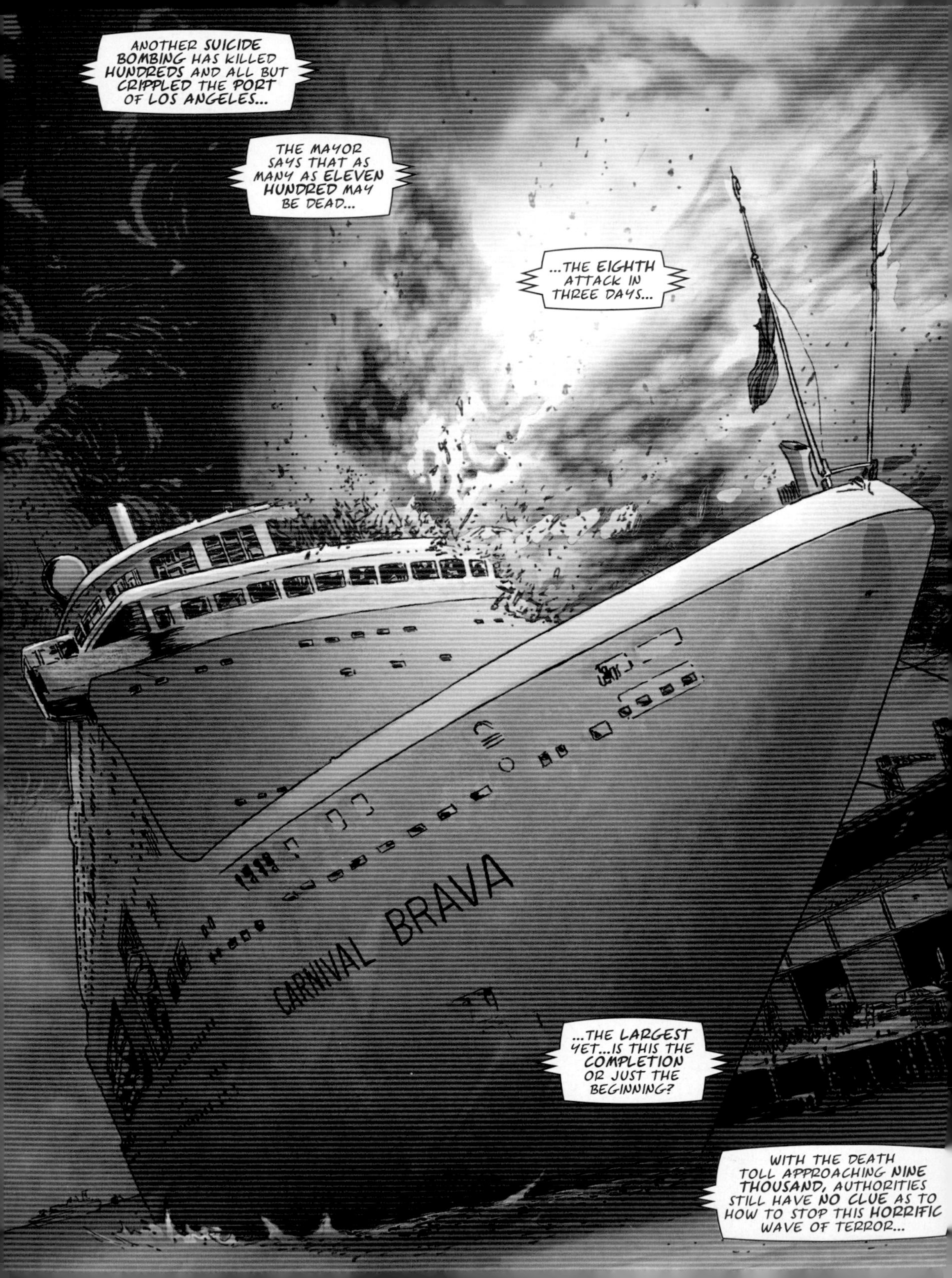
ANOTHER SUICIDE BOMBING HAS KILLED HUNDREDS AND ALL BUT CRIPPLED THE PORT OF LOS ANGELES...
THE MAYOR SAYS THAT AS MANY AS ELEVEN HUNDRED MAY BE DEAD...
...THE EIGHTH ATTACK IN THREE DAYS...
CARNIVAL BRAVA
...THE LARGEST YET...IS THIS THE COMPLETION OR JUST THE BEGINNING?
WITH THE DEATH TOLL APPROACHING NINE THOUSAND, AUTHORITIES STILL HAVE NO CLUE AS TO HOW TO STOP THIS HORRIFIC WAVE OF TERROR...

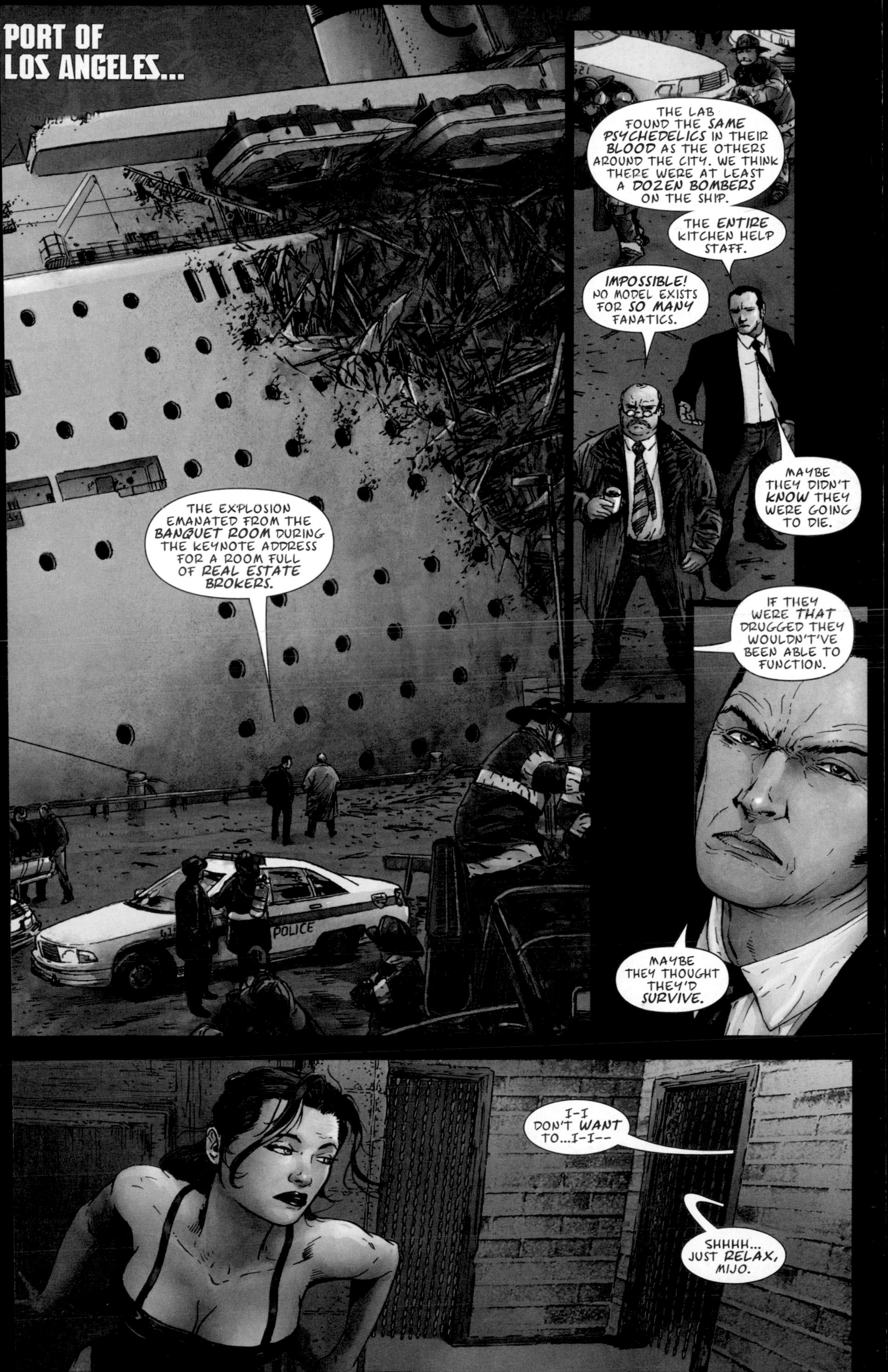
PORT OF LOS ANGELES...
THE EXPLOSION EMANATED FROM THE BANQUET ROOM DURING THE KEYNOTE ADDRESS FOR A ROOM FULL OF REAL ESTATE BROKERS.
THE LAB FOUND THE SAME PSYCHEDELICS IN THEIR BLOOD AS THE OTHERS AROUND THE CITY. WE THINK THERE WERE AT LEAST A DOZEN BOMBERS ON THE SHIP.
THE ENTIRE KITCHEN HELP STAFF.
IMPOSSIBLE! NO MODEL EXISTS FOR SO MANY FANATICS.
MAYBE THEY DIDN'T KNOW THEY WERE GOING TO DIE.
IF THEY WERE THAT DRUGGED THEY WOULDN'T'VE BEEN ABLE TO FUNCTION.
MAYBE THEY THOUGHT THEY'D SURVIVE.
I-I DON'T WANT TO...I-I--
SHHHH... JUST RELAX, MIJO.

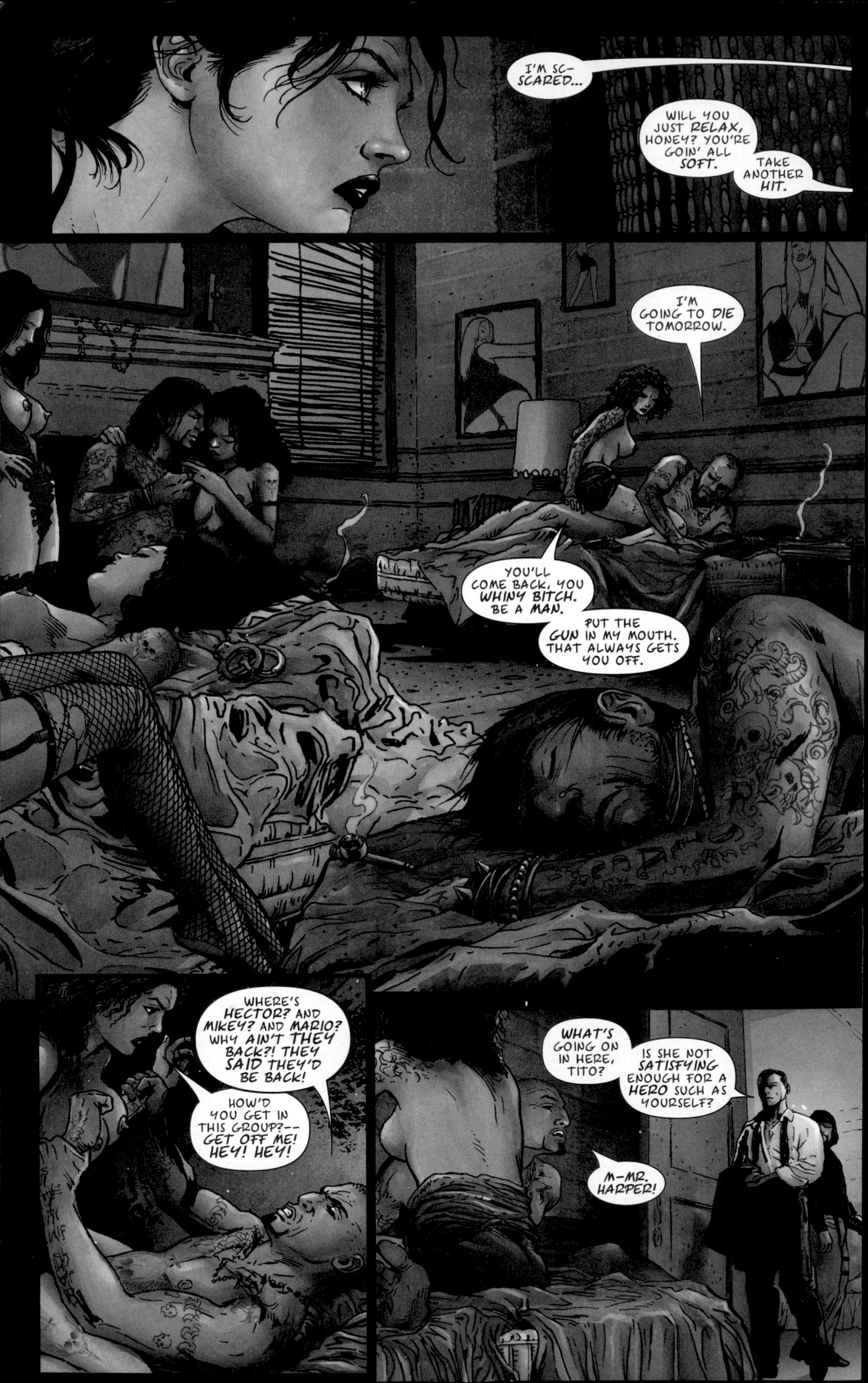
I'M SC-SCARED...
WILL YOU JUST RELAX, HONEY? YOU'RE GOIN' ALL SOFT.
TAKE ANOTHER HIT.
I'M GOING TO DIE TOMORROW.
YOU'LL COME BACK, YOU WHINY BITCH. BE A MAN.
PUT THE GUN IN MY MOUTH. THAT ALWAYS GETS YOU OFF.
WHERE'S HECTOR? AND MIKEY? AND MARIO? WHY AIN'T THEY BACK?! THEY SAID THEY'D BE BACK!
HOW'D YOU GET IN THIS GROUP?-- GET OFF ME! HEY! HEY!
WHAT'S GOING ON IN HERE, TITO?
IS SHE NOT SATISFYING ENOUGH FOR A HERO SUCH AS YOURSELF?
M-MR. HARPER!

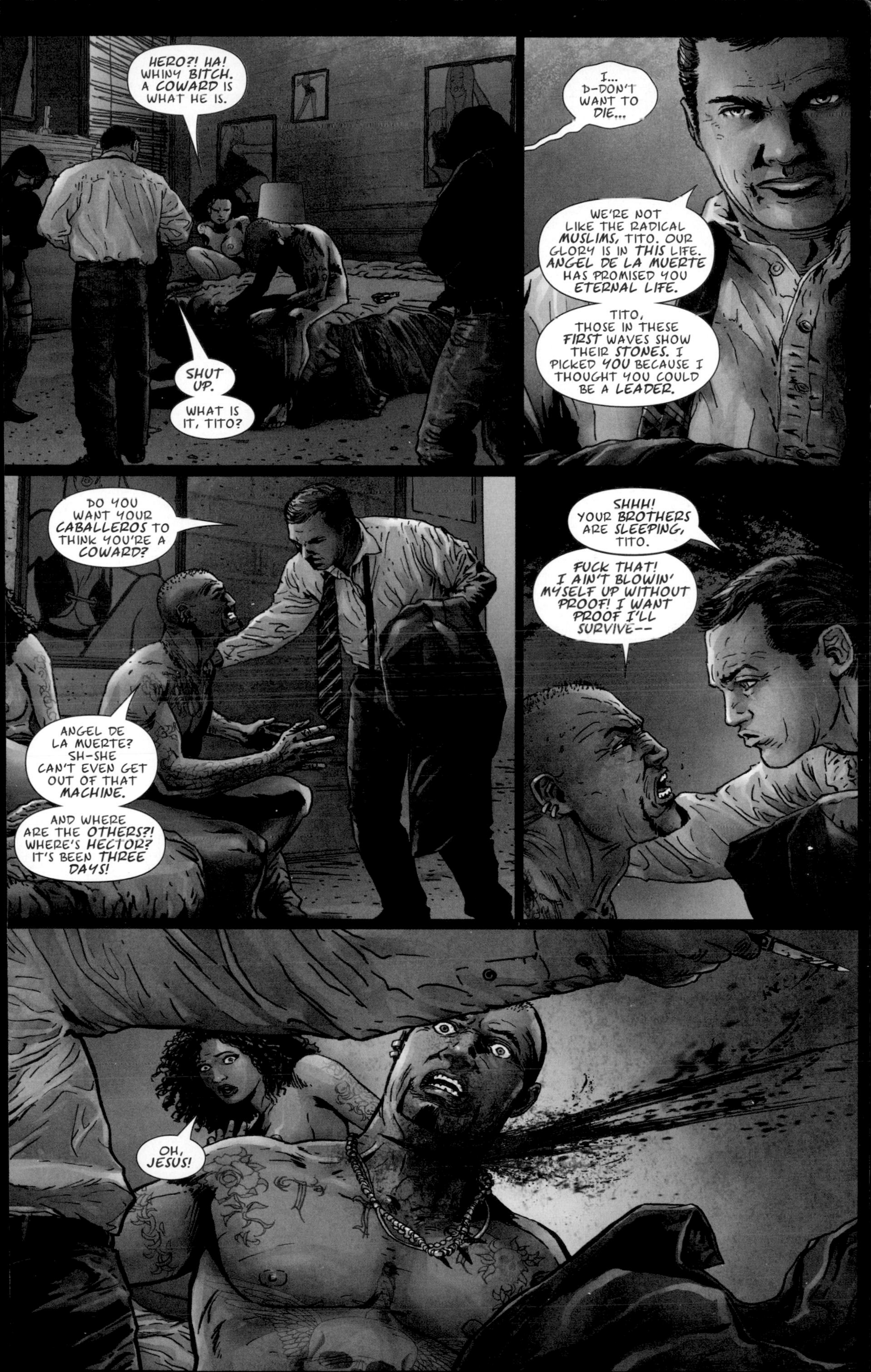
HERO?! HA! WHINY BITCH. A COWARD IS WHAT HE IS.
SHUT UP.
WHAT IS IT, TITO?
I... D-DON'T WANT TO DIE...
WE'RE NOT LIKE THE RADICAL MUSLIMS, TITO. OUR GLORY IS IN THIS LIFE. ANGEL DE LA MUERTE HAS PROMISED YOU ETERNAL LIFE.
TITO, THOSE IN THESE FIRST WAVES SHOW THEIR STONES. I PICKED YOU BECAUSE I THOUGHT YOU COULD BE A LEADER.
DO YOU WANT YOUR CABALLEROS TO THINK YOU'RE A COWARD?
ANGEL DE LA MUERTE? SH-SHE CAN'T EVEN GET OUT OF THAT MACHINE.
AND WHERE ARE THE OTHERS?! WHERE'S HECTOR? IT'S BEEN THREE DAYS!
SHHH! YOUR BROTHERS ARE SLEEPING, TITO.
FUCK THAT! I AIN'T BLOWIN' MYSELF UP WITHOUT PROOF! I WANT PROOF I'LL SURVIVE--
OH, JESUS!

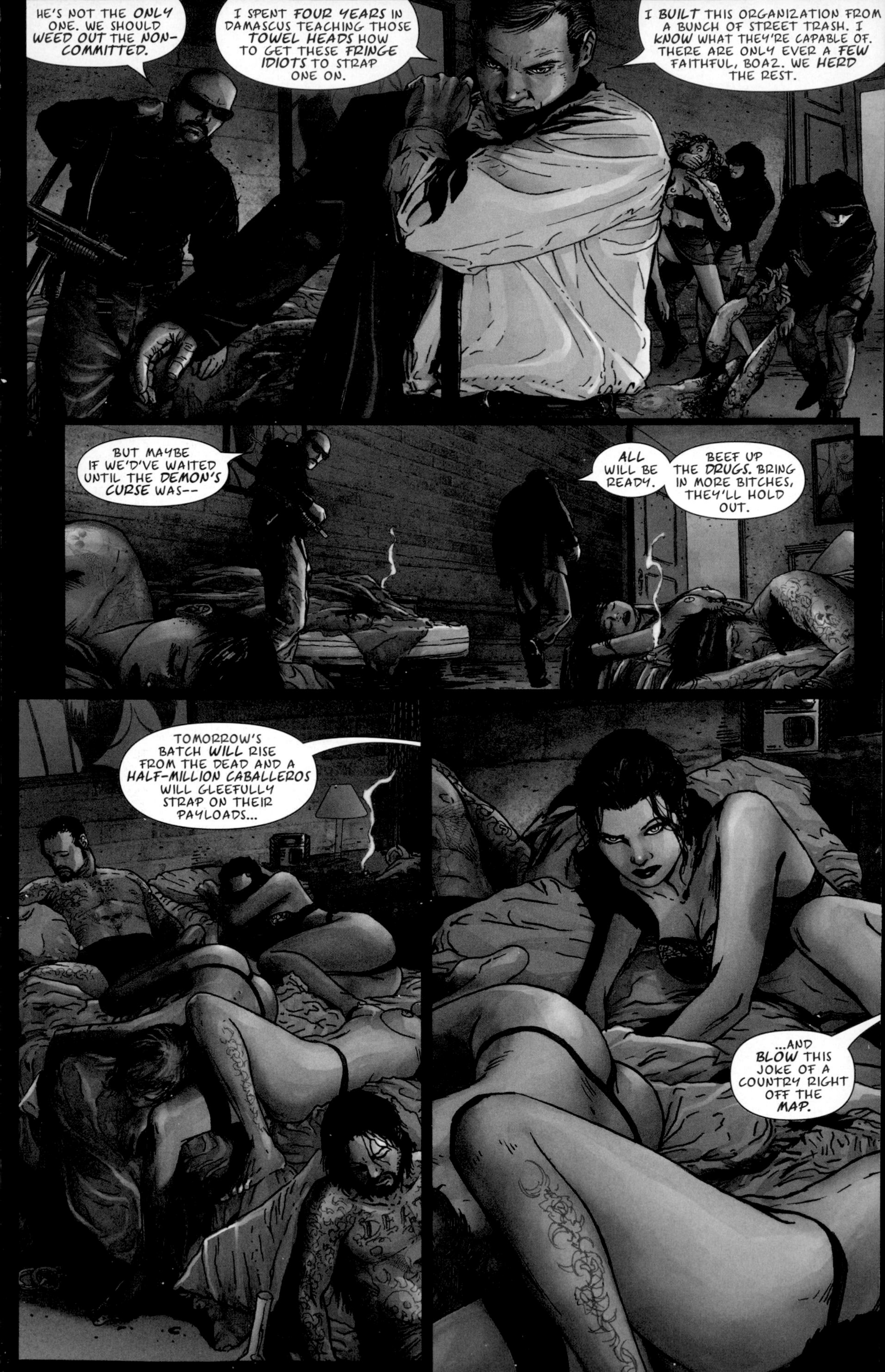
HE'S NOT THE ONLY ONE. WE SHOULD WEED OUT THE NON-COMMITTED.
I SPENT FOUR YEARS IN DAMASCUS TEACHING THOSE TOWEL HEADS HOW TO GET THESE FRINGE IDIOTS TO STRAP ONE ON.
I BUILT THIS ORGANIZATION FROM A BUNCH OF STREET TRASH. I KNOW WHAT THEY'RE CAPABLE OF. THERE ARE ONLY EVER A FEW FAITHFUL, BOAZ. WE HERD THE REST.
BUT MAYBE IF WE'D'VE WAITED UNTIL THE DEMON'S CURSE WAS--
ALL WILL BE READY.
BEEF UP THE DRUGS. BRING IN MORE BITCHES, THEY'LL HOLD OUT.
TOMORROW'S BATCH WILL RISE FROM THE DEAD AND A HALF-MILLION CABALLEROS WILL GLEEFULLY STRAP ON THEIR PAYLOADS...
...AND BLOW THIS JOKE OF A COUNTRY RIGHT OFF THE MAP.

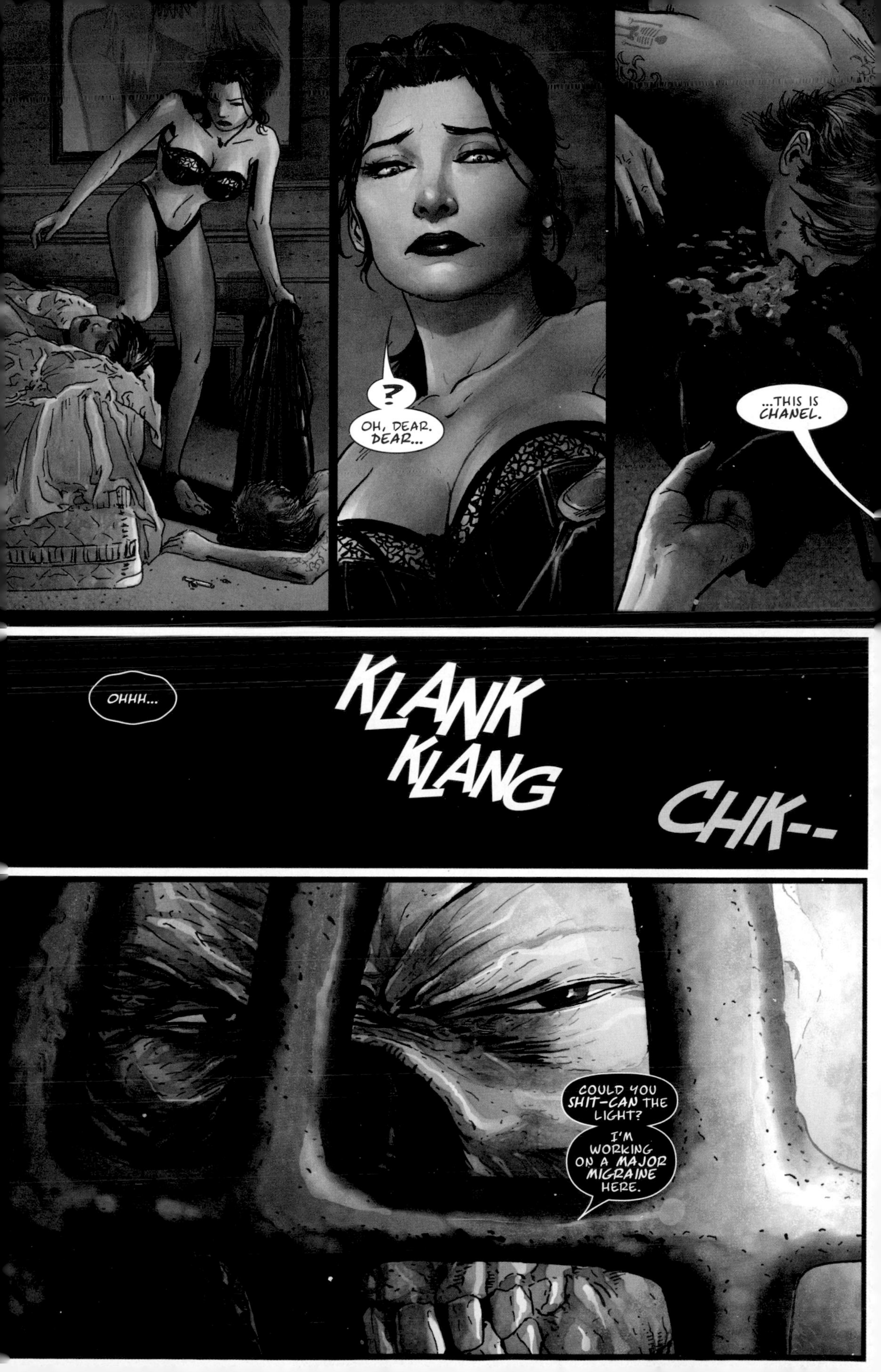
?
OH, DEAR. DEAR...
...THIS IS CHANEL.
OHHH...
KLANK
KLANG
CHK--
COULD YOU SHIT-CAN THE LIGHT?
I'M WORKING ON A MAJOR MIGRAINE HERE.

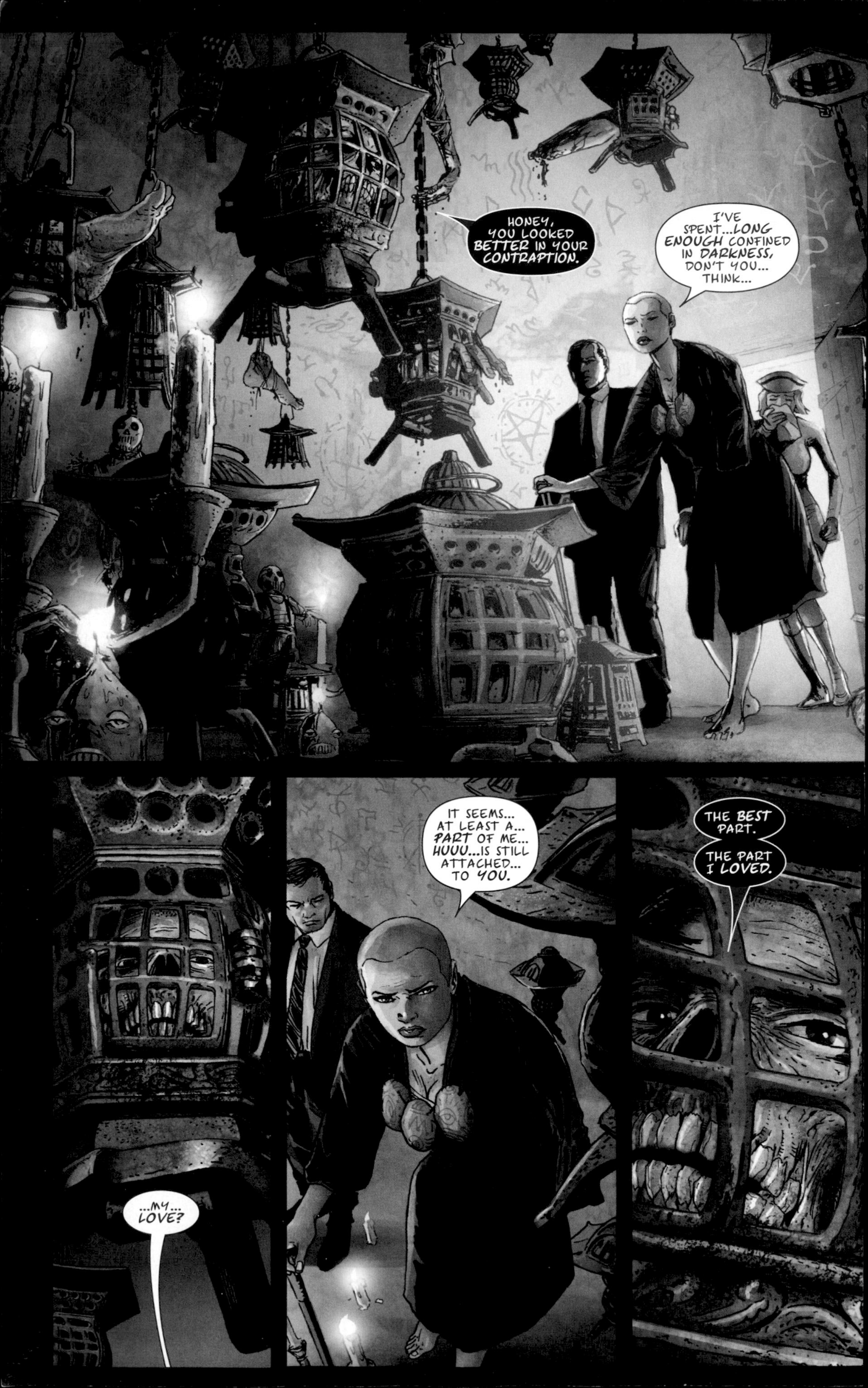
HONEY, YOU LOOKED BETTER IN YOUR CONTRAPTION.
I'VE SPENT...LONG ENOUGH CONFINED IN DARKNESS, DON'T YOU... THINK...
...MY... LOVE?
IT SEEMS... AT LEAST A... PART OF ME... HUUU...IS STILL ATTACHED... TO YOU.
THE BEST PART.
THE PART I LOVED.

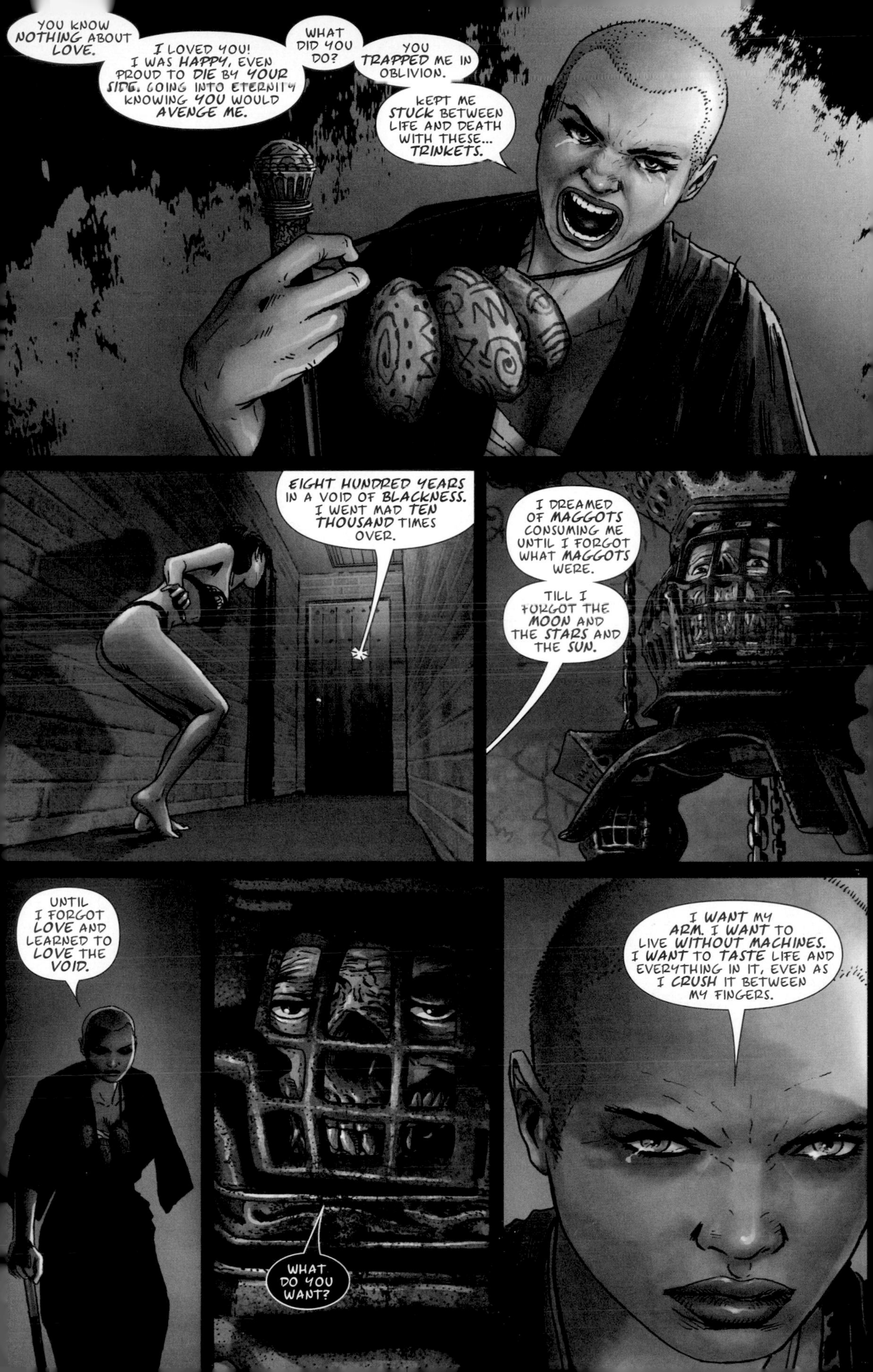

YOU KNOW NOTHING ABOUT LOVE.
I LOVED YOU! I WAS HAPPY, EVEN PROUD TO DIE BY YOUR SIDE. GOING INTO ETERNITY KNOWING YOU WOULD AVENGE ME.
WHAT DID YOU DO?
YOU TRAPPED ME IN OBLIVION.
KEPT ME STUCK BETWEEN LIFE AND DEATH WITH THESE... TRINKETS.
EIGHT HUNDRED YEARS IN A VOID OF BLACKNESS. I WENT MAD TEN THOUSAND TIMES OVER.
I DREAMED OF MAGGOTS CONSUMING ME UNTIL I FORGOT WHAT MAGGOTS WERE.
TILL I FORGOT THE MOON AND THE STARS AND THE SUN.
UNTIL I FORGOT LOVE AND LEARNED TO LOVE THE VOID.
WHAT DO YOU WANT?
I WANT MY ARM. I WANT TO LIVE WITHOUT MACHINES. I WANT TO TASTE LIFE AND EVERYTHING IN IT, EVEN AS I CRUSH IT BETWEEN MY FINGERS.

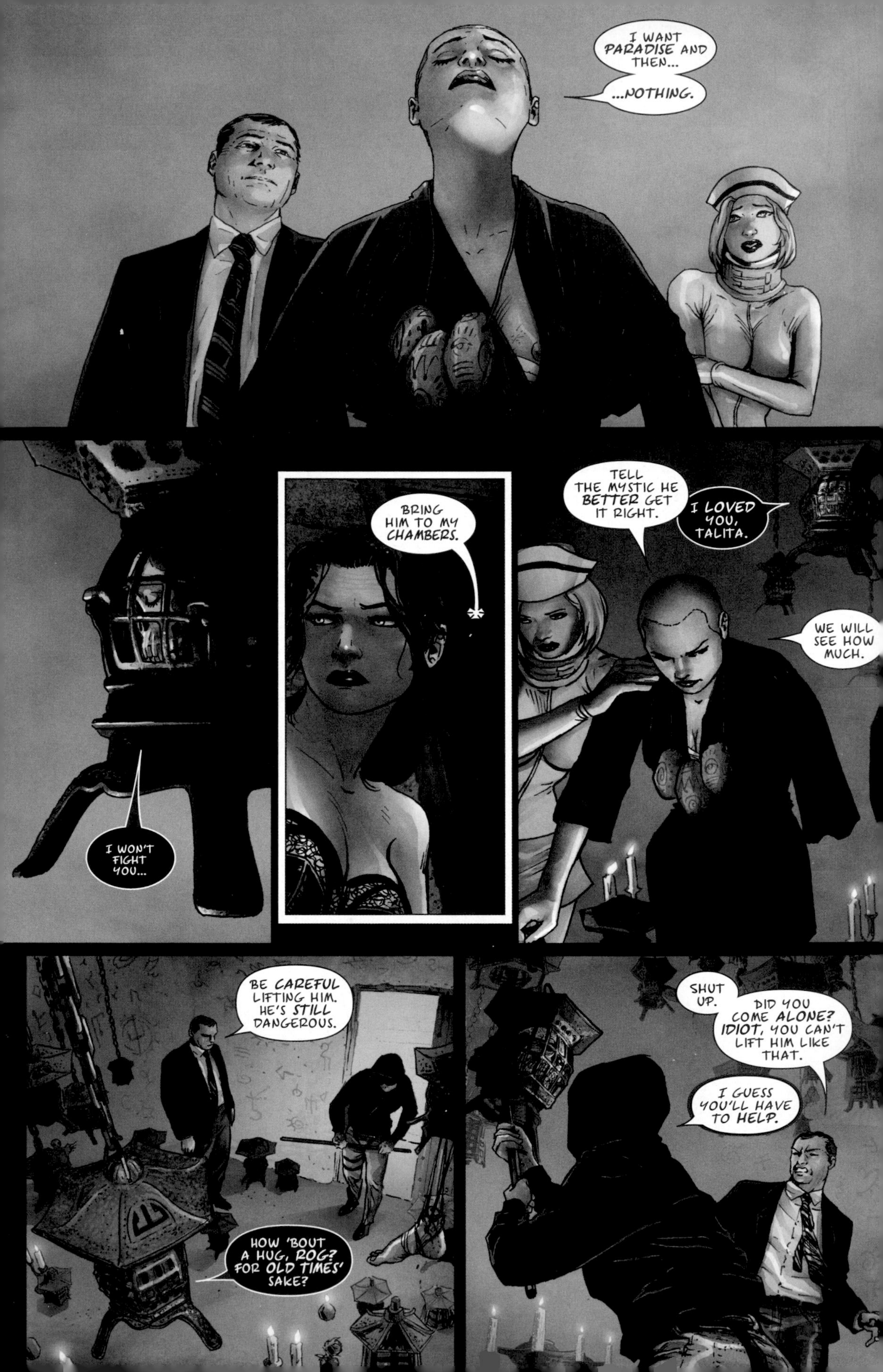
I WANT PARADISE AND THEN...
...NOTHING.
I WON'T FIGHT YOU...
BRING HIM TO MY CHAMBERS.
TELL THE MYSTIC HE BETTER GET IT RIGHT.
I LOVED YOU, TALITA.
WE WILL SEE HOW MUCH.
BE CAREFUL LIFTING HIM. HE'S STILL DANGEROUS.
HOW 'BOUT A HUG, ROG? FOR OLD TIMES' SAKE?
SHUT UP.
DID YOU COME ALONE? IDIOT, YOU CAN'T LIFT HIM LIKE THAT.
I GUESS YOU'LL HAVE TO HELP.

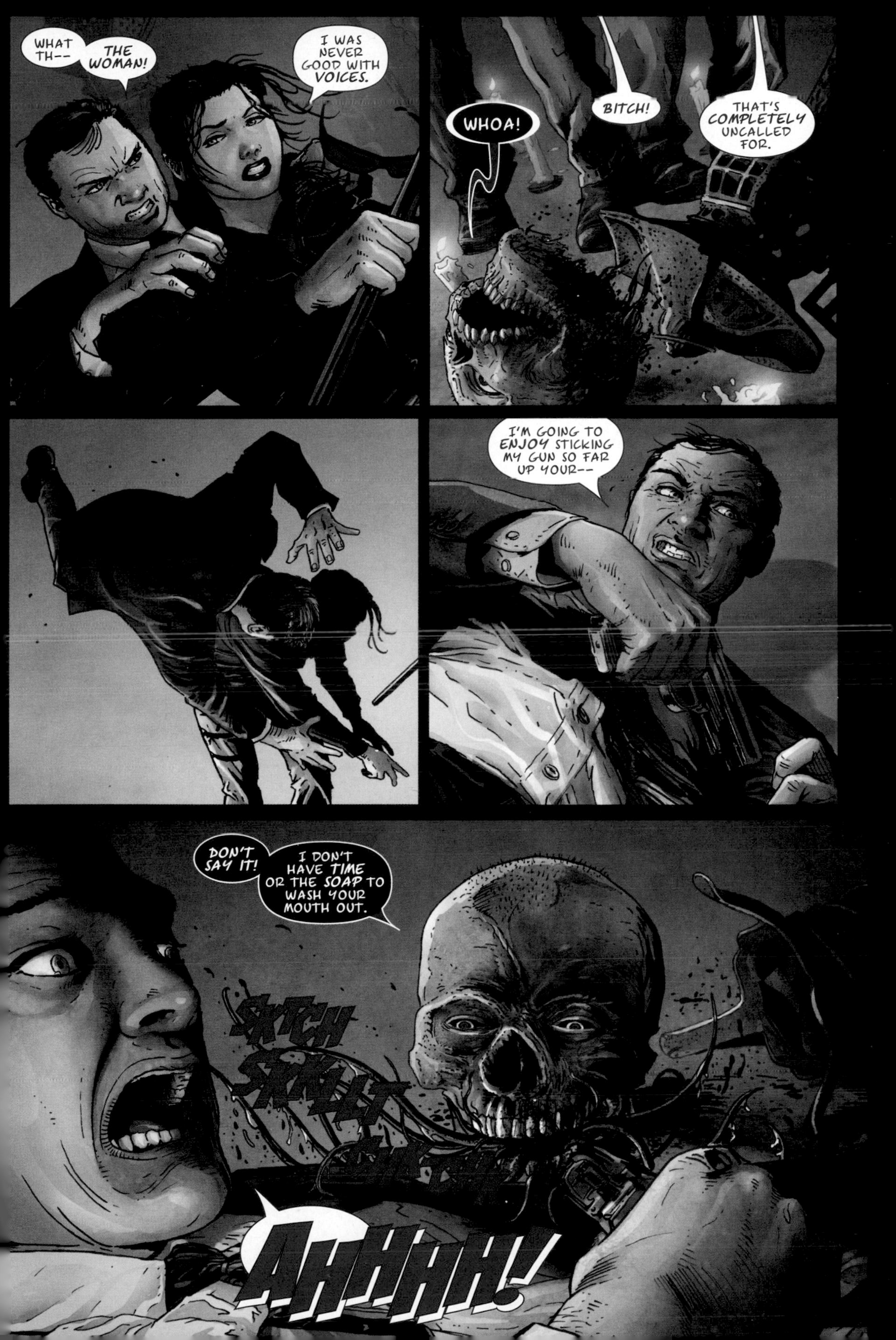
WHAT TH--
THE WOMAN!
I WAS NEVER GOOD WITH VOICES.
WHOA!
BITCH!
THAT'S COMPLETELY UNCALLED FOR.
I'M GOING TO ENJOY STICKING MY GUN SO FAR UP YOUR--
DON'T SAY IT!
I DON'T HAVE TIME OR THE SOAP TO WASH YOUR MOUTH OUT.
AHHHH!

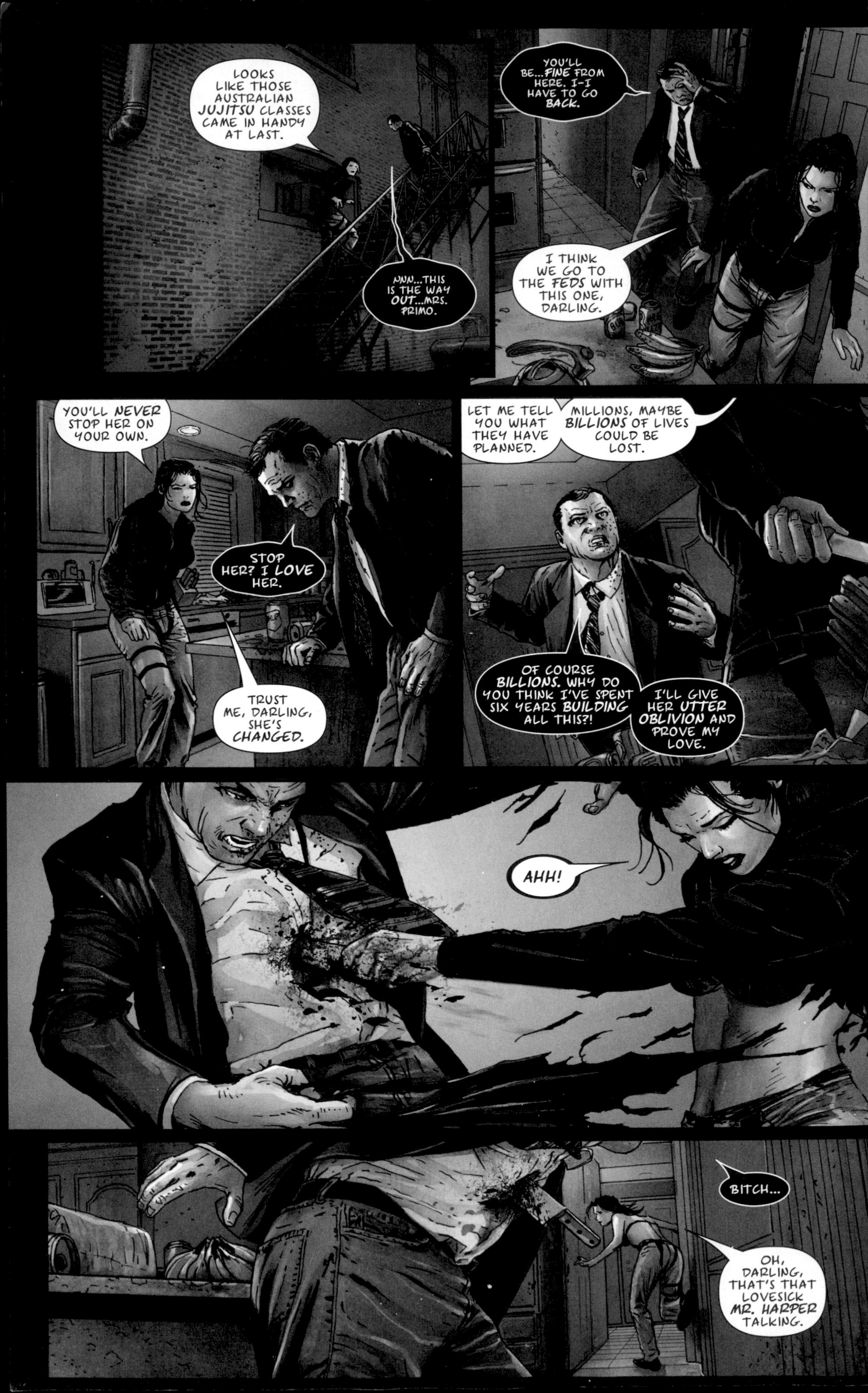
LOOKS LIKE THOSE AUSTRALIAN JUJITSU CLASSES CAME IN HANDY AT LAST.
NNN...THIS IS THE WAY OUT...MRS. PRIMO.
YOU'LL BE...FINE FROM HERE. I-I HAVE TO GO BACK.
I THINK WE GO TO THE FEDS WITH THIS ONE, DARLING.
YOU'LL NEVER STOP HER ON YOUR OWN.
STOP HER? I LOVE HER.
TRUST ME, DARLING, SHE'S CHANGED.
LET ME TELL YOU WHAT THEY HAVE PLANNED.
MILLIONS, MAYBE BILLIONS OF LIVES COULD BE LOST.
OF COURSE BILLIONS. WHY DO YOU THINK I'VE SPENT SIX YEARS BUILDING ALL THIS?!
I'LL GIVE HER UTTER OBLIVION AND PROVE MY LOVE.
AHH!
BITCH...
OH, DARLING, THAT'S THAT LOVESICK MR. HARPER TALKING.

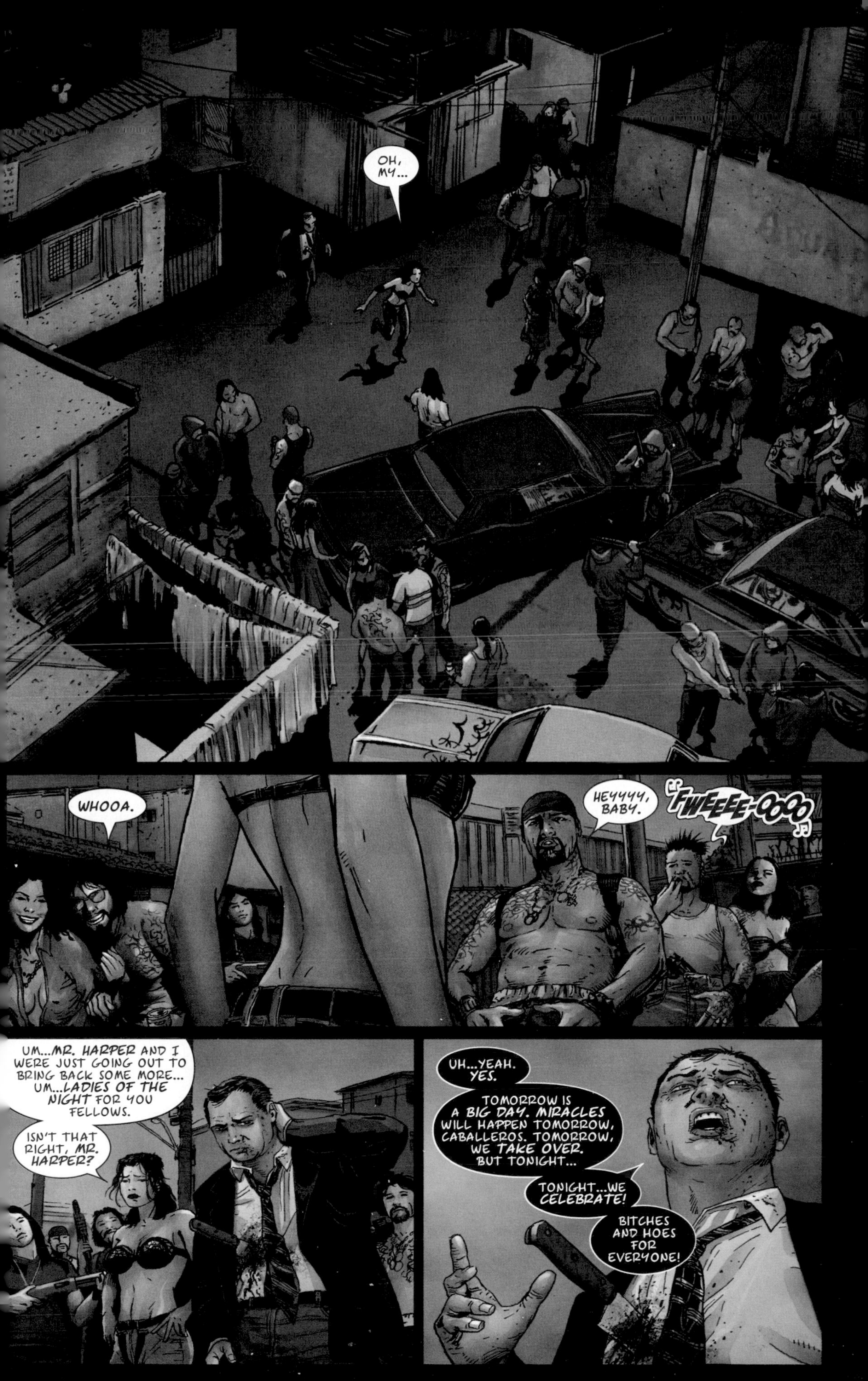
OH, MY...
WHOOA.
HEYYYY, BABY.
FWEEEE-OOOO
UM...MR. HARPER AND I WERE JUST GOING OUT TO BRING BACK SOME MORE... UM...LADIES OF THE NIGHT FOR YOU FELLOWS.
ISN'T THAT RIGHT, MR. HARPER?
UH...YEAH. YES.
TOMORROW IS A BIG DAY. MIRACLES WILL HAPPEN TOMORROW, CABALLEROS. TOMORROW, WE TAKE OVER. BUT TONIGHT...
TONIGHT...WE CELEBRATE!
BITCHES AND HOES FOR EVERYONE!

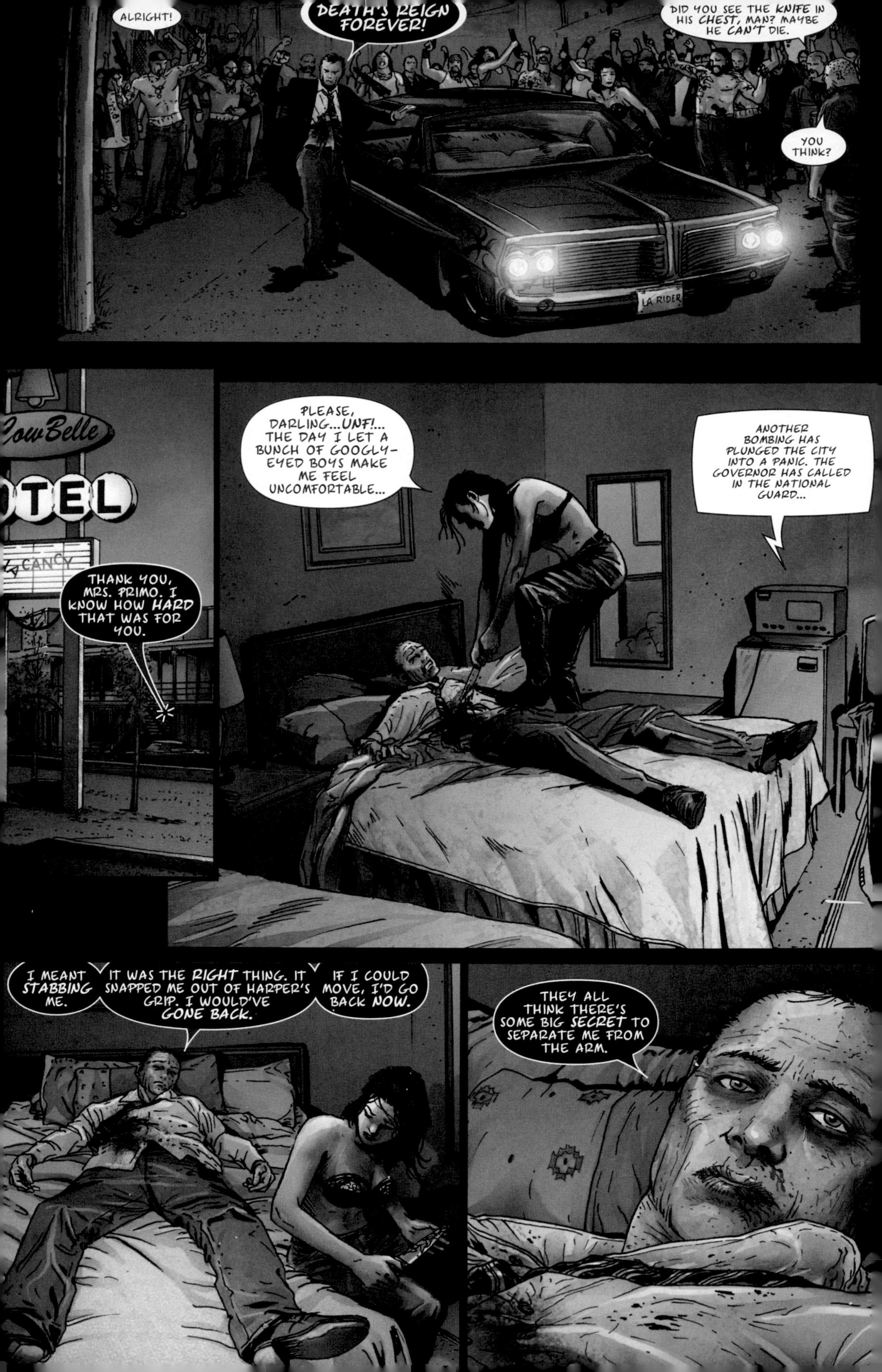
ALRIGHT!
DEATH'S REIGN FOREVER!
DID YOU SEE THE KNIFE IN HIS CHEST, MAN? MAYBE HE CAN'T DIE.
YOU THINK?
LA RIDER
CowBelle
OTEL
VACANCY
THANK YOU, MRS. PRIMO. I KNOW HOW HARD THAT WAS FOR YOU.
PLEASE, DARLING...UNF!... THE DAY I LET A BUNCH OF GOOGLY-EYED BOYS MAKE ME FEEL UNCOMFORTABLE...
ANOTHER BOMBING HAS PLUNGED THE CITY INTO A PANIC. THE GOVERNOR HAS CALLED IN THE NATIONAL GUARD...
I MEANT STABBING ME.
IT WAS THE RIGHT THING. IT SNAPPED ME OUT OF HARPER'S GRIP. I WOULD'VE GONE BACK.
IF I COULD MOVE, I'D GO BACK NOW.
THEY ALL THINK THERE'S SOME BIG SECRET TO SEPARATE ME FROM THE ARM.

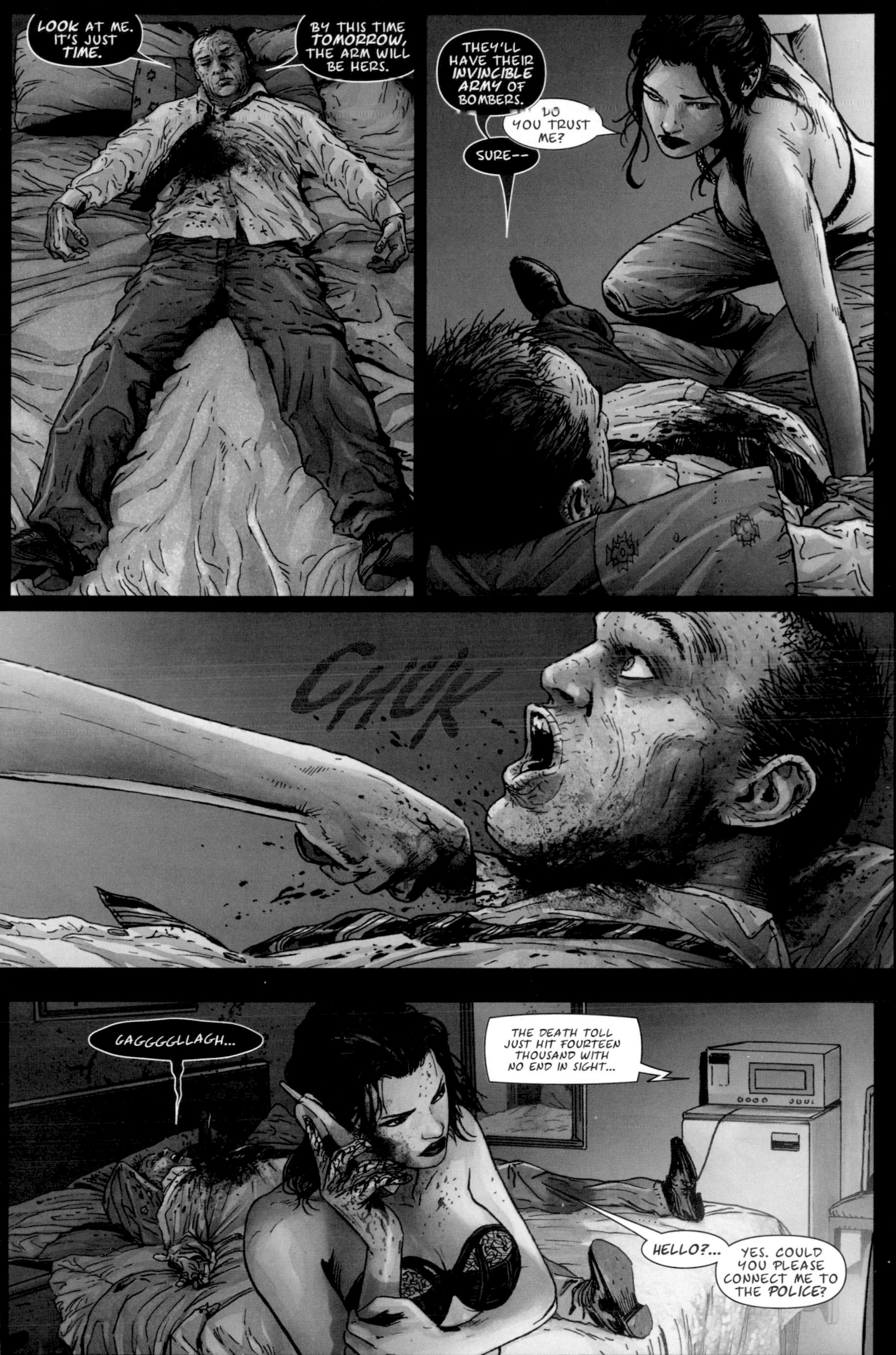
LOOK AT ME. IT'S JUST TIME.
BY THIS TIME TOMORROW, THE ARM WILL BE HERS.
THEY'LL HAVE THEIR INVINCIBLE ARMY OF BOMBERS.
DO YOU TRUST ME?
SURE--
CHUK
GAGGGGLLAGH...
THE DEATH TOLL JUST HIT FOURTEEN THOUSAND WITH NO END IN SIGHT...
HELLO?...
YES. COULD YOU PLEASE CONNECT ME TO THE POLICE?

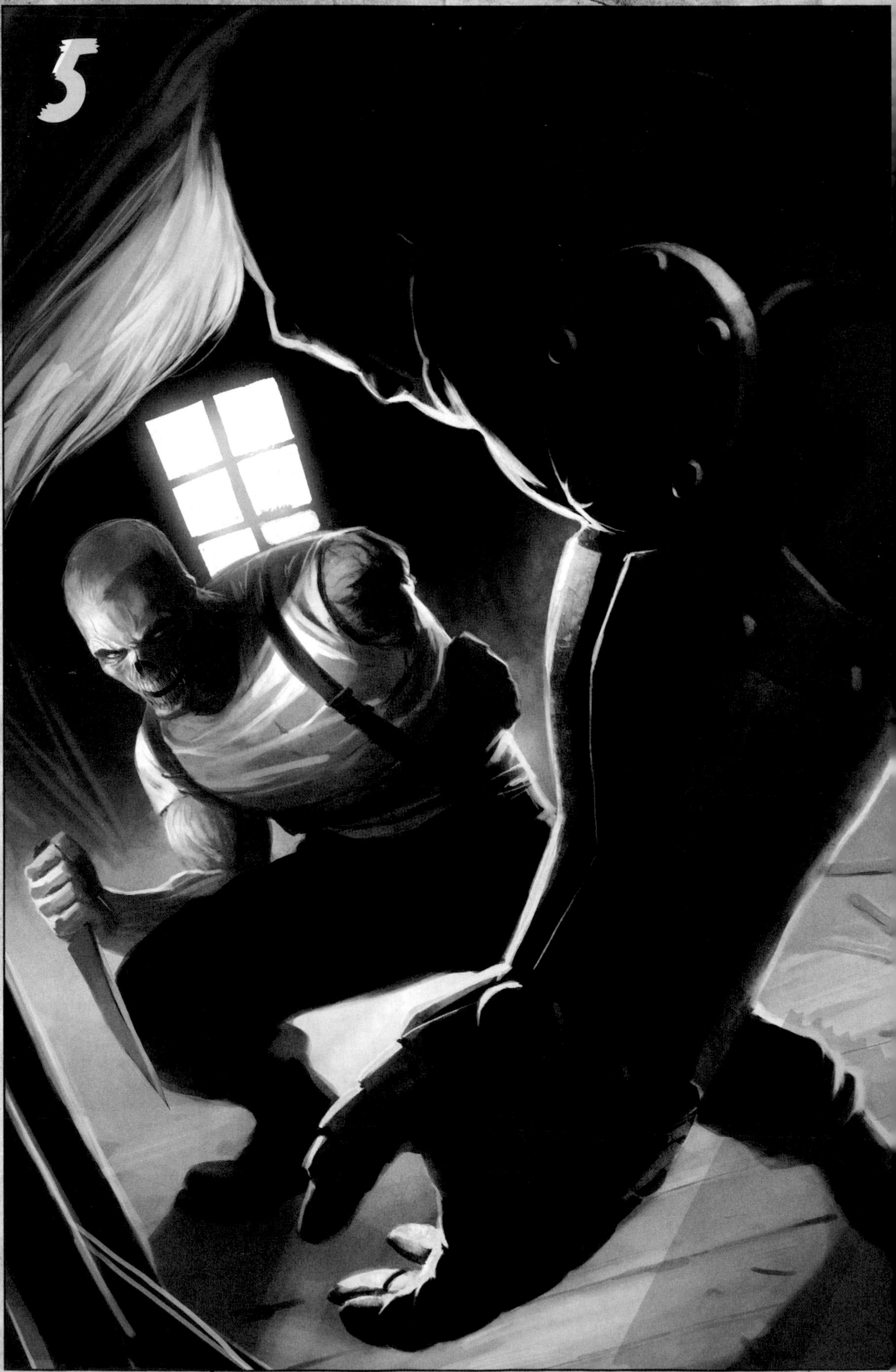
5

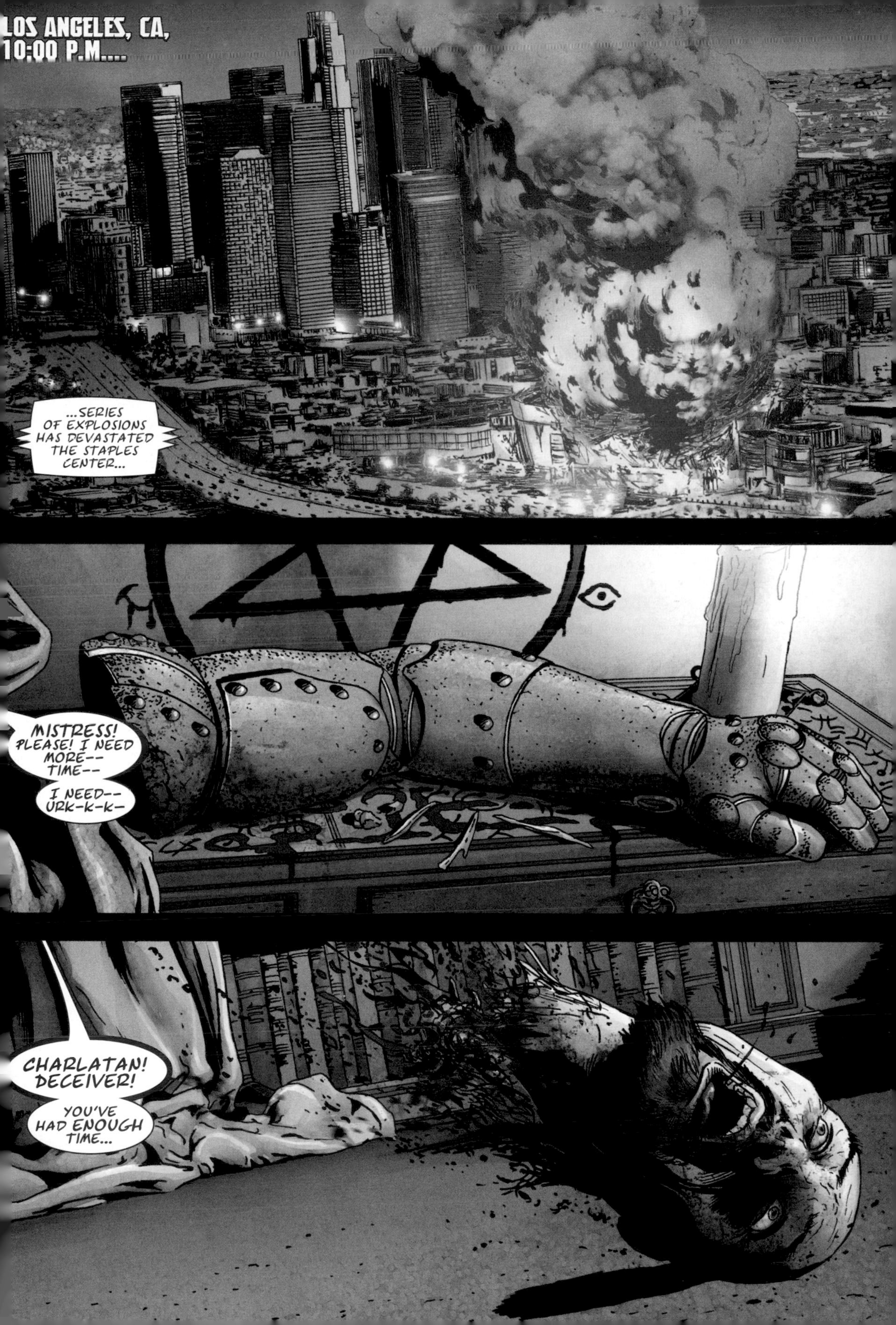
LOS ANGELES, CA, 10:00 P.M....
...SERIES OF EXPLOSIONS HAS DEVASTATED THE STAPLES CENTER...
MISTRESS! PLEASE! I NEED MORE-- TIME--
I NEED-- URK-K-K-
CHARLATAN! DECEIVER!
YOU'VE HAD ENOUGH TIME...

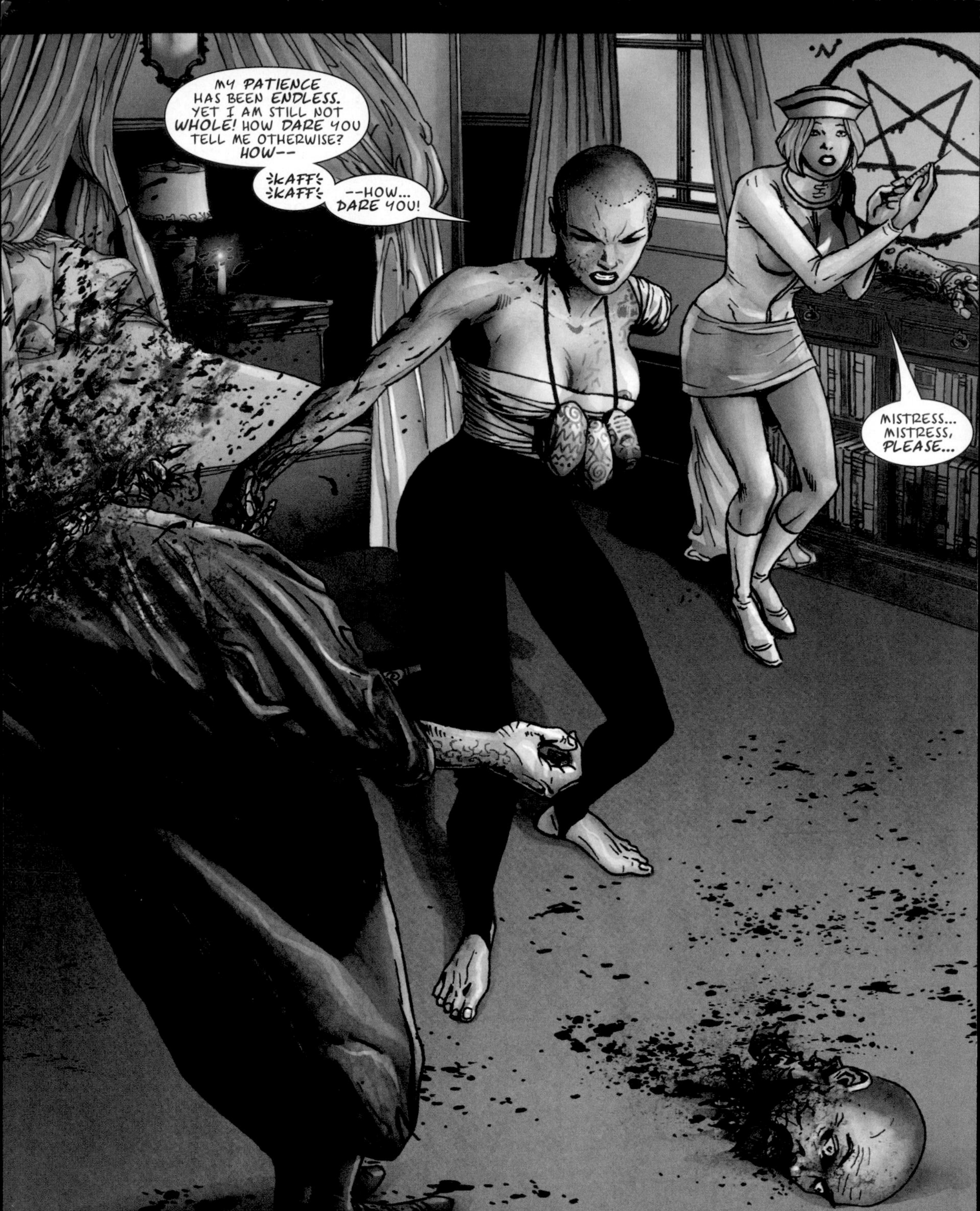
MY PATIENCE HAS BEEN ENDLESS. YET I AM STILL NOT WHOLE! HOW DARE YOU TELL ME OTHERWISE? HOW--
KAFF KAFF
--HOW... DARE YOU!
MISTRESS... MISTRESS, PLEASE...

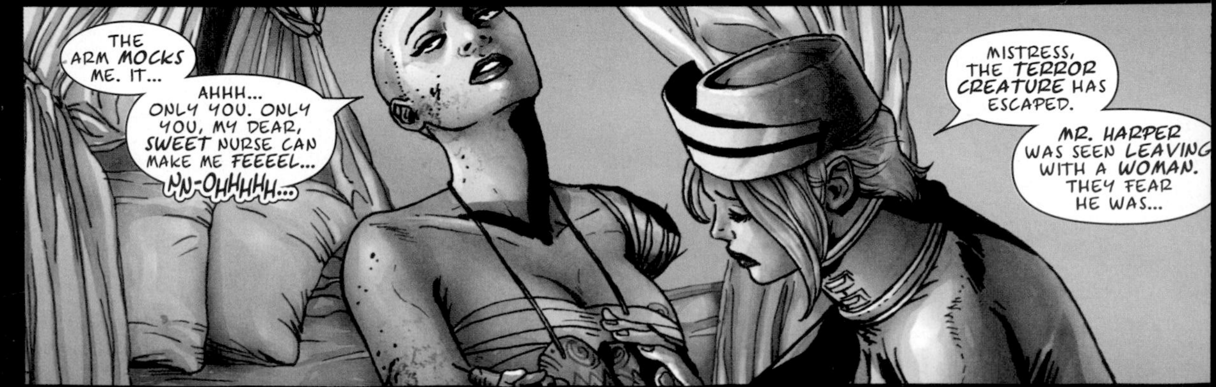
THE ARM MOCKS ME. IT...
AHHH... ONLY YOU. ONLY YOU, MY DEAR, SWEET NURSE CAN MAKE ME FEEEEL...
NN-OHHHHH...
MISTRESS, THE TERROR CREATURE HAS ESCAPED.
MR. HARPER WAS SEEN LEAVING WITH A WOMAN. THEY FEAR HE WAS...

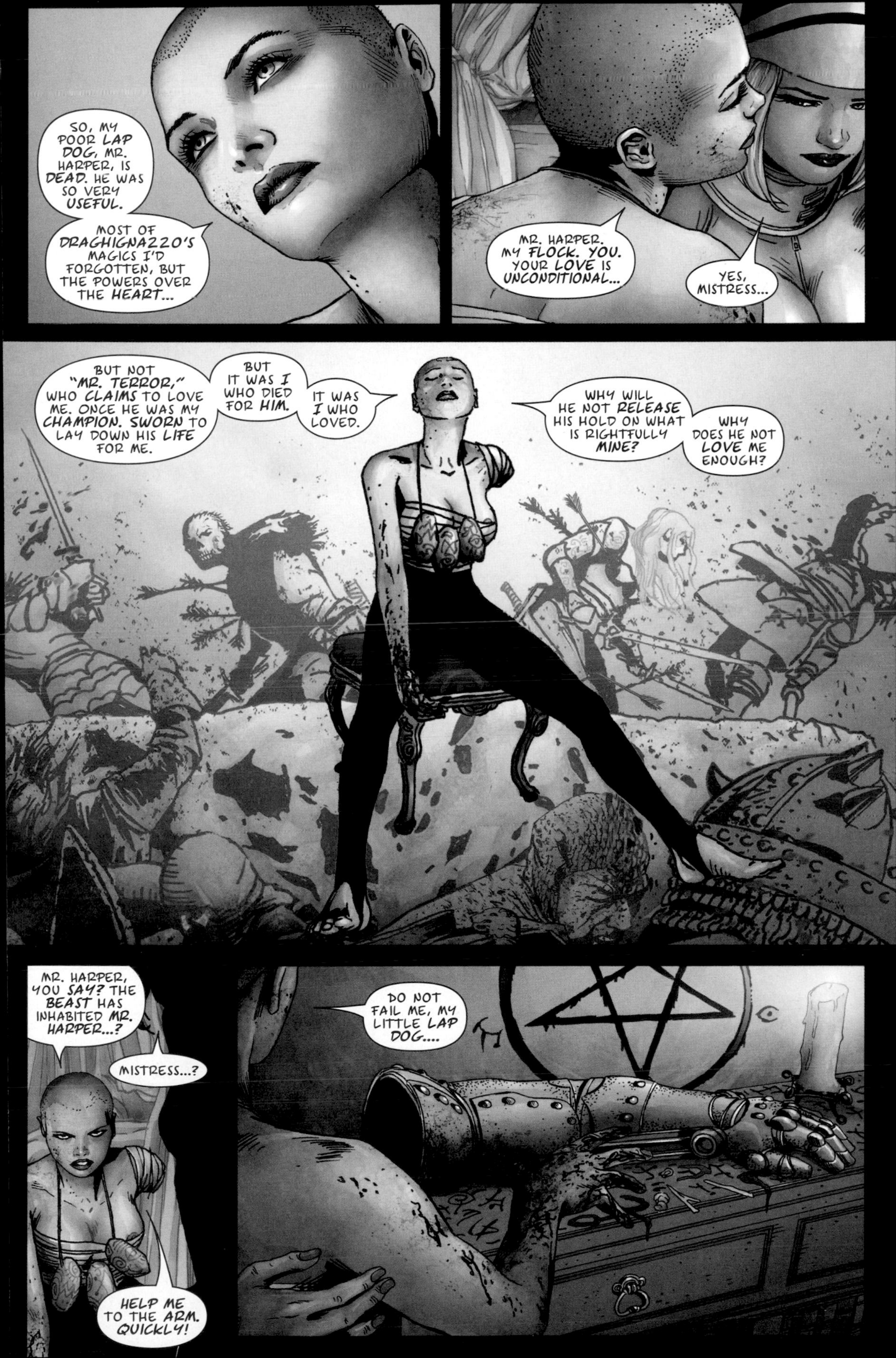
SO, MY POOR LAP DOG, MR. HARPER, IS DEAD. HE WAS SO VERY USEFUL.
MOST OF DRAGHIGNAZZO'S MAGICS I'D FORGOTTEN, BUT THE POWERS OVER THE HEART...
MR. HARPER. MY FLOCK. YOU. YOUR LOVE IS UNCONDITIONAL...
YES, MISTRESS...
BUT NOT "MR. TERROR," WHO CLAIMS TO LOVE ME. ONCE HE WAS MY CHAMPION. SWORN TO LAY DOWN HIS LIFE FOR ME.
BUT IT WAS I WHO DIED FOR HIM.
IT WAS I WHO LOVED.
WHY WILL HE NOT RELEASE HIS HOLD ON WHAT IS RIGHTFULLY MINE?
WHY DOES HE NOT LOVE ME ENOUGH?
MR. HARPER, YOU SAY? THE BEAST HAS INHABITED MR. HARPER...?
MISTRESS...?
DO NOT FAIL ME, MY LITTLE LAP DOG....
HELP ME TO THE ARM. QUICKLY!

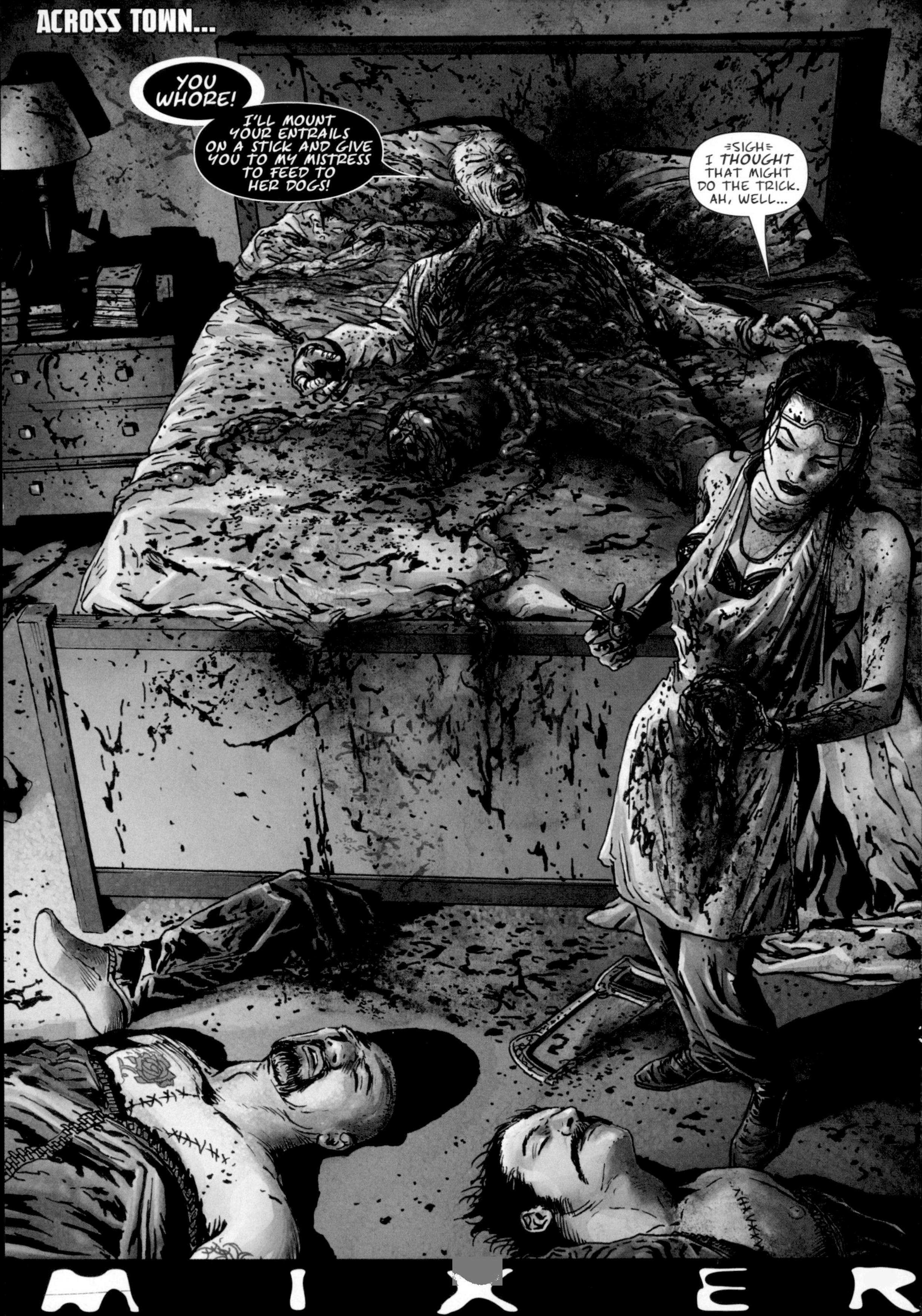
ACROSS TOWN...
YOU WHORE!
I'LL MOUNT YOUR ENTRAILS ON A STICK AND GIVE YOU TO MY MISTRESS TO FEED TO HER DOGS!
=SIGH= I THOUGHT THAT MIGHT DO THE TRICK. AH, WELL...
M I X E R

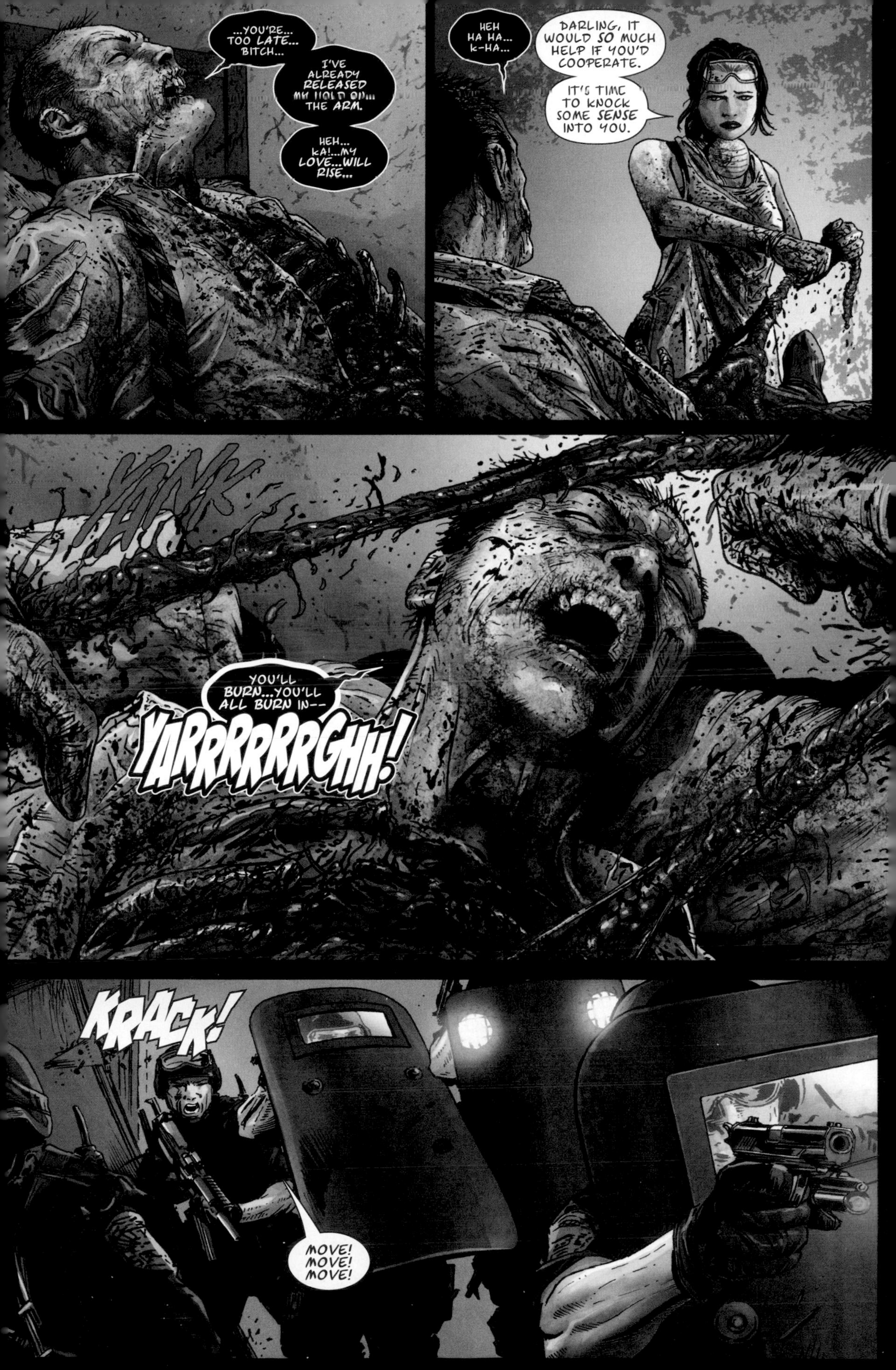
...YOU'RE... TOO LATE... BITCH...
I'VE ALREADY RELEASED MY HOLD ON THE ARM.
HEH... KA!...MY LOVE...WILL RISE...
HEH HA HA... K-HA...
DARLING, IT WOULD SO MUCH HELP IF YOU'D COOPERATE.
IT'S TIME TO KNOCK SOME SENSE INTO YOU.
YANK
YOU'LL BURN...YOU'LL ALL BURN IN--
YARRRRRRGHH!
KRACK!
MOVE! MOVE! MOVE!

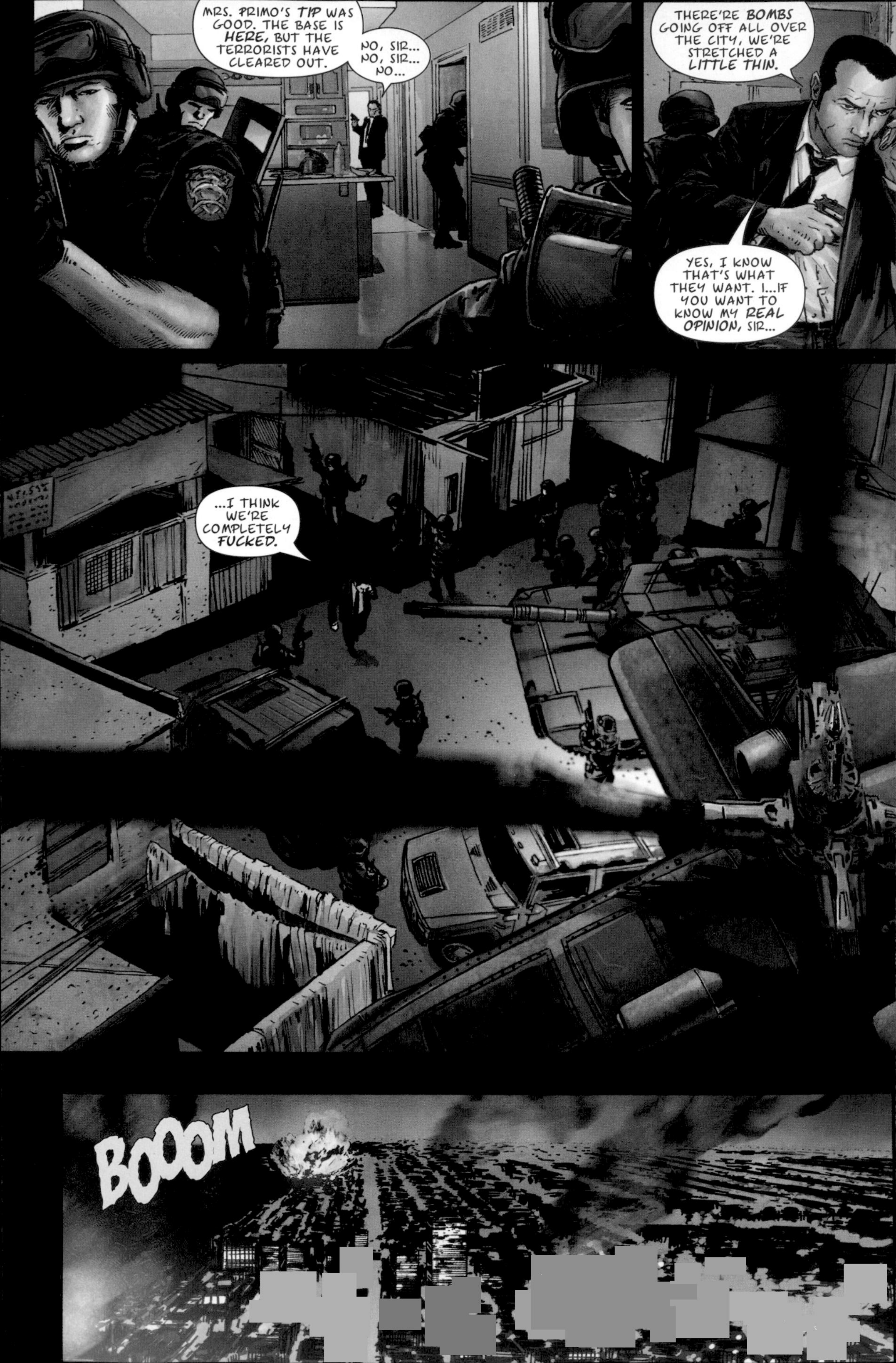
MRS. PRIMO'S TIP WAS GOOD. THE BASE IS HERE, BUT THE TERRORISTS HAVE CLEARED OUT.
NO, SIR... NO, SIR... NO...
THERE'RE BOMBS GOING OFF ALL OVER THE CITY, WE'RE STRETCHED A LITTLE THIN.
YES, I KNOW THAT'S WHAT THEY WANT. I...IF YOU WANT TO KNOW MY REAL OPINION, SIR...
...I THINK WE'RE COMPLETELY FUCKED.
BOOOM

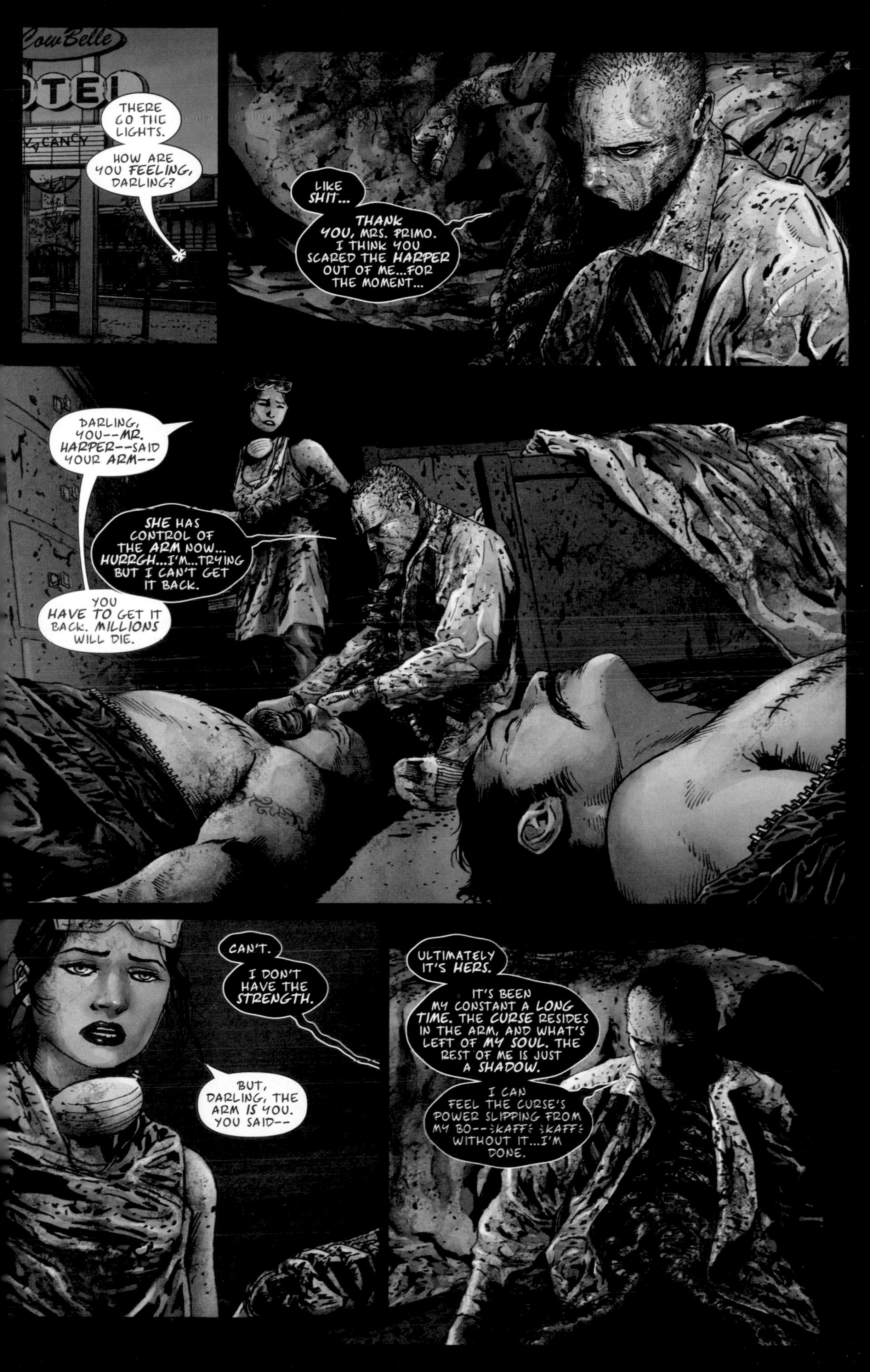

THERE GO THE LIGHTS.
HOW ARE YOU FEELING, DARLING?
LIKE SHIT...
THANK YOU, MRS. PRIMO. I THINK YOU SCARED THE HARPER OUT OF ME...FOR THE MOMENT...
DARLING, YOU--MR. HARPER--SAID YOUR ARM--
SHE HAS CONTROL OF THE ARM NOW... HURRGH...I'M...TRYING BUT I CAN'T GET IT BACK.
YOU HAVE TO GET IT BACK. MILLIONS WILL DIE.
CAN'T.
I DON'T HAVE THE STRENGTH.
BUT, DARLING, THE ARM IS YOU. YOU SAID--
ULTIMATELY IT'S HERS.
IT'S BEEN MY CONSTANT A LONG TIME. THE CURSE RESIDES IN THE ARM, AND WHAT'S LEFT OF MY SOUL. THE REST OF ME IS JUST A SHADOW.
I CAN FEEL THE CURSE'S POWER SLIPPING FROM MY BO--KAFF KAFF WITHOUT IT...I'M DONE.

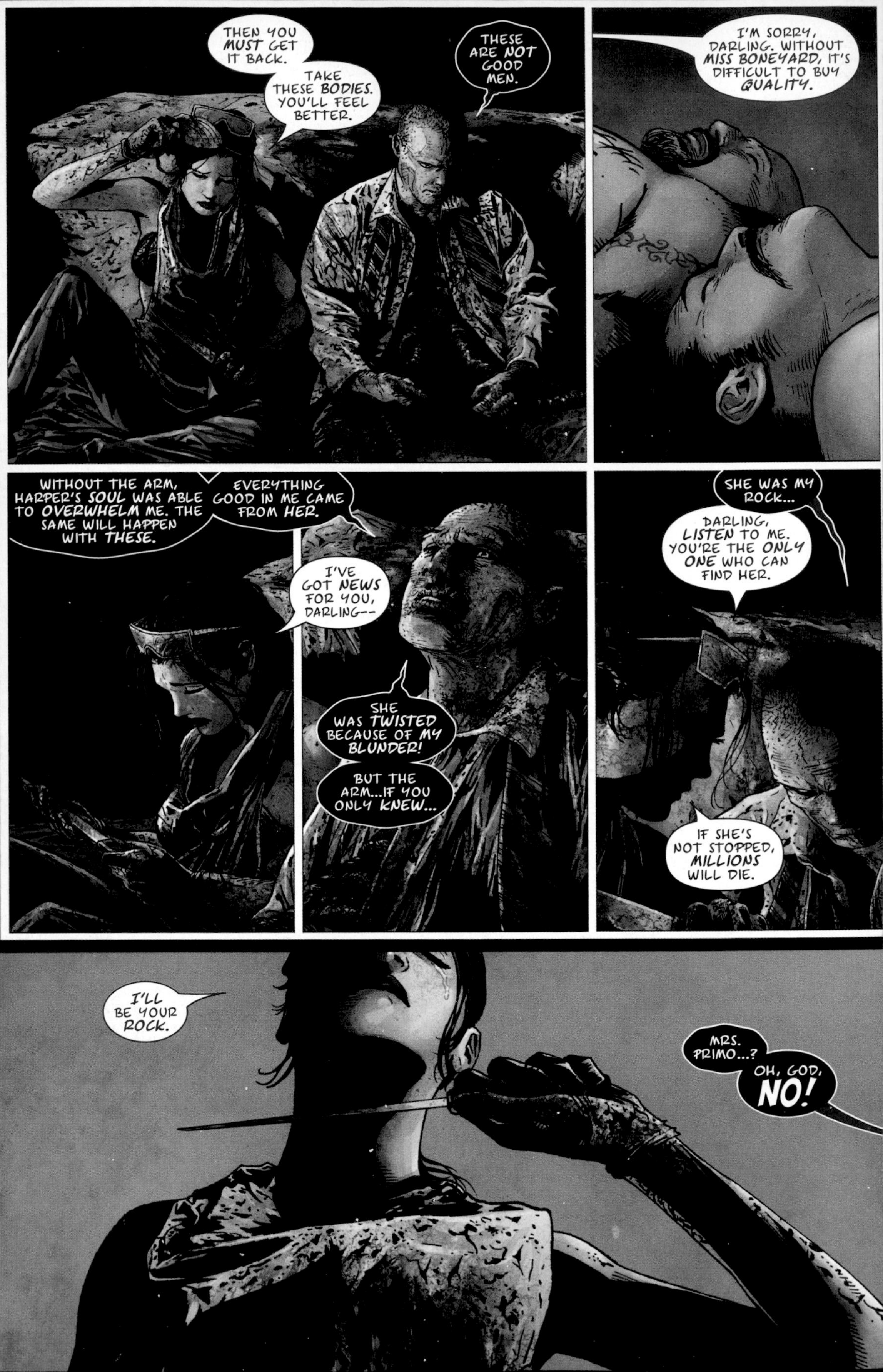

THEN YOU MUST GET IT BACK.
TAKE THESE BODIES. YOU'LL FEEL BETTER.
THESE ARE NOT GOOD MEN.
I'M SORRY, DARLING. WITHOUT MISS BONEYARD, IT'S DIFFICULT TO BUY QUALITY.
WITHOUT THE ARM, HARPER'S SOUL WAS ABLE TO OVERWHELM ME. THE SAME WILL HAPPEN WITH THESE.
EVERYTHING GOOD IN ME CAME FROM HER.
I'VE GOT NEWS FOR YOU, DARLING--
SHE WAS TWISTED BECAUSE OF MY BLUNDER!
BUT THE ARM...IF YOU ONLY KNEW...
SHE WAS MY ROCK...
DARLING, LISTEN TO ME. YOU'RE THE ONLY ONE WHO CAN FIND HER.
IF SHE'S NOT STOPPED, MILLIONS WILL DIE.
I'LL BE YOUR ROCK.
MRS. PRIMO...?
OH, GOD, NO!

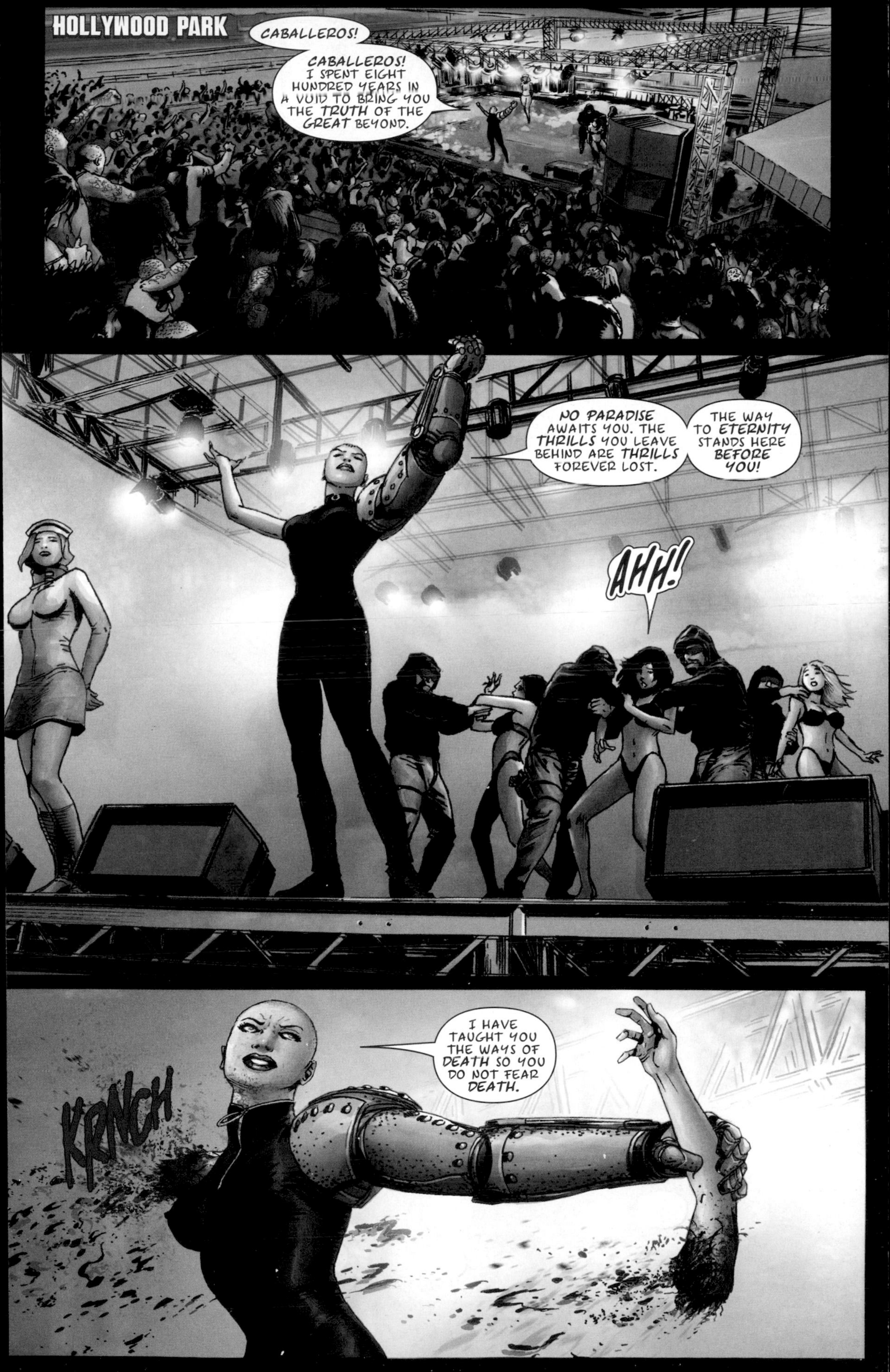
HOLLYWOOD PARK
CABALLEROS!
CABALLEROS! I SPENT EIGHT HUNDRED YEARS IN A VOID TO BRING YOU THE TRUTH OF THE GREAT BEYOND.
NO PARADISE AWAITS YOU. THE THRILLS YOU LEAVE BEHIND ARE THRILLS FOREVER LOST.
THE WAY TO ETERNITY STANDS HERE BEFORE YOU!
AHH!
I HAVE TAUGHT YOU THE WAYS OF DEATH SO YOU DO NOT FEAR DEATH.
KRNCH

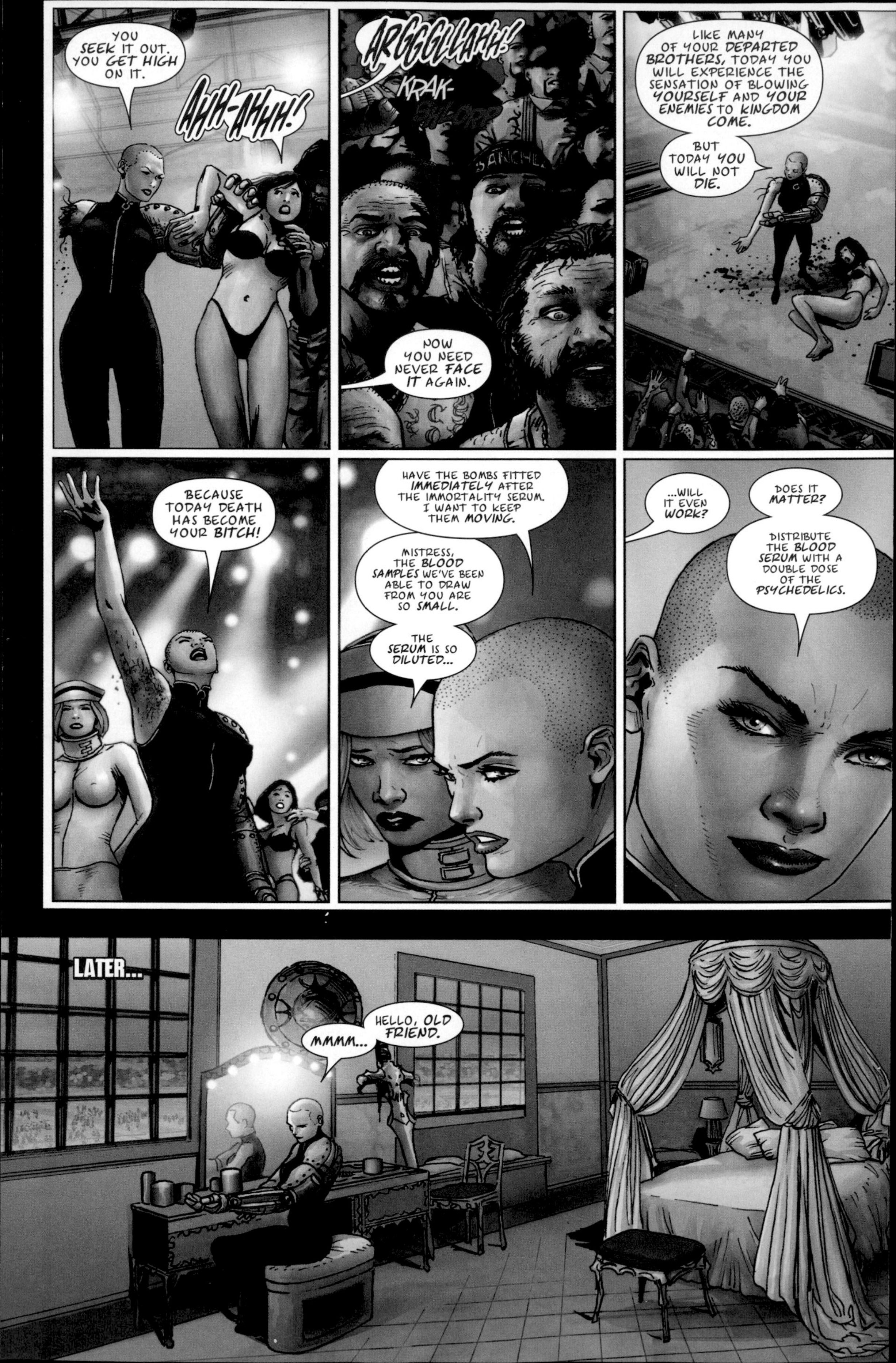
YOU SEEK IT OUT. YOU GET HIGH ON IT.
AHH-AHHH!
ARGGGLAHH!
KRAK-
NOW YOU NEED NEVER FACE IT AGAIN.
LIKE MANY OF YOUR DEPARTED BROTHERS, TODAY YOU WILL EXPERIENCE THE SENSATION OF BLOWING YOURSELF AND YOUR ENEMIES TO KINGDOM COME.
BUT TODAY YOU WILL NOT DIE.
BECAUSE TODAY DEATH HAS BECOME YOUR BITCH!
HAVE THE BOMBS FITTED IMMEDIATELY AFTER THE IMMORTALITY SERUM. I WANT TO KEEP THEM MOVING.
MISTRESS, THE BLOOD SAMPLES WE'VE BEEN ABLE TO DRAW FROM YOU ARE SO SMALL.
THE SERUM IS SO DILUTED...
...WILL IT EVEN WORK?
DOES IT MATTER?
DISTRIBUTE THE BLOOD SERUM WITH A DOUBLE DOSE OF THE PSYCHEDELICS.
LATER...
HELLO, OLD FRIEND.
MMMM...

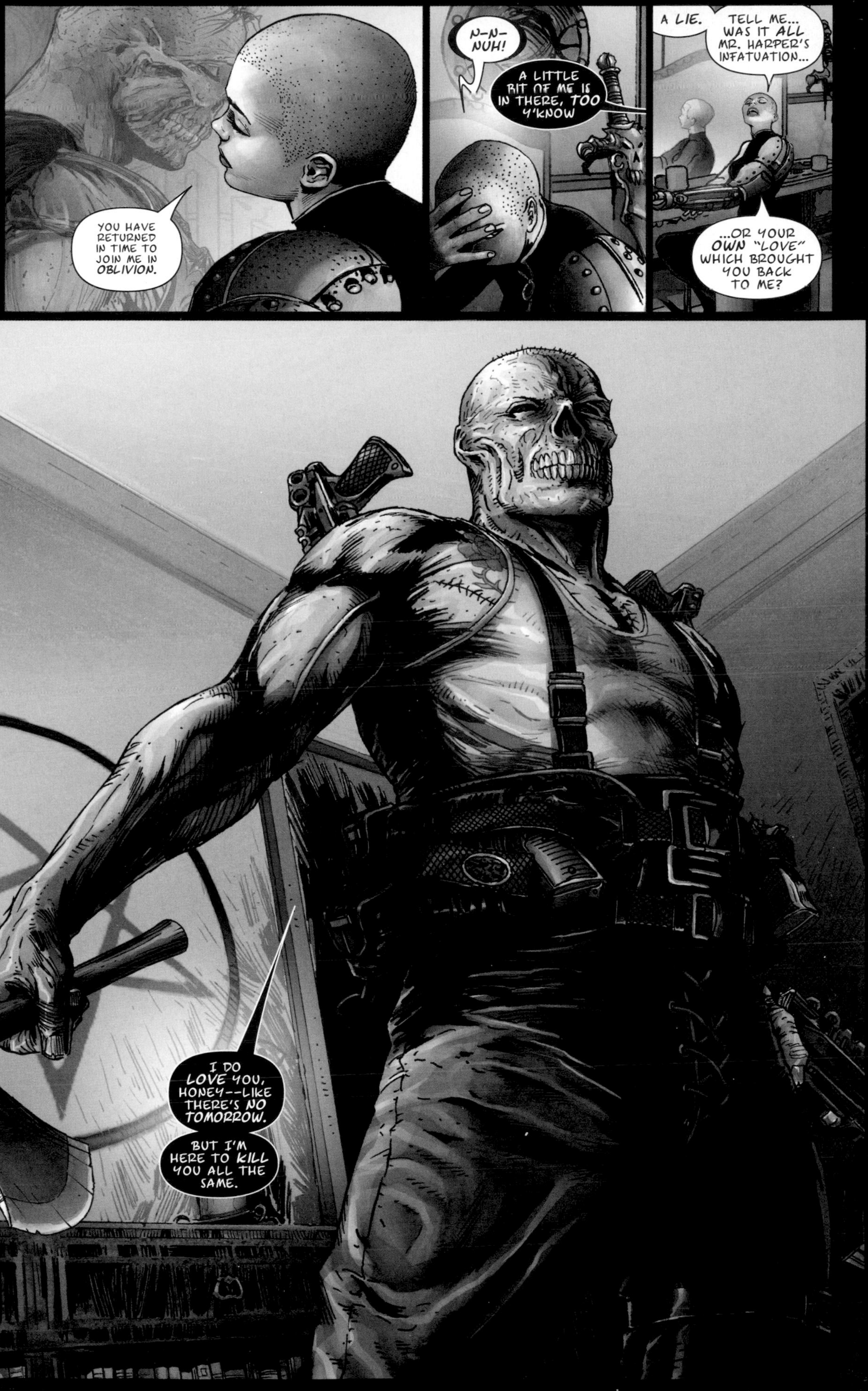
YOU HAVE RETURNED IN TIME TO JOIN ME IN OBLIVION.
N-N-NUH!
A LITTLE BIT OF ME IS IN THERE, TOO Y'KNOW
A LIE.
TELL ME... WAS IT ALL MR. HARPER'S INFATUATION...
...OR YOUR OWN "LOVE" WHICH BROUGHT YOU BACK TO ME?
I DO LOVE YOU, HONEY--LIKE THERE'S NO TOMORROW.
BUT I'M HERE TO KILL YOU ALL THE SAME.

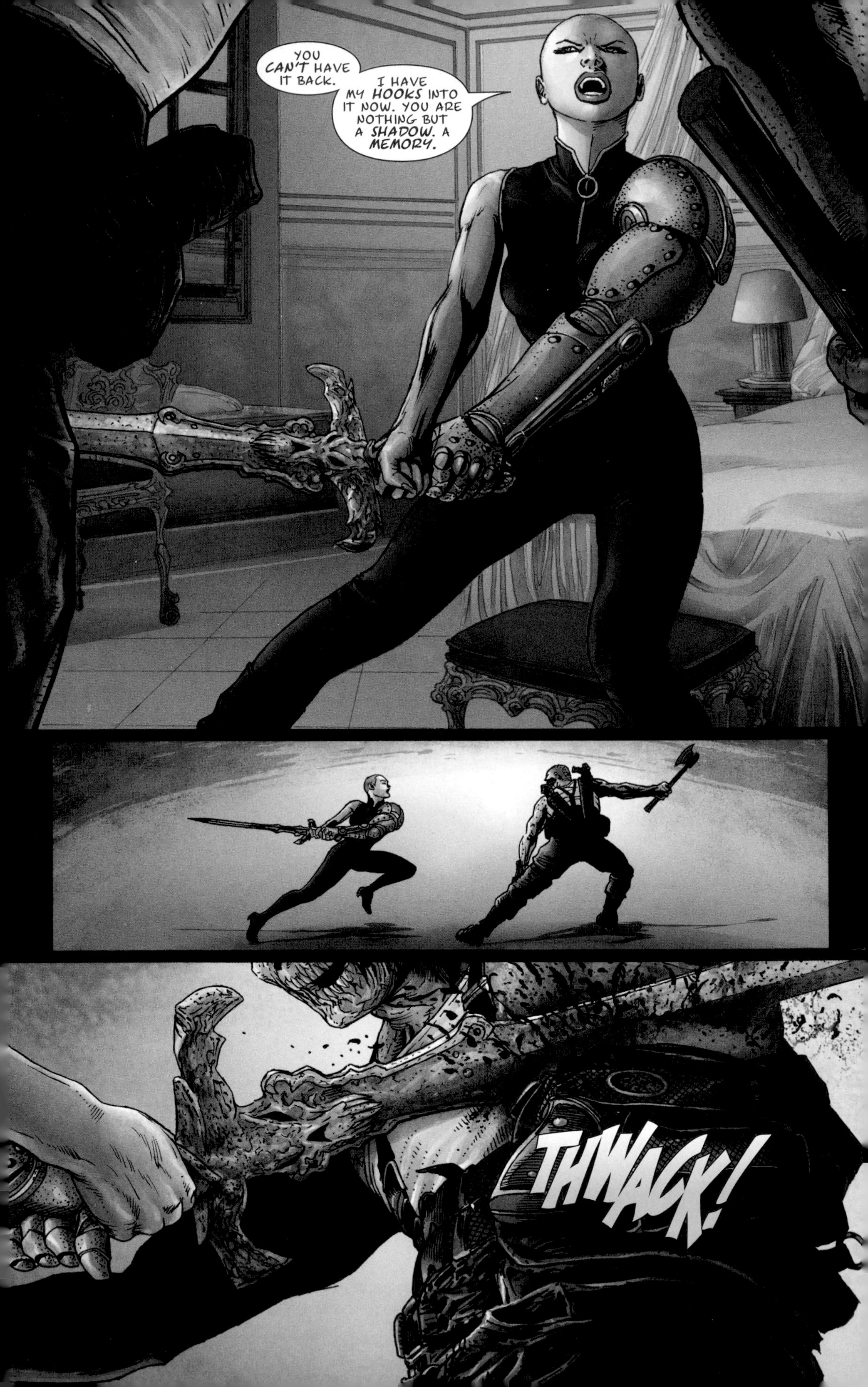
YOU CAN'T HAVE IT BACK.
I HAVE MY HOOKS INTO IT NOW. YOU ARE NOTHING BUT A SHADOW. A MEMORY.
THWACK!

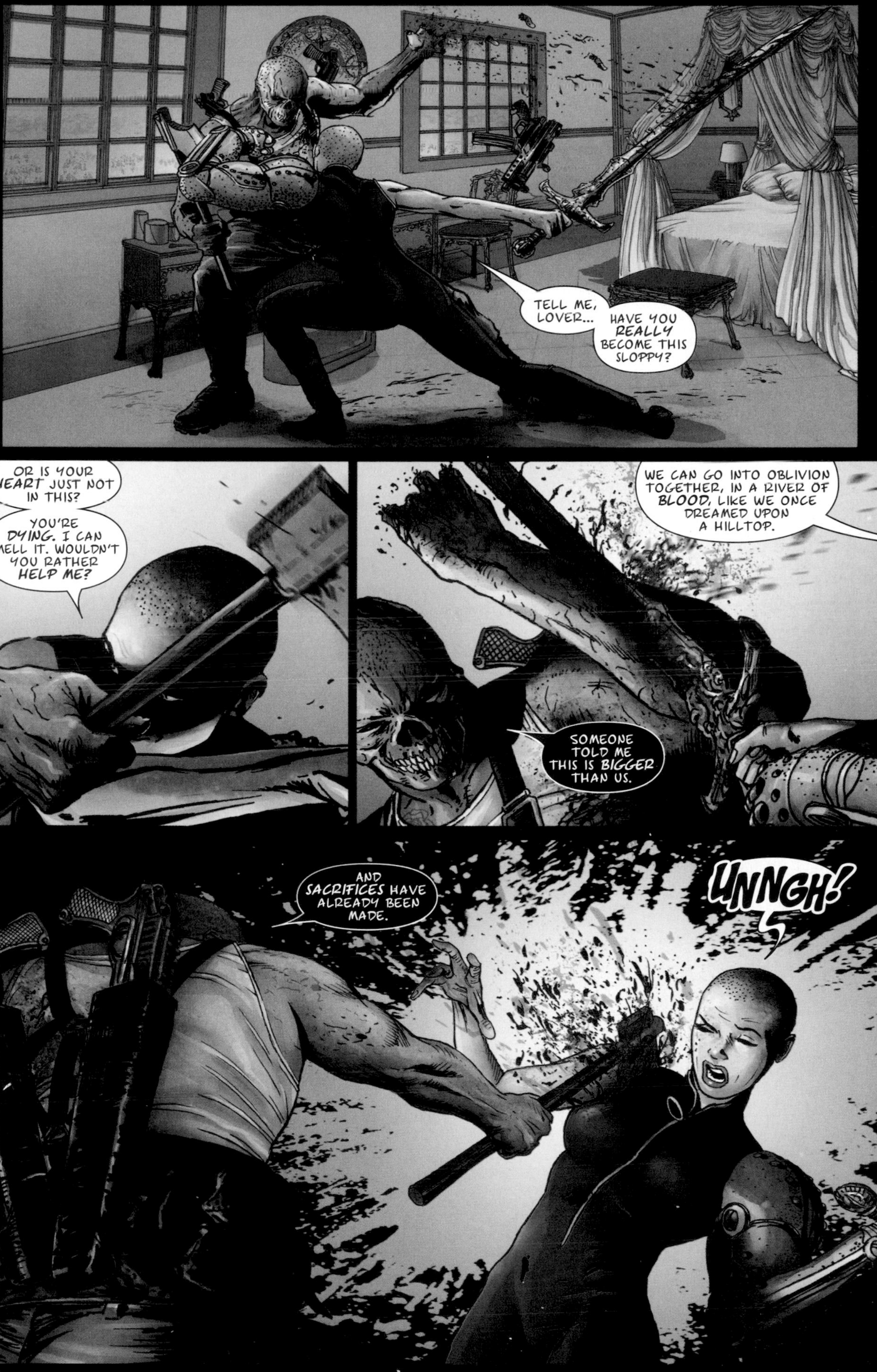

TELL ME, LOVER...
HAVE YOU REALLY BECOME THIS SLOPPY?
OR IS YOUR HEART JUST NOT IN THIS?
YOU'RE DYING. I CAN MELL IT. WOULDN'T YOU RATHER HELP ME?
WE CAN GO INTO OBLIVION TOGETHER, IN A RIVER OF BLOOD, LIKE WE ONCE DREAMED UPON A HILLTOP.
SOMEONE TOLD ME THIS IS BIGGER THAN US.
AND SACRIFICES HAVE ALREADY BEEN MADE.
UNNGH!

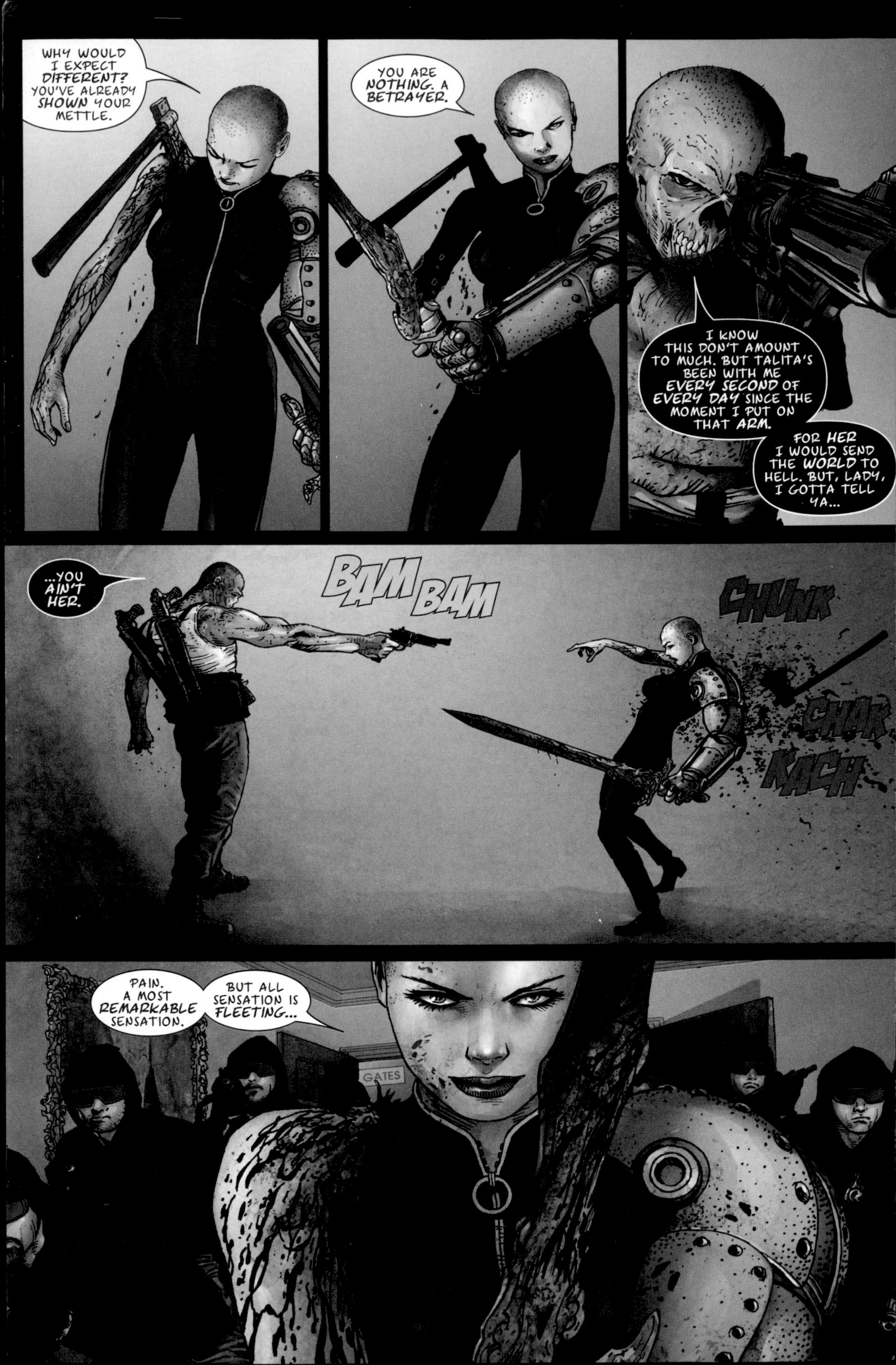
WHY WOULD I EXPECT DIFFERENT? YOU'VE ALREADY SHOWN YOUR METTLE.
YOU ARE NOTHING. A BETRAYER.
I KNOW THIS DON'T AMOUNT TO MUCH. BUT TALITA'S BEEN WITH ME EVERY SECOND OF EVERY DAY SINCE THE MOMENT I PUT ON THAT ARM.
FOR HER I WOULD SEND THE WORLD TO HELL. BUT, LADY, I GOTTA TELL YA...
...YOU AIN'T HER.
BAM BAM
CHUNK
CHAK KACH
PAIN. A MOST REMARKABLE SENSATION.
BUT ALL SENSATION IS FLEETING...
GATES

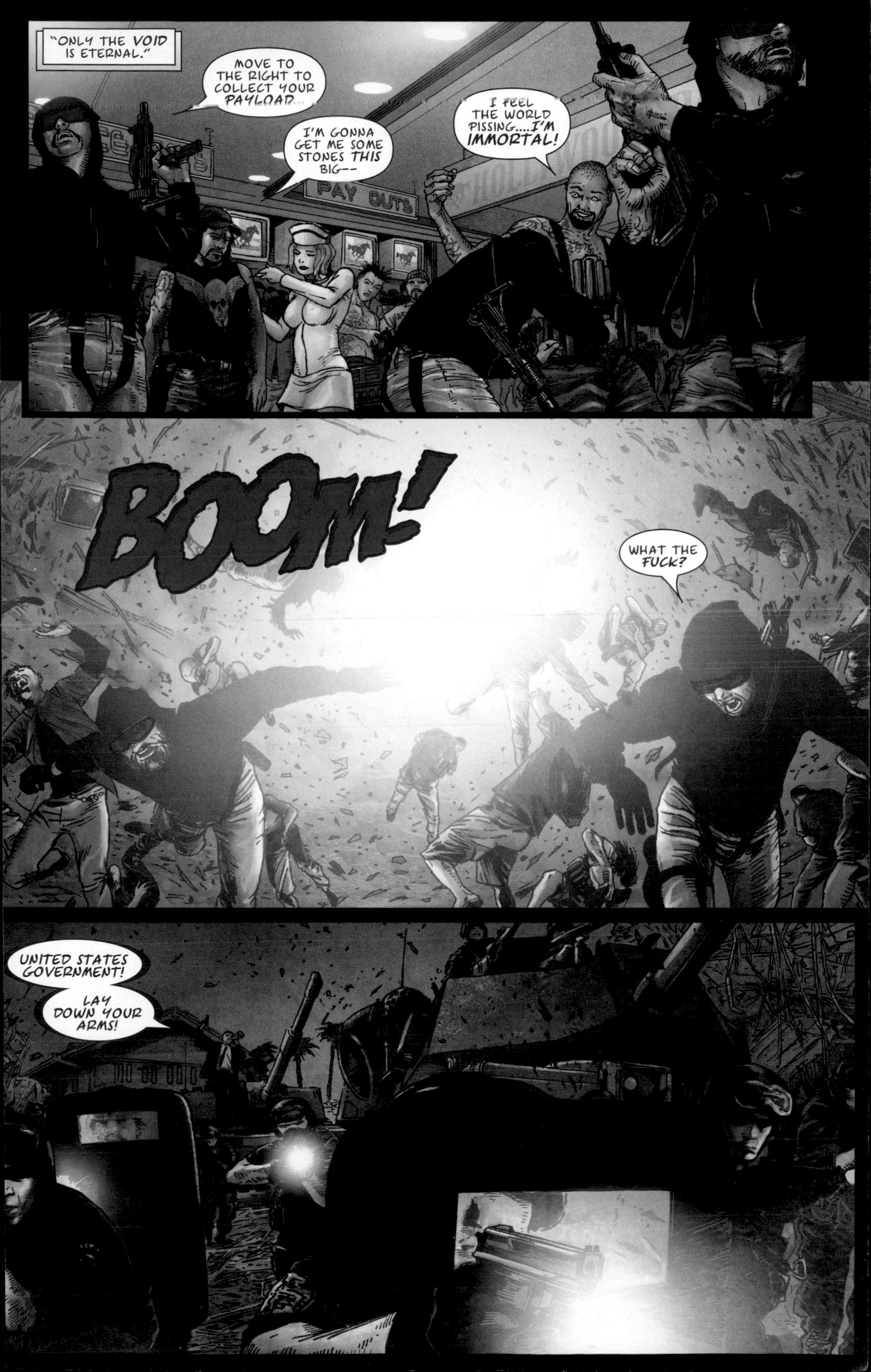
"ONLY THE VOID IS ETERNAL."
MOVE TO THE RIGHT TO COLLECT YOUR PAYLOAD...
I'M GONNA GET ME SOME STONES THIS BIG--
I FEEL THE WORLD PISSING....I'M IMMORTAL!
PAY OUTS
BOOM!
WHAT THE FUCK?
UNITED STATES GOVERNMENT!
LAY DOWN YOUR ARMS!

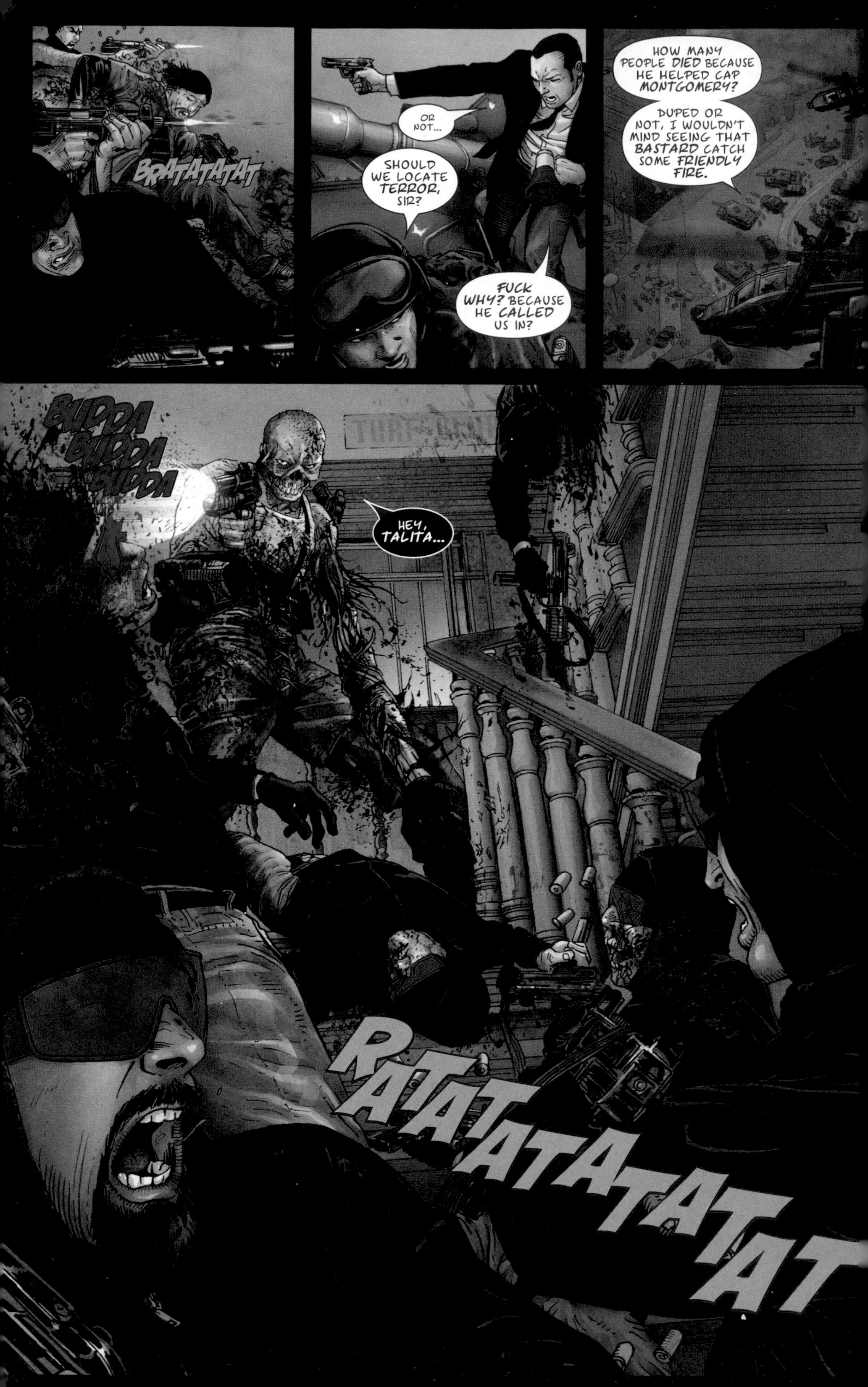
BRATATATAT
OR NOT...
SHOULD WE LOCATE TERROR, SIR?
FUCK WHY? BECAUSE HE CALLED US IN?
HOW MANY PEOPLE DIED BECAUSE HE HELPED CAP MONTGOMERY?
DUPED OR NOT, I WOULDN'T MIND SEEING THAT BASTARD CATCH SOME FRIENDLY FIRE.
BUDDA BUDDA BUDDA
HEY, TALITA...
RATATATATATAT

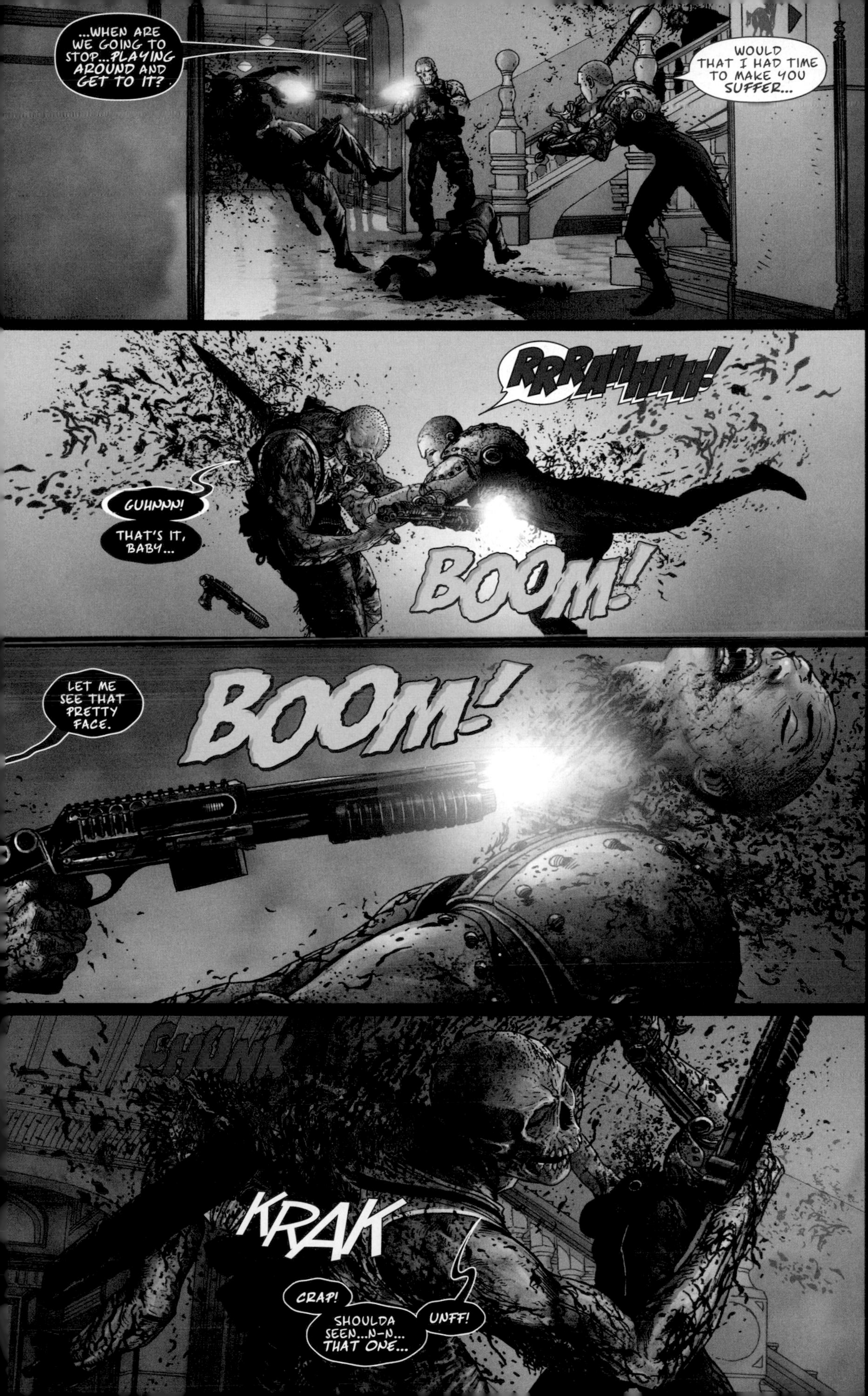
...WHEN ARE WE GOING TO STOP...PLAYING AROUND AND GET TO IT?
WOULD THAT I HAD TIME TO MAKE YOU SUFFER...
RRRAHHHHH!
GUHNNN!
THAT'S IT, BABY...
BOOM!
LET ME SEE THAT PRETTY FACE.
BOOM!
KRAK
CRAP!
SHOULDA SEEN...N-N... THAT ONE...
UNFF!

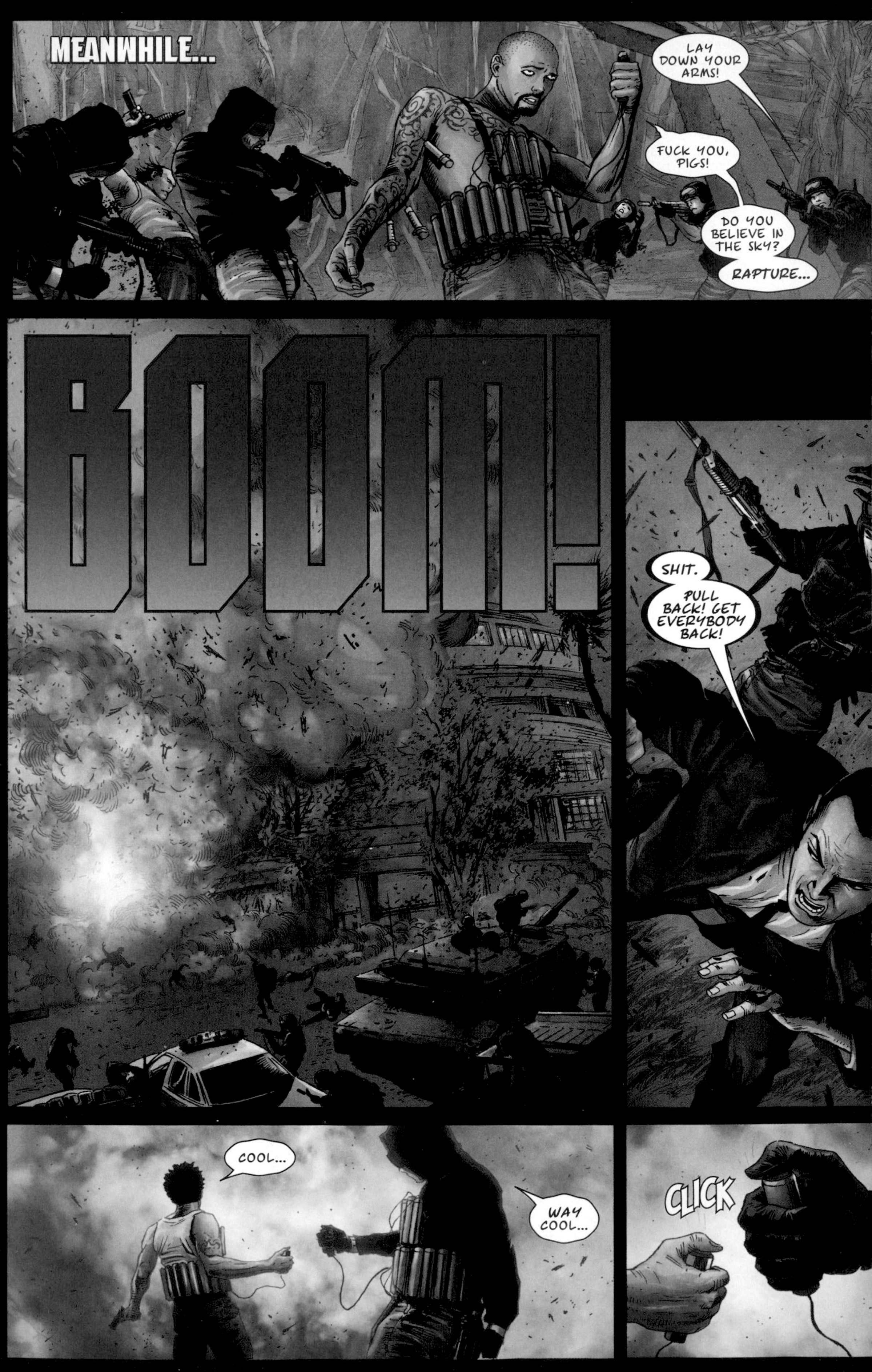
MEANWHILE...
LAY DOWN YOUR ARMS!
FUCK YOU, PIGS!
DO YOU BELIEVE IN THE SKY?
RAPTURE...
BOOM!
SHIT.
PULL BACK! GET EVERYBODY BACK!
COOL...
WAY COOL...
CLICK

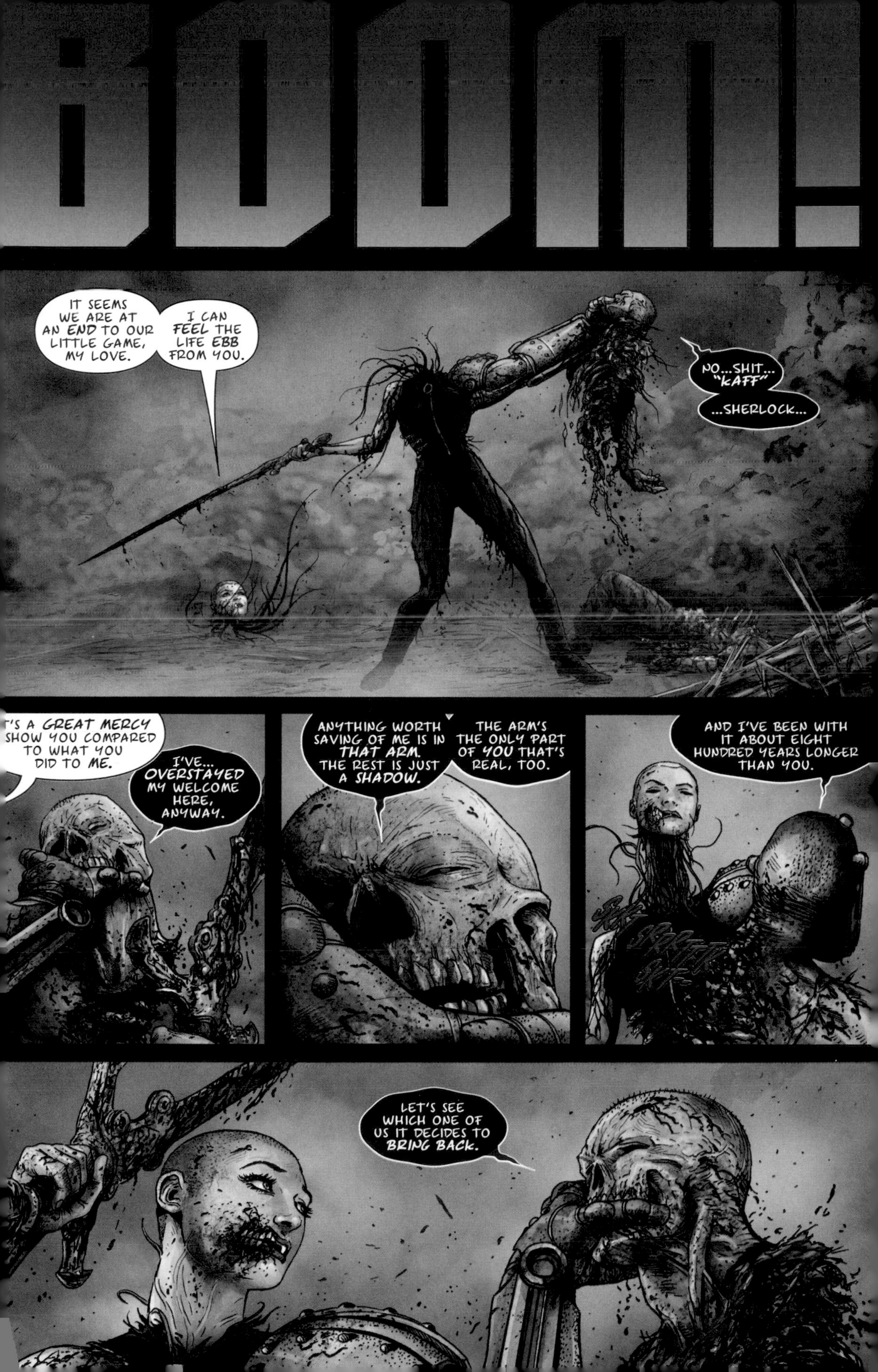
BOOM!
IT SEEMS WE ARE AT AN END TO OUR LITTLE GAME, MY LOVE.
I CAN FEEL THE LIFE EBB FROM YOU.
NO...SHIT... "KAFF"
...SHERLOCK...
'S A GREAT MERCY SHOW YOU COMPARED TO WHAT YOU DID TO ME.
I'VE... OVERSTAYED MY WELCOME HERE, ANYWAY.
ANYTHING WORTH SAVING OF ME IS IN THAT ARM. THE REST IS JUST A SHADOW.
THE ARM'S THE ONLY PART OF YOU THAT'S REAL, TOO.
AND I'VE BEEN WITH IT ABOUT EIGHT HUNDRED YEARS LONGER THAN YOU.
LET'S SEE WHICH ONE OF US IT DECIDES TO BRING BACK.

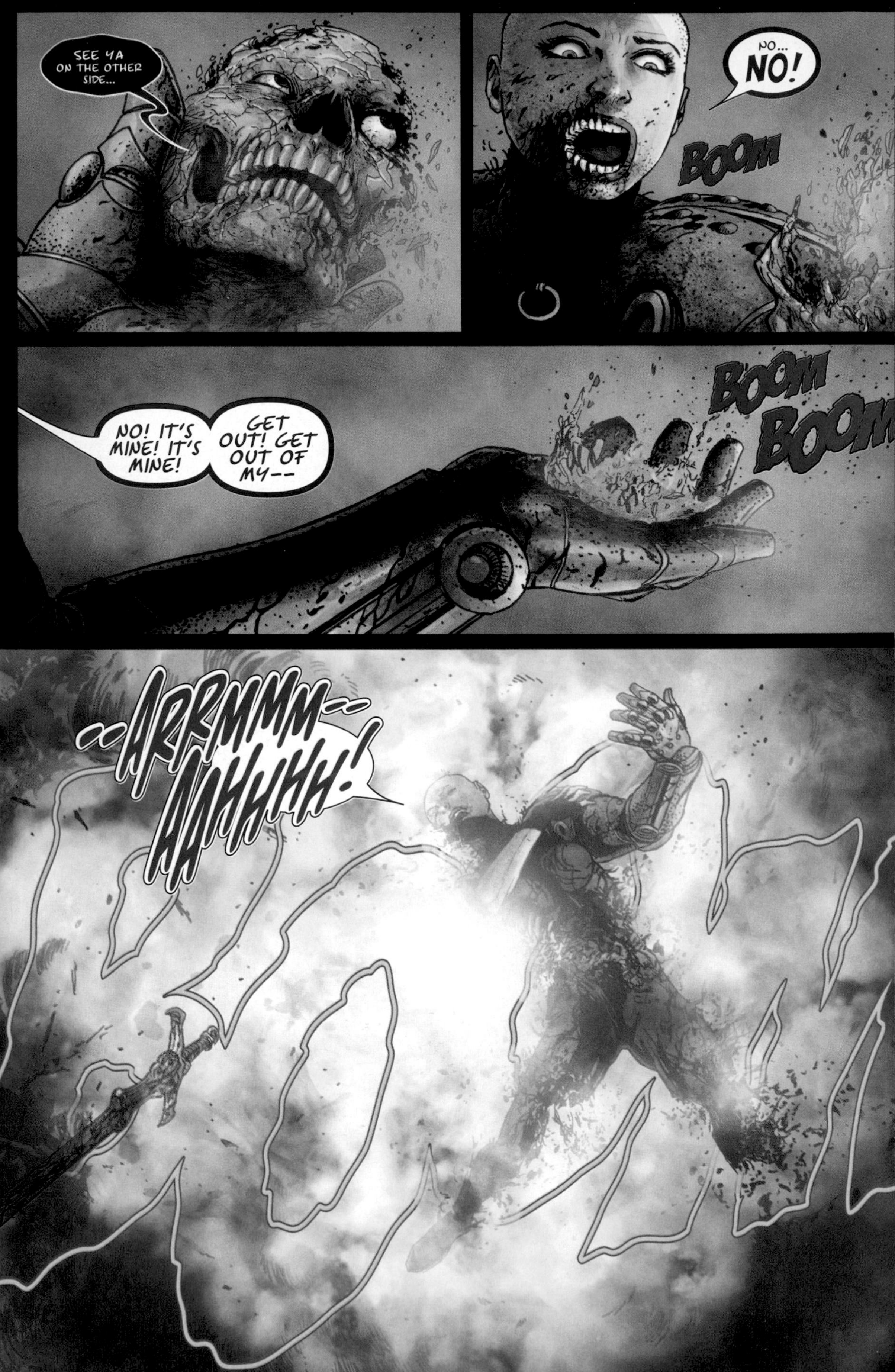
SEE YA ON THE OTHER SIDE...
NO... NO!
BOOM
NO! IT'S MINE! IT'S MINE!
GET OUT! GET OUT OF MY--
BOOM
BOOM
--ARRMMM--AAHHHH!

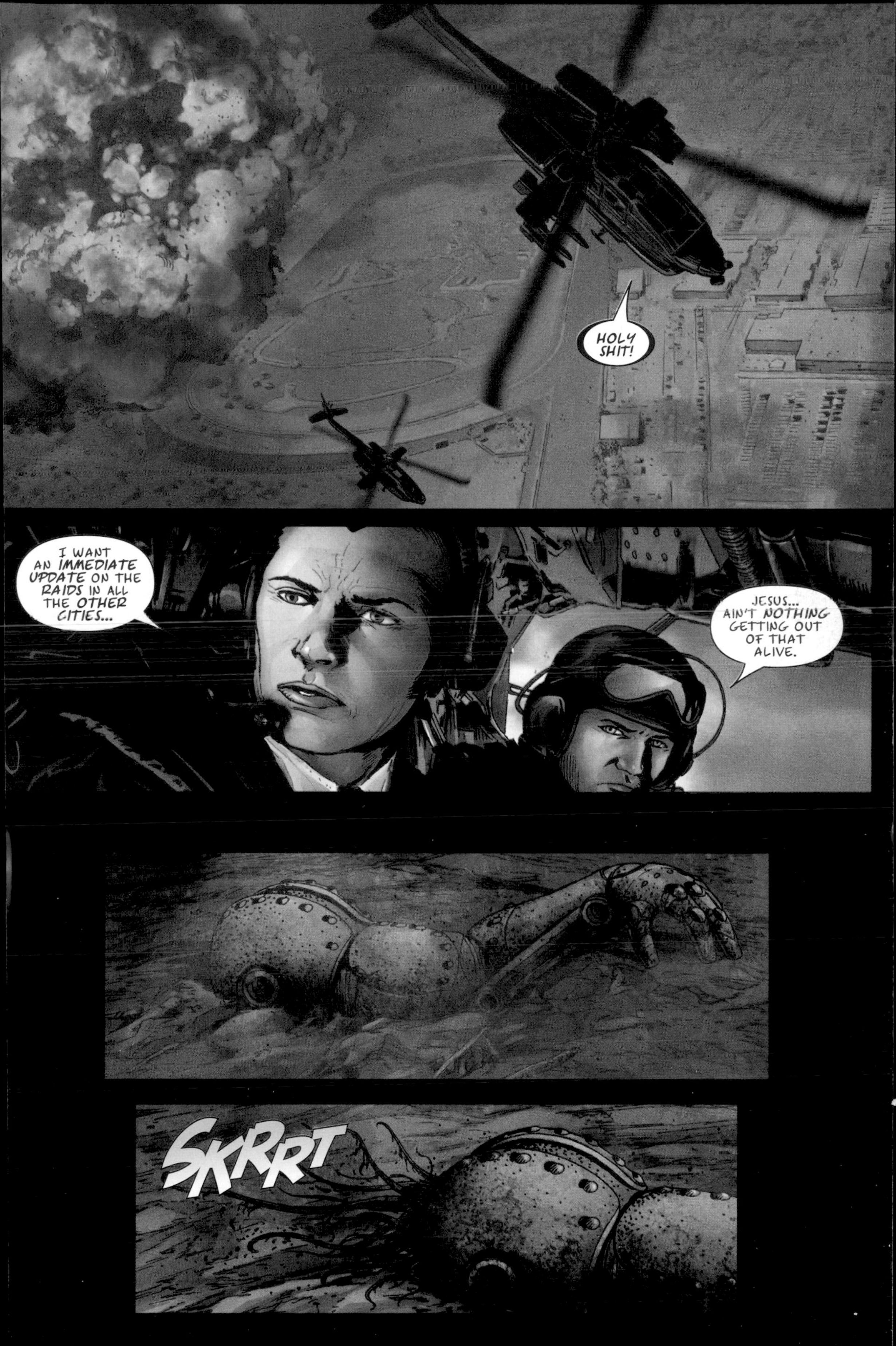
HOLY SHIT!
I WANT AN IMMEDIATE UPDATE ON THE RAIDS IN ALL THE OTHER CITIES...
JESUS... AIN'T NOTHING GETTING OUT OF THAT ALIVE.
SKRRT

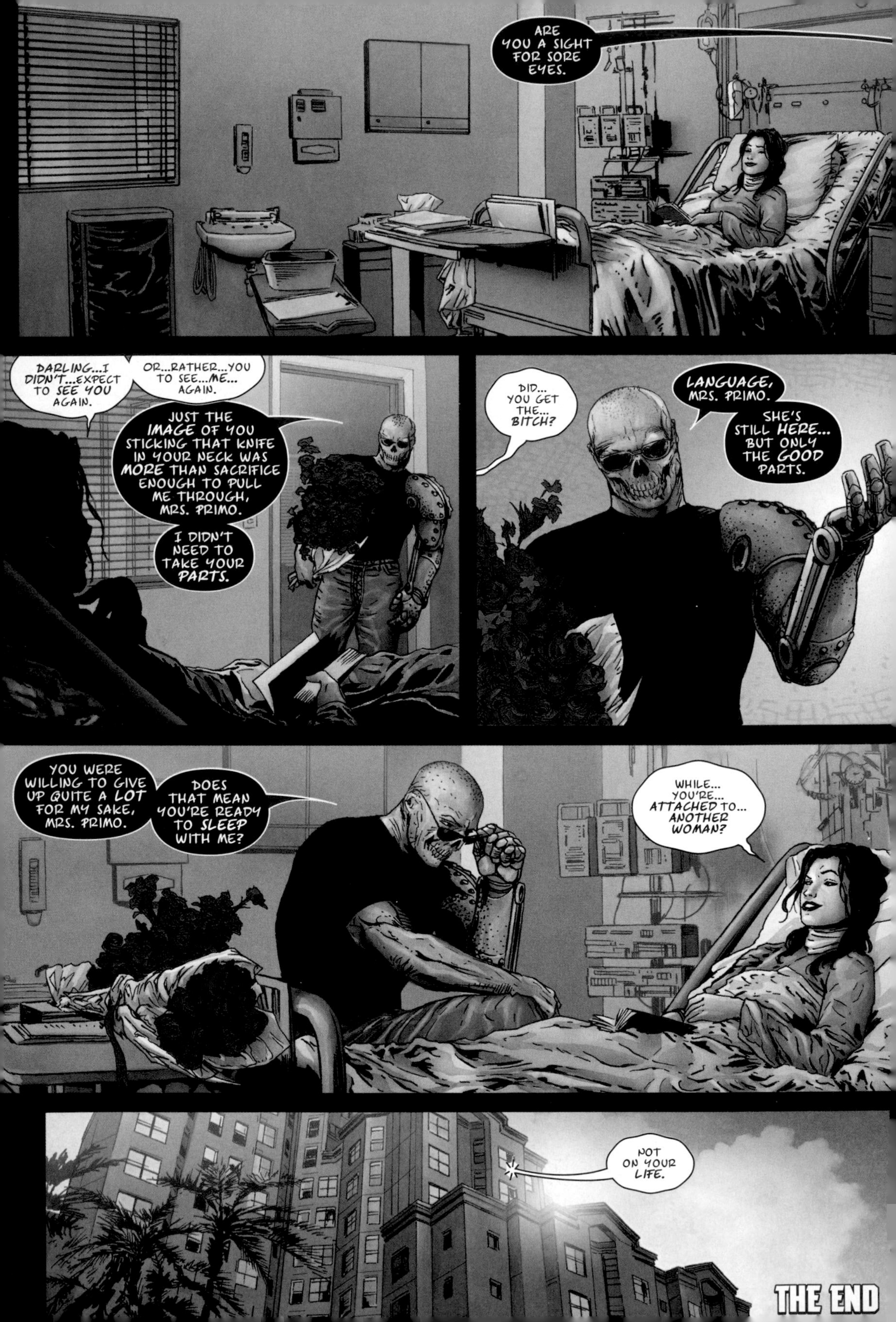
ARE YOU A SIGHT FOR SORE EYES.
DARLING...I DIDN'T...EXPECT TO SEE YOU AGAIN.
OR...RATHER...YOU TO SEE...ME... AGAIN.
JUST THE IMAGE OF YOU STICKING THAT KNIFE IN YOUR NECK WAS MORE THAN SACRIFICE ENOUGH TO PULL ME THROUGH, MRS. PRIMO.
I DIDN'T NEED TO TAKE YOUR PARTS.
DID... YOU GET THE... BITCH?
LANGUAGE, MRS. PRIMO.
SHE'S STILL HERE... BUT ONLY THE GOOD PARTS.
YOU WERE WILLING TO GIVE UP QUITE A LOT FOR MY SAKE, MRS. PRIMO.
DOES THAT MEAN YOU'RE READY TO SLEEP WITH ME?
WHILE... YOU'RE... ATTACHED TO... ANOTHER WOMAN?
NOT ON YOUR LIFE.
THE END

CHARACTER SKETCHES

BY PATRICK ZIRCHER

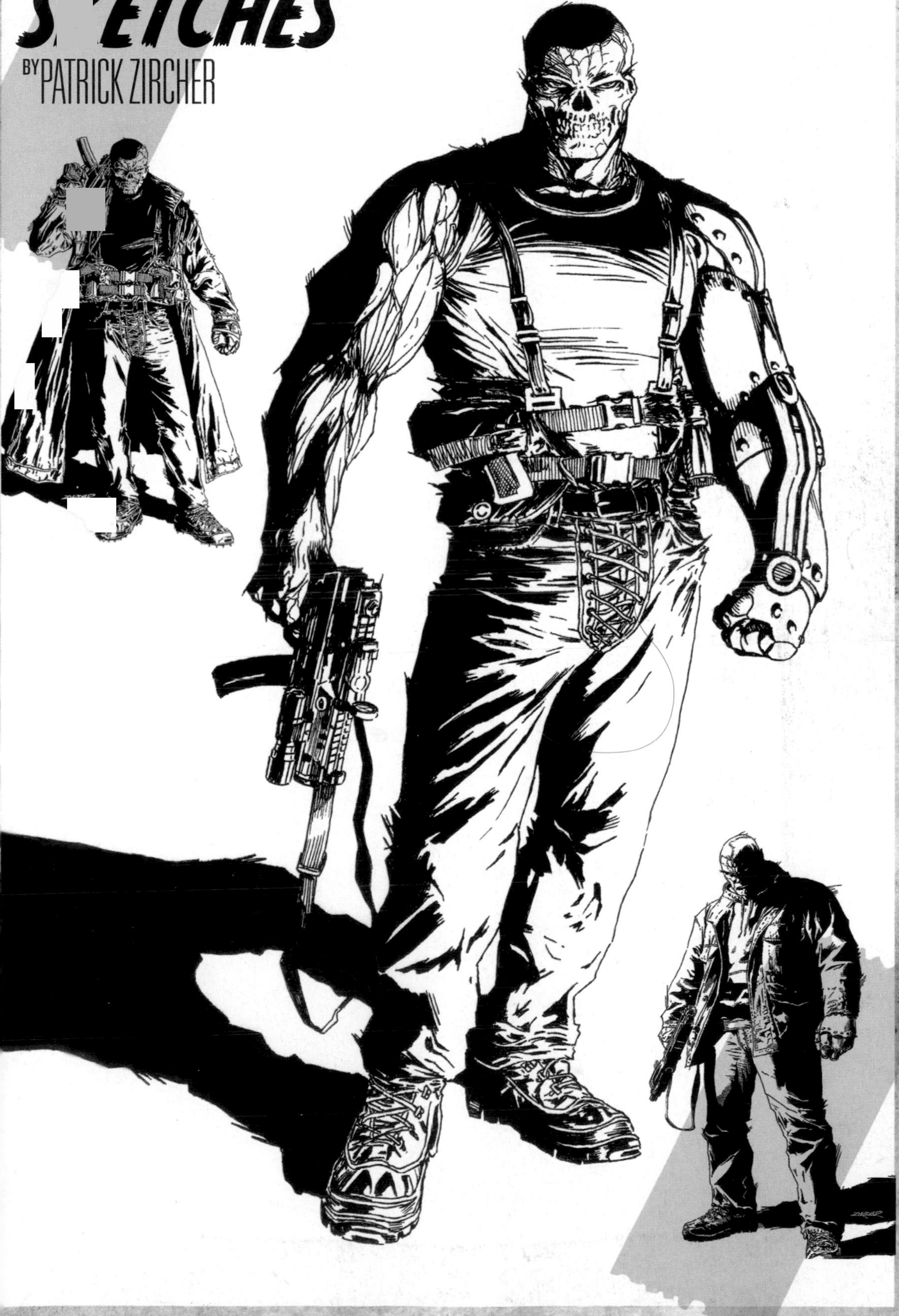

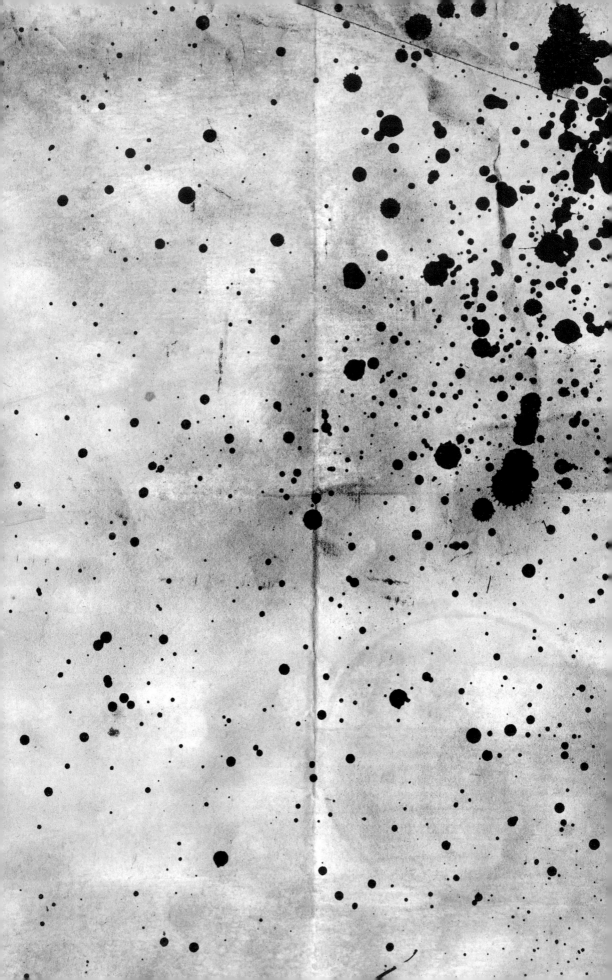